Towards a Gay Communism

Towards a Gay Communism

Elements of Homosexual Critique

Mario Mieli

Translated by David Fernbach
and Evan Calder Williams

Introduction by Massimo Prearo

Foreword by Tim Dean

First published as *Elementi di critica omosessuale* in 2002
by Giangiacomo Feltrinelli Editore, Milan, Italy

This edition first published 2018 by Pluto Press
345 Archway Road, London N6 5AA

www.plutobooks.com

British Library Cataloguing in Publication Data
A catalogue record for this book is available from the British Library

ISBN 978 0 7453 9952 2 Hardback
ISBN 978 0 7453 9951 5 Paperback
ISBN 978 1 7868 0053 4 PDF eBook
ISBN 978 1 7868 0055 8 Kindle eBook
ISBN 978 1 7868 0054 1 EPUB eBook

This book is printed on paper suitable for recycling and made from fully managed and sustained forest sources. Logging, pulping and manufacturing processes are expected to conform to the environmental standards of the country of origin.

Typeset by Stanford DTP Services, Northampton, England

Simultaneously printed in the United Kingdom and United States of America

Contents

Foreword
'I Keep My Treasure in My Arse'

Tim Dean

Rereading Mario Mieli today, I am catapulted back to the time when I first encountered his manifesto, published then in an abridged version under the title *Homosexuality and Liberation* by London's Gay Men's Press in 1980. I read Mieli alongside other works of gay liberation, psychoanalytic theory, and feminism during those heady days of university in the late eighties. AIDS cast a shadow, but not dark enough to obscure the radical ideas that were expanding the consciousness – if not completely blowing the mind – of this first-generation college student from the provinces. Mieli's book wasn't part of any syllabus; there were no gay studies or queer theory courses at universities in those days – though there would be soon. We were gearing up to invent queer theory, and Mieli offered a template for how it might be done. Yet because queer theory turned out to be 'Made in America,' its European history was largely erased. Reconsidering *Towards a Gay Communism* now, in this unabridged English translation, provides an opportunity to rewrite the origin myth of queer theory and politics in a more international frame.

Although I was unaware of it then, the world from which Mieli's book emerged had vanished almost completely by the time I came upon it – and Mieli himself had committed suicide in 1983. The 1980 English edition gave no hint of these changes. Nothing dates *Towards a Gay Communism* more than its unavoidable ignorance of AIDS, which initially gained medical notice in 1981 but was not named as such until a year later. The onslaught of the epidemic and the reactionary political climate of the eighties altered gay liberation's trajectory in ways Mieli couldn't have predicted or foreseen. In hindsight, the divide between pre- and post-liberation eras of gay existence (conventionally denoted by the date June 1969, when drag queens and others fought back against police persecution at New York's Stonewall Inn) was matched barely more than a decade later by the chasm that opened between pre- and post-AIDS epochs of gay life. Mieli wrote during that glorious decade of gay liberation, when so much seemed newly possible. His book is a testament to an era that already felt a lifetime away for gay men of my generation, who came of age during the eighties and thus never knew sex without the attendant pressure of mortality. Having no direct memory of sex in the seventies, I remain fascinated by accounts such as Mieli's that capture those years so ebulliently. *Towards a Gay Communism* documents a crucial historical moment, at the same time as it offers fresh inspiration for us today.

Mieli articulated something that has mostly got lost in contemporary queer theory: the foundational significance of sex. He put his finger on the cultural antipathy towards anal sex – an antipathy that the AIDS epidemic intensified, that Leo Bersani[1] analysed ten years after Mieli, and that paradoxically, queer theory's newfound respectability has compounded:

> What in homosexuality particularly horrifies *homo normalis*, the policeman of the hetero-capitalist system, is being fucked in the arse; and this can only mean that one of the most delicious bodily pleasures, anal intercourse, is itself a significant revolutionary force. The thing that we queens are so greatly put down for contains a large part of our subversive gay potential. I keep my treasure in my arse, but then my arse is open to everyone . . .

The most marvelous thing about Mieli is that he really seems to mean open to *everyone*. Although the HIV/AIDS epidemic cast a pall over the original joie de vivre of such sentences, Mieli's stance embraces risk even without the spectre of viral transmission. The risks of bodily porousness and radical openness to the other remain, both before and after AIDS.[2] Appreciating the ethics of Mieli's stance, we should not miss how playfully flirtatious his punctuation is here. The ellipsis that ends the last sentence quoted above – and, in fact, closes the chapter in which this passage appears – issues a provocative invitation: my arse is open to you too, if you're interested. He leaves the sentence open-ended to signal that his own rear end stays open. His butt offers a welcoming smile to the reader.

---

1. See Leo Bersani, 'Is the Rectum a Grave?' in *Is the Rectum a Grave? And Other Essays* (Chicago: University of Chicago Press, 2010), 3–30. The essay was originally published in 1987.
2. This is what (inspired by Mieli) I tried to elaborate in *Unlimited Intimacy: Reflections on the Subculture of Barebacking* (Chicago: University of Chicago Press, 2009).

This gesture of openness to all comers betokens Mieli's radically democratic ethos. The socio-erotic economy he envisions under gay communism is about not sexual identity but erotic abundance, a world in which artificial sexual scarcity would be unknown. Based on a liberationist model of queer sexuality, Mieli drastically redefines communism as 'the rediscovery of bodies and their fundamental communicative function, their polymorphous potential for love'. In this almost Bataille-like communication of material forms, human corporeality enters into egalitarian relations with all worldly beings, including 'children and new arrivals of every kind, dead bodies, animals, plants, things, flowers, turds . . .' Again the sentence ends with ellipses, this time to indicate that the list could continue. And again the beautiful (flowers) is juxtaposed with the ugly (turds), anticipating the transvaluation that crystallises in Mieli's announcement, 'I keep my treasure in my arse.'

Turds may be regarded as treasure rather than waste because embracing queer sexuality (instead of merely tolerating it) upends the entire hierarchy of value and propriety upon which social convention rests. According to Mieli, once the full significance of homosexuality is grasped, the meaning of everything changes. He could not have anticipated how normalised gay identity would become in the twenty-first century. Mieli's vision aims to restore to adult life the 'polymorphous potential for love' that characterises childhood, before categories of identity assume their disciplinary weight. In the polymorphous pleasures of gay sex, particularly its desublimation of anal play, Mieli glimpsed the possibility that we all could return to a prelapsarian state of erotic grace, forging a utopia in which not only our arses but our most intimate beings would be open to otherness. His commitment to this vision anticipates recent queer utopianism – with the difference that he does not shy away from sex.[3]

Mieli's conviction about the potential of Eros goes further than most queer critiques, since he includes pedophilia, necrophilia, and coprophagy in his catalogue of experiences ripe for redemption. Needless to say, this is explosively controversial, more so now than in the 1970s. I find his commitment to thinking beyond the limits of revulsion particularly refreshing today, at a moment when the gay movement has become so domesticated and respectable. For me, Mieli's courage in pursuing his

3. See, for example, José Esteban Muñoz, *Cruising Utopia: The Then and There of Queer Futurity* (New York: New York University Press, 2009).

thesis way beyond socially acceptable parameters recalls Freud's moral and intellectual bravery on erotic matters. The excitement I feel reading *Towards a Gay Communism* recalls how I felt when I first read *Three Essays on the Theory of Sexuality*, especially in its original, 1905 edition. Mieli's was one of the earliest radical interpretations of that indispensable Freudian text, and many of his claims anticipate subsequent readings of Freud by Italian queer theorist Teresa de Lauretis and thinkers such as Leo Bersani. It takes a fundamentally non-American perspective to see what a valuable resource – treasure, even – Freud can be for queer politics.

Regarding psychoanalysis, Mieli saw that its institutional avatars could not legitimately lay claim to Freud's most important insights. Instead, it was up to the women's and gay liberation movements to elaborate the implications of *Three Essays*, paradoxically in opposition to the mental health establishment. This project continues on many fronts today, in the work of feminists and queer theorists who read psychoanalysis against itself, often from a position outside psychoanalytic institutions.[4] Given Mieli's own experiences at the hands of the 'psychonazis', it is all the more to his credit that he was able to distinguish the radical potential of psychoanalytic concepts from the repressive practices of those who routinely invoke Freudian authority to bolster their homophobic and normalising agendas. As a queer psychoanalytic thinker, I appreciate his acknowledging how psychoanalysis 'flinches from the logic of its own insights, from drawing "extreme" theoretical conclusions'. Mieli grasped that psychoanalytic thinking represents an unfinished – perhaps an interminable – enterprise and, indeed, that too many analysts remain inhibited by professional decorum from pursuing the unsettling implications of Freud's ideas about sexuality. Freud's observation that 'all human beings are capable of making a homosexual object-choice and have in fact made one in their unconscious' tends to be hastily cordoned off from serious investigation by clinicians.[5] Whereas institutionalised psychoanalysis domesticates the conceptual wildness of the Freudian text, Mieli

4. See *Homosexuality and Psychoanalysis*, ed. Tim Dean and Christopher Lane (Chicago: University of Chicago Press, 2001), and *Clinical Encounters in Sexuality: Psychoanalytic Practice and Queer Theory*, ed. Noreen Giffney and Eve Watson (New York: Punctum Books, 2017).

5. Sigmund Freud, *Three Essays on the Theory of Sexuality*, trans. and ed. James Strachey (New York: Basic Books, 1995), 11.

labours to queer it, drawing out the productively incoherent logics of psychoanalysis.

Redefining from a radically gay perspective the established meanings of both psychoanalysis and communism, Mieli's book belongs to the Freudo-Marxist tradition of political thinking that includes such various figures as Herbert Marcuse, Guy Hocquenghem, and Slavoj Žižek (whose writing manifests a camp sensibility congruent with Mieli's queeny wit). Unlike some thinkers in the Freudo-Marxist tradition, however, Mieli has no patience for Lacan, preferring instead Deleuze and Guattari's anti-Oedipal critique of orthodox Lacanianism.[6] But what really distinguishes *Towards a Gay Communism* methodologically from queer theory – even as the book continues to provide inspiration today – is its omission of the work of Michel Foucault. The introductory volume of Foucault's *History of Sexuality* appeared in France in 1976, too late for Mieli to take stock of it in a book that reached print just a few months afterward.[7]

Foucault's introductory volume ended up functioning as a primary source for what became Anglo-American queer theory in the nineties. It was the basic idea of sexual repression – a linchpin of Mieli's thesis – that Foucault sought to challenge in that polemic. If society does not repress desire but instead provokes it by means of proliferating discourses on sexuality, then the whole project of liberation is thrown into doubt. While Mieli wasn't a specific target of Foucault's critique, *Towards a Gay Communism* got swept up in its dragnet. His account of how heterosexuals repress their inner homosexuality can sound naïve in the wake of Foucault's argument. Since Foucault aimed to wrest discussion of sexual politics away from the terms of the Freudo-Marxist tradition, the success of his book inadvertently cast Mieli's into shadow, obscuring its significance for early practitioners of queer theory and politics.

This accident of publication history also has obscured all the ways that *Towards a Gay Communism* nevertheless anticipates queer theory. In his thoroughgoing critique of the heterosexual norm, Mieli is closer to Foucault and to many contemporary queer theorists than initially he appears. As a result of his commitment to revolutionary rather than

6. See Gilles Deleuze and Félix Guattari, *Anti-Oedipus: Capitalism and Schizophrenia*, trans. Robert Hurley, Mark Seem, and Helen R. Lane (Minneapolis: University of Minnesota Press, 1987).

7. Michel Foucault, *La volonté de savoir* (Paris: Gallimard, 1976).

reformist politics, Mieli develops a view of society that prompts him to argue not simply against heterosexism but, more broadly, against the institutions of normality as such. He sees that gay identity itself can serve the forces of normalisation and that something more radical is necessary. Like Foucault, Mieli recognises that sexual behavior is regulated as much by social norms as by laws; the repeal of anti-sodomy legislation can actually intensify the social normalisation of sexuality, as is arguably the case in the United States after the Supreme Court, in *Lawrence v. Texas* (2003), invalidated sodomy statutes. That was a great victory, but it didn't solve everything for queers. Late in his manifesto, Mieli assures straight readers that 'we are not struggling against you, but only against your "normality".' Today we would say that the problem is not heterosexuality but heteronormativity. Mieli lacks the term, but he intuits the concept.

Likewise he takes the term *gay* beyond the coordinates of identity. Too often today, as *queer* is used merely as a hipper synonym for *gay*, queerness gets reduced to an identity marker. Mieli's logic works in the opposite direction, by loosening gayness from an exclusively sexual orientation to something more capacious. Sexual orientation is itself a normalising idea whose temporary benefits he could see past even in the seventies. In this respect, Mieli was considerably ahead of his time. He understood that shoring up lesbian or gay identities in opposition to heterosexuality misapprehends how identity categories themselves constrain subjectivity, desire, and relationality. It is not the particular content of any identity category but identity as a form of intelligibility – a framework governing our understanding – that limits us in so many ways. We need a revolutionary perspective now, no less so than in the seventies, to break apart the comfortable boundaries of identitarianism. We don't need a proliferation of gender and sexual identities, as many contemporary queers seem to believe, but instead to obliterate the mindset of identity altogether.

Mieli adopts from Wilhelm Reich the derisive term *homo normalis* to designate those who – whatever their gender or sexuality – remain committed to the status quo. Today the term applies to all those homos who want nothing more than to get married and 'be normal'. It would have been interesting to hear Mieli's view on the campaign for same-sex marriage and its impact on those of us who eschew the white picket fence. When assimilationist gays pass as normal, presenting themselves as 'just like everyone else', the social pressure to comply with normative models intensifies against anyone who still counts as queer or somehow beyond the pale. In other words, the social opprobrium that gay conformists manage to evade does not simply disappear. It falls with greater weight on the transgendered, sex workers, leatherfolk, SM enthusiasts, HIV-positive people, fetishists – all those who still are stigmatised by sex/gender norms. Mieli, like queer theorist Michael Warner, perceives acutely 'the trouble with normal'.[8]

If he were writing today, Mieli doubtless would present himself and his perspective as queer. No small part of the force of *Towards a Gay Communism* stems from its author's explicit desire not to be normal, his delight in being a 'crazy queen', flamboyant and outrageous. Much of the book's pungency comes from Mieli's capacity for being intellectually serious and very funny at once – as in his line about keeping his treasure in his arse. His book is psychoanalytic not only in its conceptual formulations but also in its understanding that comedy offers a unique form of insight. Mieli's humour frequently targets gender norms, especially those of machismo. In his time and place, a primary way not to be normal was through cross-dressing, or what today we might call *genderfuck*, a stylistic means of disrupting the categories of gender normativity to unsettling and often humorous effect. The point is not to conform to – or make fun of – the 'opposite' gender, but to highlight the absurdity of every attempt at gender conformity.

Given transgender politics today, we need to think about how Mieli uses the term *transsexuality*. Borrowing from Luciano Parinetto, he develops this term quite differently from contemporary usage. Whereas today transgender concerns above all questions of gender identity, for Mieli transsexuality has more to do with erotic desire than with gender presentation or performance. He may talk, in *Towards a Gay Communism*, about the mischief that cross-dressing gay men can do to the normative social order, but that is not what Mieli means by transsexuality. It is necessary to clarify this distinction since the term he uses affirmatively now connotes pathology – or at least is understood by most transgendered people as pejorative. I've suggested that today Mieli would present himself as queer; but I believe he also would be involved with trans activism. He'd grasp the connections between queer and trans, while also acknowledging the strong political tensions between them. I cannot imagine what pronoun Mieli would choose for himself, though I'm confident he'd be alive to the issues involved in pronoun usage, and

8. Michael Warner, *The Trouble with Normal: Sex, Politics, and the Ethics of Queer Life* (New York: Free Press, 1999).

I'm hopeful that trans readers will draw inspiration from his thinking, as queer readers continue to do.

Mieli's vision of 'transsexuality' entailed breaking down the barriers that separate us from each other. It was the opposite of shoring up an identity. David Fernbach suggests, in his introduction to the 1980 edition, that for Mieli, '"transsexuality" and communism are one and the same'[9] – a claim that already indicates just how differently he is deploying these terms in *Towards a Gay Communism*. The prefix *trans-* means across; by *transsexuality* Mieli refers to crossing the borders of sexual difference without normative heterosexuality. What motivates that crossing is desire, understood as Eros in the Freudian sense. He speaks of 'gay communism' because, in his political vision, the borders that separate socioeconomic classes also are traversed by 'transsexual' desire. In crossing these borders, Mieli's 'transsexuality' dissolves hierarchies too. He regards this prospect not as a terrifying loss of boundaries but as a multiplication of pleasures, a radical expansion of access to what we all really want.

It may be worth noting that the word *queer* also shares an etymological root meaning 'across'. Queer and trans, though far from identical, share an affinity that sometimes gets lost when the differences between them degenerate into identity politics, or when trans is consistently subordinated to queer. Local differences are important, as are the differences among Italian, British, North American, and other national traditions of sex/gender politics. A complete map of the criss-crossing influences remains to be drawn. But, following Mieli, I would suggest that the connections and affinities are ultimately more significant than the differences. Queer politics emerged in North America via recognition of a commonality between those who do not adhere to social norms based on their sexuality and those who do not fit a universalising idea of social subjectivity based on racial or class status. It is not that everyone excluded from heternormativity and its privileges is the same; but they share something politically precious in common. Like Mieli's sweeping critique of society as we know it, queer politics aspires to connect sexual oppression with gender discrimination, racism, ethnic chauvinism, immigration status, and many other vectors of social exclusion. The capaciousness of queer as a rubric for political mobilising – its commitment

9. David Fernbach, 'Introduction', in Mieli, *Homosexuality and Liberation: Elements of a Gay Critique* (London: Gay Men's Press, 1980), 12.

to forging alliances between otherwise quite disparate constituencies – effectively countermands the boundedness of identity categories. And *that* is what Mieli meant by transsexual desire.

Where Mieli differs from many contemporary queer thinkers and activists is in his never forgetting the motive force of Eros. Foucault cautioned that 'we must not think that by saying yes to sex, one says no to power,' since the two are interwoven rather than opposed.[10] Yet, if it is facile to resort to simple-minded formulations about the revolutionary power of sex, nevertheless it has seemed a little too convenient, in the academic precincts of queer theory, to lose sight of the erotic altogether. Sometimes one gets the impression that she is dealing with nuns. At North American academic conferences in queer studies, the piety is so overwhelming that it feels like being in church. In that context, Mieli offers a breath of fresh air.

Extrapolating from Freud's universalisation of homosexual desire, Mieli claims that even straight men long to be queens: their machismo forms a closet concealing their true desire. Certainly there are heterosexual men who love to get fucked in the arse. But Mieli pushes the psychoanalytic theory of repression to implausible conclusions, and it is symptomatic that in reasoning thus he has recourse to Jungian archetypes involving the soul's essential bisexuality. In the end, however, it is unimportant whether contemporary readers agree with the details of Mieli's conceptual formulations. What matters is whether we still can be inspired by him. *Towards a Gay Communism* belongs to a visionary tradition of ecstatic utopianism. Showing familiarity with English literary history, Mieli manifests the revolutionary enthusiasm characteristic of bardic Anglophone poets from William Blake through Walt Whitman and Allen Ginsberg, all of whom articulated connections among non-normative sexuality, madness, and social critique. For Whitman and Ginsberg, as for Mieli, revolution begins with sex between men, preferably more than a couple. These poets' Dionysian visions of radical democracy don't provide a blueprint for social reorganisation; instead they offer avant-garde inspiration for it. In a similar vein, *Towards a Gay Communism* engages our attention not only as a fascinating document of its departed moment, but also as renewable inspiration for our contemporary desire to envision a future that is foreign to today.

---

10. Michel Foucault, *The History of Sexuality*, Vol. 1: *An Introduction*, trans. Robert Hurley (New York: Random House, 1978), 157.

Introduction

Massimo Prearo

I

In one of the rare pieces of footage[1] in which Mario Mieli talks about the publication of this book, from 1977, the author is presented as a leader of the Italian gay movement and appears *en travesti*, as a way to strategically perform homosexual femininity. Mieli introduces the core of his theoretical and political views, that is, the erotic multitude of desire. The latter, described as transsexual desire, is a polymorphic drive that displaces the boundaries between the feminine and the masculine, and undoes, at the same time, all categories of sexual orientation. The erotic multitude of desire is, according to Mieli, a revolutionary tool against heterosexual patriarchy and its political regime.

Mieli's choice of cross-dressing in public can be seen as strategic, not in the sense that it helps him to hide his personal life beneath the mask of fabulousness, but because it unravels the absurdity of the heterosexual norm which imposes gender and sexual roles that are generated by capital. People who knew him before he became an activist could testify to his passion for makeup, for his relentless enthusiasm, and for his eagerness to provoke. All of this resulted, for him, in a confrontation between everyday normality and the figure of the deviant that he himself embodied, thereby denouncing the hyper-dressed rigidity of femininity and masculinity. Later, the encounter between Mieli and the Gay Liberation Front in London (1970–71) marked the beginning of a quest that was not just personal, for it was experienced by him as a collective debate, if not as a political struggle. In London, Mieli participated in the assemblies of the movement, and discovered revolutionary forms of homosexual activism and socialisation that were grounded both in one's own life and in the life of the self within the collective. To build a united front meant to reject the condition of marginality, in order not so much

1. Interview with Mario Mieli, 'Come mai?', 1977. https://www.youtube.com/watch?v=5i2xnoKaB8Q

to assume a majoritarian, comfortable position, as to assert the refusal of the majority's normalised point of view. This translated, for Mieli, into the full and radical embodiment of the marginalised position, for the sake of contaminating the realm of heterosexuality through a homosexual standpoint.

The homosexual revolutionary moment, which started with the Stonewall riots of 1969, was in fact one of consciousness raising and it aimed to challenge everything – the heteronormative structure of society as well as all assimilationist projects promoted by pre-Stonewall movements, such as *Mattachine Society* or the French homophile movement *Arcadie*. These movements wanted to normalise 'homosexuality'. To do so, they invited homosexuals to strive for more self-control and less craziness, faggotry, fairy, queen – and queer. The homosexual revolutionary project promoted by the post-'68 generation aimed, on the contrary, at breaking what Monique Wittig would call the *straight* contract, in order to rewrite the entire social vocabulary starting from the experience of homosexuals themselves.

In those same years, the Fronte Unitario Omosessuale Rivoluzionario Italiano (Unitarian Revolutionary Homosexual Front) emerged in Italy – more precisely, it was founded in 1971 in Milan, at writer Fernanda Pivano's home. The shortened name and acronym of the movement was *Fuori!*, which means 'out' (as in 'come out'), and it was crucial to Mieli's activist formation. Their first public event in 1972 was organised to counter the first International Conference of Sexology in the city of Sanremo. Activists of the homosexual revolutionary French movement (FHAR) were also demonstrating alongside their Italian comrades. Archival pictures show Mieli and other members of *Fuori!* holding banners in front of the conference venue, with slogans such as 'Homosexuals proudly come out', 'Put the electrodes in your brain', and 'This is the first and last conference on sexophobia'. As this is his first public appearance, Mieli is wearing a queer battledress with high-heel shoes, lipstick, a turban and glamorous sunglasses – words alone cannot bring about a revolution in the same way that a publicly and dangerously exposed body does.

Such a disturbing, intransigent and uncomfortable position is the one Mieli will assume all along. In his first article, titled 'For a critique of the homosexual question', published in the *Fuori!* magazine, Mieli underscores the continuities between the project of political emancipation pursued by the homosexual movement and the co-optative force of capitalist democracies:

> In most capitalist countries, the *freedom to be homosexual* is recognized as a right. [...] In fact, such legal *freedom* means freedom to be excluded, oppressed, repressed, ridiculed, become victims of moral and physical violence, and be isolated into *ghettoes*, which additionally are so dangerous and shabby in Italy.

And he goes on: 'Thus, the homosexual is *legally free* in most advanced capitalist countries with a more or less *democratic* constitution, yet he still suffers as a member of the ghetto.' Mieli understood the logics of capitalism as not limited to a repressive power that denies homosexual desire, but as a machine capable of metabolising all experiences that exceed the heterosexual norm and to recast them into the market, thanks to 'leftist parties in Parliament [which] specialise in channeling all revolutionary initiatives towards the bourgeoisie'. According to him, formal and legal emancipation, i.e., *political* emancipation, 'is a strange thing: the more you get of it, the more your hands are empty. In reality, it vanishes, but it remains codified in abstract laws, appeasing the conscience of bourgeois oppressors and giving legal recognition to the sad life (and shabby death) of hysterical fags'.[2]

The tone of his writings, which will later become a stylistic mark, was so merciless that many of his articles published in the *Fuori!* magazine were preceded by a note from the editorial staff taking distance from him. According to Mieli, the desire for emancipation is an illusion, an oasis in the desert, a fake reward for homosexuals, the siren song of capital. Yet, his theoretical and political reflections do not just review or rephrase in homosexual terms the communist project for revolution, but call for a mutation in homosexuals themselves, or, as Mieli puts it, for 'a critical process'.

II

For Mieli, writing is a way of positioning himself within the space of homosexual revolutionary activism, which allows him to put into political

2. Mario Mieli, 'Per la critica della questione omosessuale', *Fuori!*, n. 3, September 1972, p. 1–2.

practice his theoretical reflection, and, at the same time, to translate his political experience into theoretical research. In the meanwhile, Mieli starts studying philosophy at the University of Milan, broadening the activist experience to every sphere of his existence. Still, Mieli is not interested in covering the role of intellectuals within the movement, but rather in promoting a public and collective experience of the movement and his being in movement. Taking his own experience as a starting point, he steadily works to disseminate critical reflections suggesting both a critique *based on* the homosexual perspective, along with a critique *of* the homosexual perspective – in the same way as the collectives did during their meetings, where the specificities of the everyday life were analysed and collectively discussed to produce a transformative self-consciousness. In this sense, the publication of this book – a revised version of his MA dissertation – constitutes the culmination of this homosexual trajectory. Made of and producing a whole set of discourses, practices, and theories that have been thought and experienced within the movement, the homosexual revolutionary project acted in order to break through the boundaries of the revolutionary imaginary itself and eventually contaminate the left, the class struggle, the homosexual ghetto, and knowledge.

Towards a Gay Communism, more than being an essay or a political manifesto, is an experimental roadmap of sexual politics that alternates theoretical arguments and intuitions with virtually ethnographic observations about homosexual activism in the 1970s, along with experiential narratives, at the crossroads of autobiography and auto-fiction. From its first publication, the book's polymorphic character has certainly contributed to propel the content and the author, already a leading figure of the Italian homosexual revolutionary movement at the time, into the legacy of gay and queer studies. The Spanish and the Dutch translations of *Elementi di critica omosessuale* (the original Italian title), in 1979 and 1981 respectively, and the first publication in English in 1980, in an edited version, are part of a prolific body of homosexual knowledge, and theoretical insights about homosexuality. In this liminal context of wanting *theories* and yet not *studies*, Mieli's book is, however, paradoxically late and yet remarkably ahead of its time.

Despite being considered and celebrated as a common good by the homosexual movement, the philosophical and experiential nature of the book has largely prevented it from breaking through to academic circles. Indeed, already in 1968 and before Foucault's *History of sexuality*

(1976), Mary McIntosh, amongst other authors in the field of sociology, published her foregrounding essay 'The Homosexual Role', arguing for a social constructionist approach to sexuality that would soon become a source of inspiration for future works, such as the pioneering *Coming Out: Homosexual Politics in Britain from the Nineteenth Century to the Present* (Quartet Books, 1977) by Jeffrey Weeks. Although these works preserved an activist dimension, their academic-scientific-disciplinary nature inevitably introduced an *objectifying* methodology of analysis. In fact, they came to define 'homosexuality' (and all its declinations: practices, movements, communities, identities, etc.) through a scientific paradigm and, together with it, a system of concepts, theories, and models – while reforming and renewing the existing ones. Without denying its revolutionary impact at the epistemological level, the foucauldian method (as discussed in the foreword by Tim Dean) followed the same proceeding. Foucault studied the processes through which homosexuality is objectified to understand how the social, historical and political construction of homosexuality could bring about the existence of a homosexual subjectivity, not only by repressing or denying it, but rather producing it. It is precisely in this logic that lies his most original contribution.

From this point of view, Mieli's book follows a different direction. Starting from a historical, philosophical and psychoanalytical analysis shedding light on the repression phenomenon of homosexuality, *Towards a Gay Communism* proposes an exploration of the experiential dimension of homosexuality in the historical context of the revolution and the ongoing capitalistic counter-revolution. While Mieli keeps trying, he does not aim for theoretical coherence, scientific ambition, or the willingness to turn his book into a critical step of an academic career. The knowledge from which Mieli is driven and which puts his reflection in motion is not made of concepts, but rather of experiences that the author elaborates, discusses, reformulates and disseminates:

> In women as subjected to male 'power', in the proletariat subjected to capitalist exploitation, in the subjection of homosexuals to the Norm and in that of black people to white racism, we can recognise the concrete historical subjects in a position to overthrow the entire present social, sexual and racial dialectic.[3]

---

3. See page 251 of the current edition.

Probably, this is the reason why, in the late 1970s, the book is referenced in the emerging literature on homosexuality as an example of homosexual revolutionary knowledge, together with the texts of other authors, such as Guy Hocquenghem. Still, the experiential material on which Mieli builds a proposal of gay communism remains silenced in the academic debate. Not only because his erotic-political extremism could be considered inappropriate for the gentle writing of scientific knowledge, but also because the content of his critical thought does not aim at cultivating discussions within the academic environment. Rather, Mieli favours cross-fertilisation with the knowledge that already exists and circulates across the spaces of homosexuality: saunas, discos, cruising spots, factory or highway lavatories, as well as meetings, assemblies, streets and movements.

However, this is probably also the reason why Mieli's book anticipates the recent developments of gay and lesbian studies, finding in the archipelago of queer theories, and especially in the philosophically and politically anti-social versions proposed by Leo Bersani or Lee Edelman,[4] a new opportunity for discussion. On this library shelf, we find the major issues introduced by Mieli in the wake of the already quoted Guy Hochquengem's *Homosexual Desire* (published in 1972): the central role of desire, anality as symbolic and as a practice of anti-sociality, along with homosexuality as a principle of anti-heteronormative negativity. The renewed interest for Mieli's book, which is also brought about in this new full translation, does not represent the author's public consecration in the realm of queer studies, but, once again, goes beyond the boundaries of academic and legitimate knowledge (while being often hampered and contested).[5] It meets the theoretical, experimental practices of queer politics in the space of activists' self-experimentation, in the workshops of drag king and drag queen, in the *gender bender*[6] performances of contemporary artistic studios where Mieli's transqueer-feminist thought achieves a powerful appeal.

Precisely because Mieli's reflection is fuelled by homosexual activists' everyday experience and collective work of self-consciousness, through the book – although to a lesser extent with respect to the forthcom-

4. See the connection that Lorenzo Bernini proposes in his book, *Queer Apocalypses. Elements of Antisocial Theory*, Palgrave Macmillan, 2017.

5. As David Halperin lucidly relates in the introduction of *How to Be Gay*, Belknap Press, 2014.

6. This is the name of an International Queer Festival held every year in Europe.

ing poetical, theatrical and narrative productions – Mieli irrigates the practices of homosexual activism with a critical and radical thought permanently matched by experimental turns, within the interstices and the orifices of his intuitions, and of his own body. The liberation of Eros, as he states in Reichian and Marcusian Freudo-marxist terms, aiming at the revolutionary destruction of the heterosexual and heterosexist geography and economics of the social body, applies to current queer critiques of the *neoliberal neoliberation* of sexuality, and democratic promotion of gay and lesbian rights. An unexpected alliance and, I would say, an unexpected genealogy. Indeed, if we assume that without Michel Foucault, Judith Butler, Teresa de Lauretis and Eve Kosofsky Sedgwick, queer theories would not have existed in their present form, currently at the basis of numerous PhD dissertations, then without Mario Mieli, we could delight ourselves for hours and hours quibbling about a theoretical queer, granting ourselves the luxury not to confront the obscure material of a denied, repressed or even scared desire at which the queer marginality always stares.

III

After the publication of the book, Mieli acquires public visibility, within the movement and within the Italian intellectual environment. He participates in TV shows and releases interviews to the media. Nevertheless, his work is not limited to this book and spreads across a wide range of initiatives. Together with other comrades, Mieli founds a theatrical collective, writes and creates a *pièce,* which is played in several Italian cities: *La traviata Norma: ovvero vaffanculo... ebbene sì!* [The deviated Norma: or fuck you ... well, let's do it!]. Between 1976 and 1977, many queer theatrical collectives were born, giving life to a homosexual theatre season, whose themes reflects Mario Mieli's book contents: critique of heterosexuality and public exhibition of the erotic perversion of homosexual desire, of which some aspects nowadays would be considered unacceptable, such as pederasty – intended as the liberation from what Mieli calls the 'educastration' of children, and not as a praise for pedophilia. However, this clamour of revolutionary flavour does not seem to involve the larger movement. As had already happened in France after 1974 with the disappearance of FHAR, clearing the way for alternative groups of homosexual liberation – whose project was far less oriented towards revolution and much more towards building a large, organised and structured movement – between 1974 and 1978, the leaders of the Italian *Fuori!* decide to turn to parliamentary politics and to federate with the Radical Party. In 1978, they organised a Congress focussed on homosexual liberation and civil rights. This turn generates a deep fracture between the movement's reformist and revolutionary factions, which will progressively lead to the integral rewriting of *Fuori*'s political program. A core issue revolves around formal and political emancipation within the fields of law and rights. The revolutionary collectives, reduced to a minority and demobilised, will disappear to be replaced by other collectives that saw the revolutionary horizon no longer as a historical rupture with the past, but rather as a motivational discourse allowing the foundation of a new homosexual movement in the present.

To the extent that in 1979, during an interview for the journal *Lambda*, Mieli asserts that 'he is no longer part of the gay movement', a movement that is going in the direction of institutionalisation and normalisation. Moreover, these years mark the commercial remodelling of the 'ghetto', involving the consecration of gay virility and the refusal of gender crossing. In 1981, after a night out in a gay club in Milan, Mieli writes an article in which, in the guise of queer ethnographer, he accounts the failing hegemony of homosexual masculinity:

> Some of them are dancing with open pants exposing their butt, some of them are half naked, others dressed in Indian clothes, others as cowboys. Not the stuff of a saloon girl. The cocks that I'm sucking taste all the same. I don't know who's fucking me, if he's young or old, cute or ugly: I'm still looking ahead, with legs and cocks under my nose. Me, the sissy boy they didn't want to let in because I wasn't soldierlike enough, I'm animating the place. I despise all of them. They expose their own goods following the competitive market rules. No one looks at you in the eyes, or hardly. They just give a look-over. There's a big sense of guilt. It's impressive how in this virile acting, cocks fail.

And he tersely concludes:

> Damned men, they accept the ghetto rule and they can't even enjoy it. They have never heard of the metaphysics of sex. Tell them that if they can benefit from ghettoes like this one, they owe it to our

courage. Firstly, we act to let homosexuality come out of the closet! Those idiots let capital make a craze of this.[7]

While he continued to be politically engaged, in such matters as ecology and the dangers of nuclear war, Mieli is disappointed and enraged by what he sees as a movement's involution, and more generally, by what the public experience of homosexuality has become. His research of homosexual critique is turning into a poetical activity rather than a theoretical or political one. While he continues writing poems, he works on a novel, participates in a TV screenplay and performs some of his theatrical texts in several experimental theatre festivals in Milan.

In the early 1980s, Mieli is shifting in a kind of ascetic and esthetic mysticism, aiming at staying politically connected with the Italian intellectual scene while following a more spiritual route and research. He is looking for the solution to the hermetical and alchemical equation of himself being part of the real world. This search leads him to a journey in India, where he appears to be working on a second book, which unfortunately was lost. Perhaps, such loss is a sign of Mieli's own loss of sense during these years. In the poems written during the last months of life, his style becomes disconnected, uncertain, and unstable. The fragile queer marginality that Mieli could translate in political theories and practices seems now to generate a black hole, swallowing his gay genius, even going so far as to erode his body of existence from any possible foothold. It is no longer possible to love, fight or resist, to enjoy, write or maybe simply to think. The desire to build alternative realities, still radically queer, vanishes too.

On 12 March 1983, Mieli commits suicide in his flat, after having already performed his death in a tragically anticipatory text: *Ciò detto, passo oltre* [That said, I'm moving on]. The book is only a small part of the author's masterpiece, which contributed to design the matrix of queer theories and politics, even if the random architecture of this queer anticipation of the queer is revealed only *après-coup*. Reading *Towards a Gay Communism* in times of equal rights is without any doubt an invitation to think about how to resist the tautological symbolic of #LoveIsLove or the promotional rhetoric of #LoveWins. Reading Mieli today perhaps also means to rediscover the path that leads to those forms of political

7. Mario Mieli, 'La sagra dell'impotenza. Una serata al One Way', *Grattacielo*, March 1981, p. 36.

enjoyment, which do not feed victories – easy or difficult as they might be – but rather the failing positioning of critique and minority subjectivities, never completely coherent, never completely satisfactory and always deeply frustrating. Reading again Mieli's work, from a queer perspective, is somehow a renewed occasion to resist the discreet appeal of gay normativity, this feeling of existential power that comes from the formal and institutional recognition of a certain kind of homosexuality made of nuptial celebrations, familiar constrictions, natalist injunctions and nationalist pride. Perhaps, this is Mieli's queer legacy, a fucking invitation to think against, and first and foremost, against ourselves.

Massimo Prearo

Translator's Preface

Evan Calder Williams

Like any translation, this one is a product of several minds trying to find a language in common or, perhaps more importantly, the generative friction that comes from what always seems to elude the right combination of words. More often than not, that sort of messy confluence takes shape most explicitly between the author and the translator, even as they are shadowed by, and hopefully attuned to, all the echoes and traces of those whose dialogue, critiques, friendship, and influence irrevocably mark a text but too often go unnamed. In the case of this specific translation, there's another layer, as my work was to return to David Fernbach's excellent first rendering of the book into English. What I did was to translate chapters and chunks that had not been included in the version he published with Gay Men's Press in 1980; to thoroughly annotate the text as a whole, attending to Mieli's slippery puns and wordplay and especially to those newly added parts whose Italian cultural and political references might be otherwise obscure; and to cast fresh eyes over it, some 37 years later. In this way, what you'll read represents a fusion of David's and my approaches not only to trying to translate this incendiary and brilliant text, but also more generally to the questions and concerns given such unmistakable force, lucidity, and humour throughout it.

One consequence of this joint translation, with its main efforts separated by three and a half decades, is that it might let us read Mieli anew, as each of our efforts are surely marked by the relevant currents of those moments and what feels urgent to us. By reading anew, however, I don't mean from scratch, and certainly not according to a model of disinterested interpretation or some purportedly neutral 'objective' approach. That would fly straight in the face of so much of what this book does, in its genre-blurring prose that joins rigor to jokes, bilious and snarky anger to careful close reading, and especially in its insistence that all critique is corporally embodied, suffused with desire and loss in historically and personally precise ways, even if too few of us admit this fully. Rather, through the interval formed by the years between the book's appearance in 1977 (as well as the preceding years in which it took shape and David's translation three years later) and the appearance of this new edition in 2018, a parallax takes shape, and it is this span that might cast different light on Mieli's project. I won't remotely try to offer a full litany of the shifts and eddies of social history in those intervening decades, and perhaps it is enough to note with horror how relevant and timely much of the book still feels, given that this signifies how much has remained the same that deserved to be abolished forever. There have been four more decades of capital's persistence, four decades of ravages, crises, and mutations that, at the end of the day, leave its fundamental social relations intact and continually retrenched by mechanisms of racial policing, debt, social shaming, surveillance, border security, politics as usual, neofascist yearning, and all the rest of the manifold, lethal, and contradictory apparatus that constitutes the general defense system of a catastrophic status quo. Moreover, for all the gains made against the sanctioned tyranny of gendered, homophobic, and transphobic violence and control, it is all too clear both how prevalent it still is and how unevenly it is applied, particularly as an operation and logic never distinct from race and class but rather embedded within the ongoing threat and application of force aimed to bolster social order, the accumulation of capital, and the perpetuity of nations.

Towards a more modest end, then, I want to note shifts in two specific fields of inquiry within which this book seems likely to be situated and read. First, especially in the past decade, there has been a marked surge in interest amongst American and British left orbits in histories of Italian radicalism, especially of the years in which Mieli and *Fuori!* were active. We have seen extensive new investigations into Italian extraparliamentary formations, *operaismo* and autonomist Marxism, ultra-left critiques, 'worker's inquiries,' and, perhaps most crucially, the Marxist feminism of the 1970s associated with Lotta Femminista and Wages for Housework as well as individual figures such as Leopoldina Fortunati, Silvia Federici, and Mariarosa Dalla Costa. Especially in the portions of the text not included in the previous translation (in part because they are indeed highly particular to an Italian situation and resist transposition beyond that), Mieli's proximity to, and distance from, far-left currents of these years become more evident, revealing him to be a razor-sharp and engaged critic of his own moment. This can be seen, for instance, in the equally furious and mournful chapter on the murder of Pier Paolo Pasolini and in his extended theoretical devastation of the dangerous pablum of Franco Fornari, an influential Italian psychiatrist who was head of the Italian Psychoanalytic Society during the very years when Mieli was writing. Perhaps most compelling of these highly specific engagements, however, is the attempt to reckon with extraparliamentary and far-left formations at the time, as he blasts the preservation of patriarchal and homophobic structures reinforced within them, as well as the complicity with those of many who called themselves comrades.

Second, reading Mieli now necessarily means reading him not only in the history of gay liberation but also within contemporary constellations of queer theory and transgender studies more widely, fields whose development may be partially presaged by his book but were in no way as robust (and often institutionally sanctioned) as they are now. Bringing Mieli into contact with these strands is not a new endeavor, as his work has been a key touchpoint for many since the book was first published, but the timing of this edition brings it into a field that has seen not only crucial work on gender performativity and the lived histories of the AIDS epidemic (that temporal matrix of survival and mourning that makes the present haunted, 'the future of our past' in Didier Eribon's words). It also involves more recent tendencies of queer and trans theory centred around race and indigeneity, the hormonal and biochemical, animal studies, the impasses of heteronormative futurity, decolonisation, and posthumanism. In such a context, there are undoubtedly certain elements of Mieli's work that will feel too much of another time: the continual engagement with Freudian schematics; his particular version of thinking 'transsexuality'; the potential limits of its largely binary gender schema (i.e. the focus on bisexual being), even if it opens out towards a more fluid and 'polymorphous' plane; the degree to which the category of homosexuality is transposed across history, geography, and species; and its sometimes questionable analogies (such as that between colonial uprisings and gay liberation). But despite this, *Towards a Gay Communism* feels nothing like a mere historical curiosity to me, neither politically nor theoretically. It is now, as it was then, a bracing gust of laughter, acrimony, innovation, and expansive commitment to the communist prospect of going beyond what have come to be the assumed limits of human possibility. So our hope, in this new edition, is that its potential diversions from, and frictions with, more contemporary approaches to some of its burning questions are generative and unexpected, rather than seeming dead ends. After all, as familiar and potentially dated as its more familiar hybridisation of Marx and Freud might appear, certain of its key elements have started to feel uncannily present once again, like its obstinate insistence on the revolutionary necessity of gender abolition, its advocacy for a dramatically re-configured libidinal economy, its attention to traps of pleasure and complicity that bind us to calcified subject formations, or the transsexual future it sketches. Consider, for instance, the 'Letter from a Trans Man to the Old Sexual Regime', published by Paul B. Preciado, author of *Testo Junkie*, in *Le Monde*, some of whose lines could come straight from the pages of *Towards a Gay Communism* without missing a beat:

> This will be a 1000-year war – the longest of all wars, given that it will affect the politics of reproduction and processes through which a human body is socially constituted as a sovereign subject. It will actually be the most important of all wars, because what is at stake is neither territory nor city, but the body, pleasure, and life.[1]

Indeed, insofar as there is a substantive difference between this and Mieli's claim that 'we must either decide openly for life, for pleasure, or else accept the tragic scenario that capital has in store', it may lie above all in what has *not* vanished or become outmoded but rather so omnipresent as to vanish into plain sight. As Preciado's necessary work in recent years has shown, many of the mechanisms we must contest in this '1000-year war' are rarely as obvious as direct political antagonism or social exclusion. Rather, they are constituted at biological, technological, and libidinal levels that structure and rewire the very categories of visibility, engagement, and attention that they use to cloak themselves and their continued confining force.

The last element that I want to address here, one that I think our new translation draws out more fully due to materials not included previously, concerns precisely this point about how social control functions without being seen to do so. Specifically, it is about Mieli's relation to Marxism and to the *gay communism* that we've chosen to use as the overall title (rather than a literal translation of the original Italian title, *Elements of Homosexual Critique*). There's no doubt that *Towards a Gay Communism* is no work of 'orthodox' Marxism, even if I'd argue that designation is far

1. An English translation of the letter was published at 'Letter from a Trans Man to the Old Sexual Regime', Texte zur Kunst Online at: www.textezurkunst.de/articles/letter-trans-man-old-sexual-regime-paul-b-preciado/

less meaningful than its frequent deployment would indicate. The book is decidedly scornful, albeit often in an acidly playful way, of many of the predominant tendencies amongst the Italian and European left, from Maoism to centrist socialism, even as it remains undeniably committed to revolutionary political movements – provided that they are willing to deeply consider and unmake their own complicity with capital's reliance upon gender and heteronormativity, and, in so doing, to go beyond the affirmed limits of politics itself. Especially in its critique of persistent machismo in radical formations, Mieli shares much with the aforementioned variants of Italian Marxist feminism active in these same years, which also posed crucial challenges to the orthodoxy of what was allowed to count as *political*, let alone *militant*, even as those challenges were taken to heart far less than they deserved to be, and seemingly in inverse proportion to just how much they pointed out something deeply embedded and wholly worth tearing out.

So if *Towards a Gay Communism* is a book engaged with Marxism, just how so? It is, first of all, of an unmistakably Freudo-Marxist bent. Despite Mieli's relentless criticism of Freud, it is that criticism, and the general architecture of Freudian thought, in addition to its pathologisation of homosexuality, that drives much of the text. Indeed, one of the elements of this book that only became clearer to me during the process of translation was just how much of it is structured around a series of engagements with texts that Mieli doesn't merely disagree with but openly loathes, and for good reason: for the homophobic violence they excuse and naturalise, for their denigration of any subjectivity other than the norm, for their deadening of pleasure's convoluted and inconstant pathways, and for their unmistakable complicity with the order of capital as such. One result of this is that the book is studded with bilious and incisive takedowns, such as that of Fornari, although many of its most compelling and joyous – *gay*, Mieli would insist – moments come when he leaves behind both the Freudian hobbyhorse and the model of textual critique more generally to trace his speculative and desirous communism of recombinatory transindividuality.

All that said, the book is not only engaged with an expanded Marxist critique of capital but also deeply involved in its stakes. This is evident in the repetition of a single pair of terms – *formal domination* and *real domination* – that recur throughout the book and without which I don't think its force can be fully grasped. An attention to these terms isn't just my own preference or interpretation, however: they appear in the first sentences of the first full chapter, as a way to situate the historical ground on which his whole project takes hold:

> Contemporary gay movements have developed in countries where capital has reached the stage of real domination.
>
> However, while still under the formal domination of capital, and for the first time in history, homosexuals had organised themselves into a movement.

These terms, which Mieli partially unpacks in a footnote so long we have included it as an appendix, come specifically to him from Jacques Camatte, a French left communist thinker with whom Mieli carried on a correspondence and who wrote a long critical appraisal of *Towards a Gay Communism* in 1978. Camatte was associated with a heterodox group of theorists often deemed 'ultra-left' and, more specifically, with the journal *Invariance*.[2] The terms themselves are extensions of key concepts in Marx's own work, the 'formal subsumption of labour to capital' and the 'real subsumption of labour to capital'. Often statically interpreted as designating successive periods or stages, especially concerning the pivot to mass industrialisation, these terms are better understood as processes of articulation by which capital incorporates labouring activities into productive enterprises and the generation of surplus value. Formal subsumption specifies a relation in which those activities themselves are not constitutively altered but whose results are commodified, like agricultural production after the enclosure that continues to function much as it had for centuries but whose crops are now exchanged on the market, rather than consumed by its growers or forfeited to feudal lords. As Marx puts it plainly, 'There is no change as yet in the mode of production itself. *Technologically speaking*, the *labour process* goes on as before, with the proviso that it is now *subordinated* to capital.'[3] With formal subsumption, the only way to substantively increase surplus-value is to make people work longer, harder, and faster, and in this way, it suggests

2. Both Camatte and *Invariance* more generally drew especially on the work of Amadeo Bordiga, a communist and engineer who was involved in the initial formation of the Italian Communist Party but whose work after the fascist period grappled with a fascinating range of topics, from peasant communes to urban planning, 'natural' disasters and capitalist temporality.

3. Karl Marx, 'Results of the Immediate Process of Production', *Capital: A Critique of Political Economy, Vol. 1* (Harmondsworth: Penguin Books, 1976), p. 1026.

a mode of capitalism predicated on 'variable capital' (i.e. human labour) and reliant upon direct political control and coercion in order to enforce discipline and productivity. Real subsumption, conversely, designates how labouring activities are themselves transformed in accordance with the appropriation of surplus value, shaped into a concrete image of the social abstraction that impels their continuity.[4] It involves a major shift towards the importance of fixed capital, such as machinery, as is made plain in the most notorious figure of real subsumption, the factory, that inhuman assemblage of machinery, material, and workers that is increasingly organised, down to the smallest gestures, around the most efficient production of commodities possible. Crucially, with the real subsumption of labour to capital forms of direct *external* control and discipline become less effective, as the control schemas become embedded in the very material and social arrangement of production itself.

What, one might fairly ask, does this long detour have to do with a theory of transsexuality and gay communism, let alone with Mieli's analyses of pop stars and cruising? The key turn, for his central incorporation of the idea lies in how Camatte as well as Gianni Collu, another thinker in the *Invariance* orbit, shift from *subsumption* to *domination*. In the simplest sense, that shift involves raising formal and real subsumption from specific historical processes to historical periods. As Camatte and Collu put it, 'The starting point for the critique of the existing society of capital must be the reaffirmation of the concepts of formal and real domination as historical phases of capitalist development'.[5] Yet this is a restricted sense, a starting point indeed, because what is ultimately crucial in their work on this question is a way to understand what happens when that process of restructuring activities in accordance with an abstraction – i.e. subsuming discrete processes and practices to the form of value – spills far beyond just waged production or the factory floor. As the translators of Camatte's major work on this question into Italian (the volume that Mieli himself cites), formal and real domination are 'the extensions to all of society of the periodization of the develop-

4. The key point, in Camatte's gloss of this, is that the 'labour process' and 'valorization process' become unified in the 'immediate process of the production of capital'. And as he says, 'The transition from formal to real domination is linked to this transformation.' *Il capitale totale: il capitolo VI inedito de «Il capitale» e la critica dell'economia politica* (Bari: Dedalo, 1976), p. 89. All translations from this text are my own.

5. 'Transition', *Invariance*, Series I, n. 8, (1969). Available online at: http://revueinvariance.pagesperso-orange.fr/Transition.html. My translation.

ment of capital that one finds at the center of the analysis in Chapter 6', Marx's unfinished draft for a chapter in *Capital* which forms the core of Camatte's extensive theory.[6] So if, as Camatte argues, the foundation of capital required both expropriation (such as the enclosure of common land and the restriction of access to modes of reproducing and caring for a community) and autonomisation[7] (the decoupling of exchange value from the limited sphere of market exchanges, so as to become a general social form), the expanding real domination of capital means that this autonomisation bleeds outwards. Real domination involves, in short, a creeping substitution: the 'human community' and its processes of interchange and political decision-making – vicious and exploitative as its results historically could be, and certainly deserving of no nostalgic sighs – is gradually supplanted and remade by what Camatte calls the 'material community' of capital itself, a tautological network of accumulation and reproduction. This network, which has increasingly little need for those more conventional forms of political control (and hence reduces representational politics to a baleful game of lesser evils), slowly absorbs all forms of life and activities and leaves nothing but a variegated surface of capital, its sanctioned relations, and its support structures.[8] This material community both becomes increasingly dematerialised, in the sense of financialisation and in that of its diffuse cultural logic, and, if we push out from Camatte's reading, materially instantiated in the physical networks that facilitate the circulation of value, information, image, and human movement.

One of the major consequences of this is what it does to the possibility of critique and revolt, for 'if capital dominates everything to the point of being able to identify itself with the social being, it appears, on this basis, to disappear'.[9] In short, it poses a genuinely fundamental problem: how do we even discern what is to be challenged, what provides oppor-

6. Giovanni Dettori and Nicomede Folar, 'Nota sulla traduzione', *Il capitale totale*, p. 5.
7. I'd suggest that we also read autonomisation, in the early formation of capital, in the sense both of forcing persons onto the market as autonomous 'free individuals' and of the decoupling of accumulation from any automatic ties to a political and religious order, as in the feudal system.
8. As Camatte puts it plainly, 'if it is true that labour creates all wealth, so it is true that capital, as it appropriates surplus-value, seems to be endowed with this same ability. This occurs in the phase of real domination, in which everything appears as capital'. Camatte, *Il capitale totale*, p. 109.
9. 'Transition'.

tunities for antagonistic expansion, what is newly emerging, and what is merely the persistence of the accumulated detritus of the past? Faced with what Mieli calls 'the chameleon-like flatness that marks the real domination of capital', we stare at this camouflage of putative difference and supposed free choice, gazing at what seems at once constantly in flux and obstinately the same, and we search for some crack able to be pried open.

This, I would suggest, is the grounding understanding of the relation between capitalism and social forms that underwrite *Towards a Gay Communism*, and this is why Mieli introduces it at the very outset of his argument. What he does in the book that follows, then, is to demonstrate the utter centrality of homosexuality in both understanding and challenging this order. His approach to this is dual, involving both a history of homophobia (and its accompanying violence) and a speculative but wholly corporal horizon of generalised transsexuality and the liberation of Eros, a queer revolt in the name of pleasure against deadly and stultifying dominion. But it's worth insisting that he does not simply overlay Camatte's schematic onto a lived research into homosexuality or vice versa. Rather, this inquiry proceeds along two interrelated paths. First, he claims, we can only understand not just the structure of society in general but also the specific violence, marginalisation, and panic directed at queer populations if we adopt a framework able to detect how capital disappears by means of this autonomisation and saturation into all corners of life, especially including into those realms of pleasure and apparent transgression, unincorporability, and brief freedom. Second, however, he insists that the history of homosexuality and homophobia alike *cannot* be entirely explained within this framework. Not least of all, this is because, as he demonstrates at length, homophobia is hardly a novel invention that might be easily correlated to the enclosure of common lands and all else that follows. One would have to discount the reams of evidence that Mieli compiles of millennia of attacks on homosexual behavior in order to imagine that the horror of gay desire is simply one amongst many torqued expressions of the community of capital. Yet for Mieli, the fact that homosexuality cannot be contained wholly *within* this theoretical model and historical period doesn't mean that the model needs to be scrapped. Rather, it does not fit cleanly because homosexuality is in excess of real domination, both in its revolutionary potential and in the continual panic and retribution it engenders. So over the wandering path of the text, he insists that the prospect and practice of gay liberation bears a unique insight into the structures of capital's real domination, and that this insight – never in theory alone, always constituted by the bravery of those who desire something *other* – detects and widens several of those elusive cracks. What is that insight and force? It is capacity to disrupt what he calls the 'absurd absolutisation of contingent historical values and the hypostasis of opinions (scientific, ethico-moral, socio-political, psychological) that are in reality relative and transitory'. It is a refusal of the idea that heterosexuality is 'eternosexuality', as he puts, and that this arrangement of corporal pleasure, access, and judgment is transhistorical. It is, above all, a challenge to the calcification of a certain vision of the human, one that has been gradually molded to double and mimic the contours of the material community of capital. To call for a gay communism, as he does, isn't just to add a qualifier. It is to assert that the process of the abolition of a present cursed equally by its past and prescribed future will require a total remapping of the values of productivity, civility, usefulness, and decency that have been congealed into the model of heterosexuality and literally beaten into those who contest it.

Two final comments, on the occasion of the release of this book.

First, I undertook this project in memory and honour of our comrade Chris Chitty, whose remarkable work on the history of homosexuality Mieli would surely have loved and from which I learned deeply. I can only hope that new readership of Mieli's text will have the same vivifying, challenging, and radicalising effect on readers that Chris' work and life did on all of us.

Second, this edition will be released into a cultural and political landscape where an assemblage of neofascists, men's rights advocates, white supremacists, rape apologists, old-fashioned conservatives, and blowhard fools join together in arguing that capitalism, white supremacy, and Western civilisation itself are under assault from a subversive program of 'cultural Marxism' and postmodernism that seeks to erode cherished values and bring about the perverse reign of a queer communist abolitionary mob. I'm reminded once again of Guy Hocquenghem's precise diagnosis: 'society' is, in this respect, paranoiac: it suffers from an interpretative delusion which leads it to discover all around it the signs of a homosexual conspiracy that prevents it from functioning properly.'[10]

10. Guy Hocquenghem, *Homosexual Desire* (Durham: Duke University Press, 1993), p. 55.

(Some things never change, it seems.) So in this context, I can't help but feel a small degree of satisfaction that my efforts towards bringing about the new release of this book will contribute to offering a text that argues stridently for exactly what those joyless bores are so terrified of. As Mieli puts it in the very pages that follow: *Oh my gay God!*

Preface

> We are entirely correct when we say that the only experts on homosexuality are homosexuals. – Herbert Spiers[1]

This book grew out of a university thesis on homosexuality. That fact is responsible, I believe, for some of its limitations, and in the first place for a certain discordance of style between the stilted tones of academia and the less inhibited gay mode of expression. There is also a discordance of content in that some themes have been investigated more deeply, while others have remained more or less at the level at which they were originally drafted.

As a thesis, this book essentially focussed on male homosexuality, even if many of its arguments bear on homosexuality in general. As a gay man, I have preferred to discuss female homosexuality as little as possible; for only lesbians can really know what lesbianism is, rather than just speaking about it in the abstract.

Moreover, at a time when the homosexual question is generally understood as uncharted waters[2] that open out into the wider ocean of the women's question, I decided to limit myself to addressing six points in particular:

1) I have tackled from my own perspective, one that was matured and rejuvenated in the ambits of the gay movement, many of the most widespread anti-homosexual commonplaces and some of the best known psychoanalytic theories that bear on homosexuality. I did this because I think it opportune, even on a 'theoretical basis', to oppose the opinions of us gays to the traditional opinions of the heteros, which as a rule share – more or less deliberately, more or

---

1. Herbert Spiers, 'Psychiatric Neutrality: An Autopsy', in *The Body Politic*, no. 7, Winter 1973, pp. 14–15. [Translator's note: The epigraph was presented in English by Mieli in the Italian text.]

2. [Translator's note: Mieli here uses the Latin phrase *mare magnum*, which literally means 'great sea' (and often referred to the Mediterranean) but came to denote figuratively both a maelstrom and, crucially for this context, an unmapped zone where expected forms of navigation and cartography were of little use.]

less consciously – the prejudices of a certain reactionary rabble,[3] i.e. all those doctors, psychologists, magistrates, politicians, priests, etc. who peddle as truth on the homosexual question the crudest lies – or, more rarely, the more subtle ones. We, who refuse to identify ourselves with their 'science', base ourselves rather on a *gay science.*

2) I have briefly summarised the repression of homosexuality in history (or *prehistory*, in the Marxist sense), with the aim of recording the *historical origin* of the anti-homosexual taboo and demonstrating how terrible the persecution perpetrated against us homosexuals was in the past, and can still be today.
3) I have insisted on the *universal* presence of homosexual desire, *normally* negated by capitalist-heterosexual ideology. Still today, it is generally held that the homosexual question exclusively concerns a minority, a limited number of queers and lesbians: they don't want to take into account how as long as homosexuality remains repressed, the homosexual will be a *problem* concerning everyone, insofar as gay desire is present in every human being, congenitally so, even if in the majority of cases it is repressed or semi-repressed.
4) I have tried to cast light on the relation that exists between homoeroticism and what stands behind the 'veil of illusion' i.e. what is beyond ordinary perception and that which is commonly considered as 'normal' and hypostatised by the system. I have indicated that homosexuality is a bridge towards a decidedly other dimension of existence, sublime and profound, one that is in part revealed by so-called 'schizophrenic' experiences.
5) I have emphasised the importance of the liberation of homosexuality in the context of *human emancipation*; indeed, for the creation of communism, one of the sine qua non, among others, will be the complete disinhibition of homoerotic tendencies, which, if freed, can guarantee the attainment of a totalising communication between human beings, independent of their sex.

3. [Translator's note: The word he uses here is *canaglia*, which carries heavy echoes, particularly in its sense of a condemnation of the masses as rabble. In Italian, it also suggests a scoundrel or riffraff, linked etymologically to the word *cane* ('dog'). Here, this meaning is flipped to signify the well-heeled pack of what Mieli later terms the 'psychonazis' hounding homosexuals.]

6) I have defined as *transsexual*[4] our potential erotic availability, constrained by repression to latency or subjected to a more or less severe repression, and I have therefore indicated in *transsexuality* the telos (a genuine telos, insofar as it is *internal*) of the struggle for the liberation of Eros.

I hope this book will promote the liberation of gay desire among all who now repress it, and will aid gay people who are still enslaved by the sense of guilt induced by social persecution to free themselves from this false guilt. It is high time to root this out, as it only helps to perpetuate the deadly domination of capital. It is time to oppose both this determination and the heterosexual Norm that contributes to maintaining it by guaranteeing, among other things, the subjection of Eros to alienated labour and the divisions between men, between women, and between women and men.

I am deeply grateful to Rosa Carotti, Adriana Guardigli, Corrado Levi, Manolo Pellegrini and in particular Francesco Santini for having helped me write this book. I also want to thank: Angelo Pezzana, who advised me to publish it, Myriam Cristallo, who was the first to read it, and Walter Pagliero, who lent me books and articles which proved very helpful. And I am indebted to Silvia Colombo, Marcello Dal Lago, Franco Fergnani, Maria Martinotti, Denis Rognon, Guia Sambonet, Anna Sordini, Aldo Tagliaferri and Annabella Zaccaria for their valuable suggestions.

I have used the terms 'homosexuality' and 'homoeroticism' as synonymous, and 'gay' as a synonym for 'homosexual' or 'homoerotic'. I have used the term 'pederasty' only in its proper sense, to define erotic desire directed at a very young person.

4. [Translator's note: As Mieli does not hyphenate this word, and in order to put it in closer dialogue with contemporary trans and queer theory, I have followed his lead and left it unhyphenated.]

1
Homosexual Desire is Universal

The Gay Movement Against Oppression

Contemporary gay movements have developed in countries where capital has reached the stage of real domination.[1] However, while still under the formal domination of capital, and for the first time in history, homosexuals had organised themselves into a movement. This happened first of all in Germany, in the second half of the nineteenth century, thanks to the spread of the work of Karl Ulrichs and the subsequent foundation of the Scientific Humanitarian Committee in 1897,[2] as it did in different ways in England, and then in the first decades of this century in Holland, Austria, the USA, Soviet Russia, and other countries. The homosexual movement did not invariably take the fixed organisational form that distinguished the Scientific Humanitarian Committee and its international offshoot, the World League for Sexual Reform, but in many countries, even without producing specific formal organisations, it still gave rise to a wide debate on homosexuality that involved for the first time a considerable number of cultural and political 'personalities' and brought to light problems and arguments which had until then been passed over in silence, in deference to one of the severest of taboos.

1. See Karl Marx, 'Results of the Immediate Process of Production', published as an appendix to *Capital: A Critique of Political Economy, Volume 1* (New York: Pelican Books, 1976). [Translator's note: particularly pp. 1019–36; see also Jacques Camatte, *Il capitale totale: il <<capitolo VI>> inedito de «Il capitale» e la critica dell'economia politica* [Total Capital] (Bari, Dedalo Libri, 1976). This volume of Camatte's from which Mieli is working has not been translated into English directly, but there is a 1988 English translation by David Brown for Unpopular Books of a French volume that comprises the same texts: Jacques Camatte, *Capital and Community: The Results of the Immediate Process of Production and the Economic Work of Marx*, trans. David Brown (London: Unpopular Books, 1988). Given this, however, in Appendix B, I am translating and citing the Camatte passages from the Italian version on which Mieli himself was drawing, although I am consulting the French for accuracy.]
2. See John Lauritsen and David Thorstad, *The Early Homosexual Rights Movement (1864–1935)* (New York: Times Change Press, 1974), pp. 9ff.

The violent persecution of homosexuals by Nazism, Stalinism and fascism obliterated this movement, and with it the very memory of this first major international homosexual self-assertion, thereby re-establishing the absolute ideology of the Norm. Due to this setback, it was only through the research of the new gay movement, re-emerging in 1969 with the Gay Liberation Front in the United States, and subsequently spreading to several other countries, that those of us born in more recent decades became at all aware of the existence of an earlier gay movement, and came to see ourselves as engaged – contrary to what we had believed – in a second wave of the liberation movement and not in the first. Some of the questions that we raise today, for example, involve themes that were already tackled by the first gay movement. One of these, in particular, still concerns homosexuals today as much as those in the past: *for what reasons does society marginalise us and repress us so harshly?*

To this and other questions, we have tried to reply with a research starting from our own personal experience, whether by talking together at general meetings about our existential and social condition as homosexuals and comparing our experiences, or by committing ourselves more deeply to the analysis of individual experience, undertaking the 'work' of self-awareness in smaller consciousness-raising or 'awareness' groups. As a result, we have begun to understand better what we are, and why we have been oppressed, in the process of coming together on the basis of our common desire and with the viewpoint of liberation.

The new gay movement has also resumed the historical and anthropological investigations started by the first wave, shedding light on the persecution of homosexuals across the centuries and on the historical origin of anti-gay condemnation, a condemnation that is almost invariably peddled by the ideology of heterosexual primacy as simply *natural*. And if the old movement had a strong commitment to psychological research, in the new movement groups have formed that concern themselves instead with psychiatry, struggling against the anti-homosexual persecution perpetrated in the guise of psychiatric treatment. The gay movement totally rejects the reactionary (pre)judices against homosexuality displayed by mainstream psychiatry, yet revolutionary homosexuals also oppose the new 'progressive' but completely heterosexual view of homosexuality currently widespread in anti-psychiatry circles.[3]

3. [Editor's note from the original volume: Anti-psychiatry, or alternative psychiatry, is an orientation that challenges the repressive function of traditional psychiatry and

The work of consciousness-raising has also brought us face to face with elements of psychoanalytic theory that refers to homosexuality. We have discovered in psychoanalysis some important ideas, such as that of the unconscious, for example, and repression – ideas which we can integrate at least temporarily into our own gay science. As a result, we have reached the firm conclusion that the hatred generated towards us within heterosexual society is caused by the repression of the homoerotic component of desire in those individuals who are apparently heterosexual. The general repression of homosexuality, in other words, determines the rejection by society of the manifest expressions of the gay desire. The question now is what it is that provokes this repression; and we believe we shall discover the hidden motives for this by combatting the repression itself, i.e. by spreading the pleasure and desire of homosexuality.[4] It is in the struggle for liberation that we shall come to understand why we have up till now been slaves – and we are all slaves, both gay and straight alike.

But if repression is a psychoanalytic concept, it was also psychoanalysis, in modern times that first upheld the universality of homosexual desire. In Freud's words, 'in all of us, throughout life, the libido normally oscillates between male and female objects'.[5] Why, then, we might ask,

---

proposes a new way of treating mental illness, no longer based on the use of violence and of segregation as 'therapy' and no longer organised around the centrality of the concept of social normality. It developed on an international level between the end of the 1960s and start of the 1970s. Its most well-known representative in Italy was Franco Basaglia (1924–1980), to whose work we also owe Law 180 in 1978, which abolished mental hospitals.]

4. [Translator's note: Mieli's language here turns on an essentially untranslatable pun on the words *combattendo* (struggling) and *battendo* (cruising). While obscure in English, his original footnote in Italian explaining the sense is as follows: 'In this book I always use the term *battere* (to beat) in the gay sense of going to look for someone with whom to have sex (or making the effort, or putting one's self on display). If in the language of male and female prostitutes *battere* means looking for clients, for us homosexuals *battere* doesn't mean prostituting ourselves but rather, more simply, searching for other people 'like us'. (It can always happen, in this way, that you meet an American or a man from [the wealthy area around Lake] Como who offers you a room at the Hilton and a Baccarat pink crystal *corbeille* [fruit bowl].) In the gay sense, the Italian *battere* corresponds to the French *draguer*, *to cruise* in English, to the German . . . I don't know. (There's here with me at the moment a Viennese gay, helpless to recall the equivalent expression in his mother tongue.)']

5. Freud, 'The Psychogenesis of a Case of Homosexuality in a Woman', *Standard Edition*, Vol. 18 (London: Vintage, 2001), p. 158.

if all people are also homosexual, do so few admit this and enjoy their homosexuality?

Polymorphous 'Perversity', Bisexuality and Transsexuality

> The hermaphrodite was a distinct sex in form as well as in name, with the characteristics of both male and female, but now the name alone remains, and that solely as a term of abuse. – Plato[6]

Psychoanalysis comes to the conclusion of an infantile *'perverse' polymorphism* and *recognises in every individual an erotic disposition towards others of the same sex*. According to Freud, the child is 'constitutionally disposed' to this *'perverse' polymorphism*, and all the so-called 'perversions' form part of infantile sexuality (sadism, masochism, coprophilia, exhibitionism, voyeurism, homosexuality, etc.). In fact, 'a disposition to perversions is an original and universal disposition of the human sexual instinct and . . . normal sexual behaviour is developed out of it as a result of organic changes and psychical inhibitions occurring in the course of maturation.'[7]

Among the forces that inhibit and restrict the direction of the sexual drive are, above all, 'the structures of morality and authority erected by society.'[8] Repressive society and dominant morality consider only heterosexuality as 'normal' – and only genital heterosexuality at that. Society operates repressively on children, above all through an *educastration* designed to eradicate those congenital sexual tendencies deemed 'perverse.' (Moreover, one could say that today, more or less all infantile sexual impulses are considered 'perverse,' including heterosexual ones, the child having no right to erotic enjoyment.) The objective of educastration is the transformation of the infant, in tendency polymorphous and 'perverse', into a heterosexual adult, erotically mutilated but conforming to the Norm.

The majority of psychoanalysts recognise sexual expressions even in the very first months of life, and have established steps of sexual development that we can sum up as *autoeroticism – homosexuality – heterosexuality*.

---

6. Plato, *Symposium* (Harmondsworth: Penguin Books, 1966), p. 59.
7. Sigmund Freud, 'Three Essays on the Theory of Sexuality', *Standard Edition*, Vol. 7 (London: Vintage, 2001), p. 231.
8. Ibid.

But this is in no way a 'natural' evolution; it rather reflects the repressive influence of the child's social and family environment. There is nothing in life itself that requires the child to 'grow out' of autoeroticism and the homosexual 'stage' in order to attain this exclusive heterosexuality. The environment in which we live is heterosexual (in the first place the family, the cell of the social tissue), in that it forces the child, through a sense of guilt, to abandon the satisfaction of his auto- and homoerotic desires, obliging him to identify with a mutilated monosexual (heterosexual) model. Obviously, this does not always succeed.

Psychoanalysis defines the first expressions of eroticism as 'undifferentiated,' or only a little so. In other words, the selection of an object, for the infant, is due more to circumstances than to biological sex (and to circumstances that can change even in the course of a day). Little girls are all also lesbians, and little boys are all also gay.

To those who still wonder whether they are born homosexual or become so, we must reply that everyone is born endowed with a wide range of erotic propensity, directed first of all towards the self and the mother, then gradually turning outward to 'everyone' else, irrespective of their sex, and in fact towards the entire world. They become either heterosexual or homosexual only as a result of educastration (repressing their homoerotic impulses in the first case, and their heterosexual ones in the second).

At this point, however, we might pause to consider whether these tendencies are actually repressed in the strict sense. According to Georg Groddeck, for example, no heterosexual really represses all his homoerotic desires, even if he believes himself to have done so. Rather than repressed, the majority of people most commonly exhibit a latent homosexuality (just as the desire for the opposite sex is latent, as a general rule, in gays). According to Freud, again, 'we have two kinds of unconscious: the one which is latent but capable of becoming conscious, and the one which is repressed and which is not, in itself and without more ado, capable of becoming conscious'.[9] To be quite correct, we should therefore speak of both latent homosexual desires and others that are effectively repressed. But since it is not always easy to distinguish the two, I shall speak sometimes of latent homosexual desire and in other contexts of the repression of homosexuality, without establishing too fine a distinc-

9. Sigmund Freud, 'The Ego and The Id', *Standard Edition,* Vol. 19 (London: Vintage, 2001), p. 14.

tion and thus using the concept in a somewhat elastic sense. In any case, faced with skilled seduction by a gay person, it is not repression that wins out; sooner or later, all heterosexuals give in. All are latent queens.

In actual fact, latent homosexuality exists in everyone who is not a manifest homosexual, as a residue of infantile sexuality, polymorphous and 'perverse', and hence also gay. A *residue*, because homoeroticism has been repressed by society, condemned to latency and sublimated in the form of feelings of friendship, comradeship, etc., as well as being converted, or rather distorted, into pathological syndromes.[10]

I shall use the term *transsexuality* throughout this book to refer to the infantile polymorphous and 'undifferentiated' erotic disposition, which society suppresses and which, in adult life, every human being carries within him either in a latent state, or else confined in the depths of the unconscious under the yoke of repression. 'Transsexuality' seems to me the best word for expressing, at one and the same time, both the plurality of the erotic tendencies and the original and deep hermaphrodism of every individual. But what exactly is this hermaphrodism?

In psychoanalytic theory, the claim of 'perverse' infantile polymorphism goes hand in hand with the theory of *original bisexuality*. (And this theory will also make clearer what I mean by transsexuality and the transsexual nature of our underlying being.) The theory of original bisexuality was first put forward – among other reasons – to explain the causes of so-called 'sexual inversion' (i.e. homosexuality).[11] Its roots lay in the discovery of the coexistence in the individual of somatic factors common to both sexes. This was well summed up by Daniel Paul Schreber (even though he was not a medical man but a crazy old queen): 'In the first months of pregnancy the rudiments of both sexes are laid down and the characteristics of the sex which is not developed remain as rudimentary organs at a lower stage of development, like the nipples of the male.'[12] The same applies to the female clitoris. *Similar observations of this kind were taken to mean that sex is never unitary, and that monosexuality rather conceals a certain bisexuality (a hermaphrodism).* According to psychoanalysis, we are all bisexual beings.

10. See Chapter 3.

11. The term 'homosexuality' (from the Greek *homos*, alike) was coined in 1869 by the Hungarian doctor Benkert; Lauritsen and Thorstad, *The Early Homosexual Rights Movement (1864–1935)*, p. 6.

12. Daniel Paul Schreber, *Memoirs of My Nervous Illness* (London: Harvard University Press, 1988), p. 231.

This question has been comprehensively studied by genetic theory and endocrinology. In the words of Gilbert Dreyfus:

> Although genetic sex is determined by the composition of the fertilising spermatozoon, so that the father alone is responsible for the genetic sex of his offspring, the embryo undergoes in its early development a phase of apparently undifferentiated sexuality. It is only in the second month of foetal life that the rudimentary genitals begin to differentiate, so as to end up – after a long process and according to whether the first growth of tissue later develops or atrophies to make way for a second growth – with the formation of a testicle or an ovary. But even in adults, there remain in both sexes residues of the other, as evidence of the dual male and female development of the embryonic gonads and the double reproductive system with which the embryo is initially endowed.[13]

It can happen, in this embryonic development, that discrepancies arise between genetic and genital sex (and so, the son of Hermes and Aphrodite merges with the body of the nymph Salmacis).[14] This gives rise to combinations of male and female characteristics, causes of what is termed 'pseudo hermaphrodism', 'inter-sexuals', or, better, 'cases' of *manifest transsexuality.*[15]

But not all these 'cases' are determined simply by unusual physiological conditions. There are many conscious transsexuals, for example, who are physiologically every bit as male as the butchest heterosexual. What does it mean, then, to be manifestly transsexual today?

In general, we call 'transsexuals' those adults who consciously live out their own hermaphrodism, and who recognise in themselves, in their body and mind, the presence of the 'opposite' sex.

At the present time, the 'cases' of manifest transsexuality are still subject to the contradiction between the sexes and the repression of Eros, which

13. Gilbert Dreyfus, 'L'omosessualità vista da un medico', *Ulisse* xviii (1953), p. 642.
14. [Translator's note: Mieli is riffing off the description in Ovid's *Metamorphoses* of the rape of Hermaphroditus by the nymph Salmacis, who traps them beneath the water until the two merge into an inseparable, intersex form that is no longer distinct bodies but a 'two-fold form'. In a fitting nod to Mieli's argument here, Salmacis declares that, 'It is right to struggle, perverse one, but you will still not escape.']
15. The most informative work on this subject is Harry Benjamin, *The Transsexual Phenomenon* (New York: Warner Books, 1966).

is the repression of the universal transsexual (or polymorphous and hermaphrodite) disposition common to all human individuals. Persecuted by a society that cannot accept any confusion between the sexes, they frequently tend to reduce their effective transsexuality to an apparent monosexuality, seeking to identify with a historically 'normal' gender opposite to their genital definition. Thus a female transsexual feels herself a man, opting for the male gender role, while a male transsexual feels himself a woman. A human being of 'imprecise' sex has a much harder time just getting around than does a male person who seems, by all external signs, to be a woman, or vice versa. This is why people who recognise themselves as transsexual in the present society often want to 'change' (genital) sex by surgical operation, in Casablanca or Copenhagen, or rather more frequently, restrict themselves to strict psychological identification with the 'opposite' sex.[16] Society induces these manifest transsexuals to feel monosexual and to conceal their real hermaphrodism. To tell the truth, however, this is exactly how society behaves with all of us. *In fact we are all, deep down, transsexuals, we have all been transsexual infants, and we have been forced to identify with a specific monosexual role, masculine or feminine.* In the case of manifest transsexuals, or those rare persons who have not repressed their transsexuality in growing up, the social constraint produces the opposite effect from what it does in 'normal' people, in as much as a male person tends to identify with the feminine role, and vice versa.

As we shall see, manifest transsexualism does not necessarily involve a particular propensity for homosexuality. There are many heterosexual transsexuals. But when, for example, these are males who feel themselves to be women, but who also sexually desire other women, their heterosexuality is then, in a certain sense, homosexuality. Far from being particularly absurd, transsexualism overthrows the presently separate and counterposed categories of that sexuality considered 'normal,' revealing it to be, in fact, a ridiculous constraint.

In any case, *through those people who recognise themselves as transsexuals today, we can glimpse the transsexuality (bisexuality) that is latent in everyone.* Their particular condition has brought them more or less close

16. [Translator's note: Mieli's reference to Casablanca and Copenhagen is linked to the fact that at the time he was writing this, gender reassignment surgery was illegal in Italy; the cities named were two of the better-known alternatives in which to seek operations. Gender reassignment surgery would become legalised in Italy by 1982.]

to an awareness, potentially a revolutionary one, *of the fact that every human being, embryologically bisexual, maintains for his or her whole life, both in biological and psychological aspects, the presence of the other sex.* I believe that the resolution of the present separate and antithetical categories of sexuality will be transsexual, and that transsexuality discloses the synthesis, one and many, of the expressions of a liberated Eros. I shall often return to this argument later on.[17]

For the time being, I simply want to stress how 'our hormonal bisexuality is amply demonstrated,'[18] and how the determination of 'definitive' and manifest sex membership at birth generally signifies only the 'predominance' of this sex in the individual, and does not eliminate altogether the 'opposite' sexual presence.

From the phylogenic standpoint, registration of such biological, anatomical and endocrinological data leads to the conception of 'an originally bisexual physical disposition [which] has, in the course of evolution, become modified into a unisexual one, leaving behind only a few traces of the sex that has become atrophied'.[19]

The transposition of this conception into the mental field was of particularly great importance, leading to the interpretation of homosexuality 'in all its varieties as the expression of a psychical hermaphrodism.'[20] But if the theory of psychical hermaphrodism helped psychoanalysis to demonstrate the possibility of so-called sexual 'inversion', it also raised very far-reaching questions as to the fixation of the sexual drive in so-called 'normal' people onto 'objects' of the 'opposite' sex. 'Thus from the point of view of psychoanalysis the exclusive sexual interest felt by men for women is also a problem that needs elucidating and is not a self-evident fact based upon an attraction that is ultimately of a chemical nature.'[21] According to Groddeck, it is more difficult to explain why heterosexual impulses are averted than to understand why there exist in all

17. This book is intended, above all, for a popular audience. I am therefore not diving into all the esoteric debates over the issue of the androgynous (or the gyandromorphic). This is also because on this long path, I am taking only some first steps – and from my own experiences alone I might, if so desired, write a novel, but certainly not a scholarly study, given my ignorance. All the same, I deal in Chapter 5 with the theme of the transsexual in relation to the trip deemed as 'schizophrenic'.
18. Dreyfus, 'L'omosessualità vista da un medico', p. 643.
19. Freud, 'Three Essays', *Standard Edition,* Vol. 7 (London: Vintage, 2001), p. 141.
20. Ibid.
21. Ibid., p. 146 (note added in 1915).

people homosexual tendencies, which as he sees it, 'necessarily follows upon self-love'.[22]

Is there a close relationship, then, between hermaphrodism, physical and mental, and homosexuality? Yes, in that homosexuality is congenital in everyone and hence expresses the polymorphism of our underlying transsexual and hermaphrodite being. In the same way, too, the erotic tendencies directed towards the 'opposite' sex form part of our polymorphism, so that these are equally expressions of this underlying hermaphrodism. Both homosexual desire and desire for the other sex derive from the transsexual nature of our underlying being.

This is shown all the more clearly in the fact that heterosexuality is itself often accompanied by what the doctors, in repressive language, call 'morphological and hormonal disturbances'. Continuing to borrow this hateful medical jargon, heterosexual men can also be 'hypomasculine' and 'effeminate'. The hormonal characteristic that accompanies these forms of 'hypomasculinity' is 'a collapse of the androgen/estrogen ratio, as a result of a fall in the numerator and a rise in the denominator'.[23] Manifest heterosexuality, therefore, is often accompanied by clear expressions of physical hermaphrodism.

On the other hand, despite the stereotype that identifies the gay man as 'effeminate', a high percentage of manifest homosexuals do not show any particular form of 'hypomasculinity' or 'effeminacy'. To sum up, there is no direct correspondence between 'hypomasculinity' and male homosexuality, nor between 'hypofemininity' and female homosexuality. 'Masculine' women may be decidedly heterosexual, and very 'feminine' women can be gay.

As for the presumed relationship between 'mental effeminacy' and male homosexuality, and conversely for women, Freud noted:

> The literature of homosexuality usually fails to distinguish clearly enough between the questions of the choice of object on the one hand, and of the sexual characteristics and sexual attitude of the subject on the other, as though the answer to the former necessarily involved the answers to the latter. Experience, however, proves the contrary: a man with predominantly male characteristics and also masculine in his erotic life may still be inverted in respect to his object, loving

22. Georg Groddeck, *The Book of the It* (London: C.W. Daniel, 1935), p. 202.
23. Dreyfus, 'L'omosessualità vista da un medico', p. 644.

> only men instead of women. A man in whose character feminine attributes obviously predominate, who may, indeed, behave in love like a woman, might be expected, from this feminine attitude, to choose a man for his love-object; but he may nevertheless be heterosexual, and show no more inversion in respect to his object than an average normal man. The same is true of women; here also mental sexual character and object-choice do not necessarily coincide. The mystery of homosexuality is therefore by no means so simple as it is commonly depicted in popular expositions – 'a feminine mind, bound therefore to love a man, but unhappily attached to a masculine body; a masculine mind, irresistibly attracted to women, but, alas! imprisoned in a feminine body'.[24]

To put it more simply, contrary to every stereotype, a macho guy can just as well be a queen, while a man with a slender and refined body can be an inveterate womaniser. A pure young girl can be a lesbian, and a strapping schoolmistress can be hopelessly heterosexual. That is the way of the world.

In conclusion, we can say that neither manifest homosexuality nor heterosexuality necessarily correspond to any specific mental, somatic, or hormonal characteristics; both the gay desire and the desire for the other sex are expressions of our underlying transsexual being, in tendency polymorphous, but constrained by oppression to adapt to a monosexuality that mutilates it. But the repressive society only considers one type of monosexuality as 'normal', the heterosexual kind, and imposes educastration with the aim of exclusively conditioning heterosexuality. The Norm, therefore, is heterosexual.

The Assertion of Heterosexuality and the Misconception of the Woman Within

The theory of bisexuality was originally postulated by psychiatry as the basis for an etiology of 'sexual inversion'. We have seen how psychoanalysis, which took over this theory, was nevertheless soon forced to investigate the causes for this fixation of desire on 'objects' of the opposite sex on the part of people considered sexually 'normal' by society. The question that now arises is: *why, in the course of development, the individual passes from an 'undifferentiated' erotic disposition directed towards both*

24. Freud, 'The Psychogenesis of a Case of Homosexuality in a Woman', p. 170.

sexes, such as is characteristic of the infantile libido, to a fixation (whether hetero- or homosexual) on one sex alone as the 'object' of desire? 'The question, then, is how to opt for a unisexuality.' (Jacques Camatte)

The immediate reply is that this happens by the work of educastration, or by the influence on the individual of society and the 'external' world in which a monosexual Norm prevails, transmitting the repression from generation to generation. In any event, the monosexual Norm is decidedly heterosexual, and the educastration that seeks to universally affirm this makes it that, among the majority of people, monosexuality presently takes the form of heterosexuality. The Norm is based on the mutilation of Eros, and in particular on the condemnation of homosexuality. It is clear from this that only when we understand why the homoerotic impulse is repressed in the majority, by the whole mechanism of society, will we be able to grasp how the exclusive or at least highly predominant assertion of heterosexual desire in the majority comes about. On the other hand, the problem of the repression of homosexuality is also clearly connected, today, with the assertion of an exclusively or at least prevalently homoerotic desire in us gay men and women, because, historically, it is the repression of homoeroticism that contributes so greatly to characterising the present-day expressions of manifest homosexuality.

We know how the little boy is forced in growing up to develop, above all else, those tendencies that are an expression of his psychological 'masculinity'. It is society that forces him to do this in the first place via the family, just as, through education and the family, society forces the little girl to develop those aspects of her personality that are expressions of psychological 'femininity'. In this way, educastration tends above all else to negate the mental and biological hermaphrodism that is present in us all, in order to make the little girl into a woman and the little boy into a man according to the counterposed models of heterosexual polarity. The psychological 'masculinity' and 'femininity' that are respectively demanded from the little boy and girl in the process of education (which is above all a relation of subordination to the parents, and more generally, to all adults), simply reflect the contingent and mutilated historical forms which society makes into something absolute, and which are based on the subjection and oppression of women, the estrangement of the human being from itself, and the negation of human community.[25]

25. [Translator's note: The reference to *human community* is both an echo of Marx's notion of *Gemeinwesen* and to Camatte's extensive articulation of the term. See the Translator's Preface for a brief note on the relation of Mieli's work to Camatte's.]

The little boy is forced by society and the family to take his father as a model for his own life. He must aspire to be like him in every respect, but he can only do so at the cost of the full flowering of his own potential, i.e. by a mutilation. The father, in fact, has already suffered educastration, so that the son can only identify with him at the price of his own mutilation.

Gradually, through this identification, the child, like his father, comes to project onto the mother and other women the 'feminine' elements that exist within his own psyche, elements that are not to be admitted to consciousness, leading him to be ashamed of them, despite the deep attraction that they hold as fundamental components of his own being. This is responsible for one of the greatest disasters that has happened to our species: the refusal by the man to recognise the 'woman' in himself, i.e. to recognise his transsexuality.

In Jung's words, the father becomes the model for the son's persona: 'The persona is a complicated system of relations between individual consciousness and society, fittingly enough a kind of mask, designed on the one hand to make a definite impression upon others, and, on the other, to conceal the true nature of the individual.'[26]

Through this identification with the father, society forces the little boy to construct for himself an artificial personality, in keeping with the Norm prevailing in the 'external' world, and also providing a defence against the dangers of this world, the pitfalls that threaten on the stage where personas interact.

And yet: 'The construction of a collectively suitable persona means a formidable concession to the external world, a genuine self-sacrifice which drives the ego straight into identification with the persona, so that people really do exist who believe they are what they pretend to be.'[27] The son cannot identify with the father, and hence cannot construct a personality like his, except by sacrificing himself, his transsexuality and in particular his 'femininity': 'The repression of feminine traits and inclinations naturally causes these contrasexual demands to accumulate in the unconscious.'

A drastic repression of homosexuality takes place already in early childhood. The father (re)presents himself as a decisively heterosexual

---

26. Carl G. Jung, 'The Relations Between the Ego and the Unconscious,' *Collected Works, Vol*. 7 (London: Routledge, 1953), p. 190.
27. Ibid., pp. 191 and 187.

persona, rejecting overt erotic contact with the son (who for his part, however, desires without undifferentiation, and hence also desires the father). Other adult males, in deference to the taboo against paedophilia, similarly reject sexual relations with the little boy. In an analogous way, the mother and adult women reject sexual relations with girl children, even if the mother does generally maintain a greater erotic intimacy with children of both sexes than does the father. Sexual relations between children themselves are also repressed, and in particular homosexual relations.

The anti-homosexual taboo, which is particularly severe, very soon leads the little boy to recognise that homosexuality is forbidden, that it may only be spoken of, if at all, in a derogatory sense, and that you must be ashamed of your gay impulses, just like your 'femininity'. In the eyes of the child, homosexuality soon comes to be seen as associated with 'feminine' tendencies. It is only culturally, however, that sexual attraction between males is linked with femininity – though this culture negatively influences the child right from his birth.

The repression of homosexuality is revealed by the harshness with which the child is forced to reject his gay desire, and hence to repress it (though of course this does not always succeed).

Identification with the father is largely based on the repression of erotic desire for him. This identification forms a kind of introjection of the father, and in this respect alleviates or facilitates his rejection as a sexual object. According to Freud, 'the character of the ego is a precipitate of abandoned object-cathexes', and 'it contains the history of these object-choices'.[28] 'When the ego assumes the features of the object, it is forcing itself, so to speak, upon the id as a love-object and is trying to make good the id's loss by saying: "Look, you can love me too – I am so like the object".'[29]

With the rejection of the father as an 'object' of love for the child, and the replacement of this with identification, homosexual love is transformed into narcissistic libido. This transformation, determined by the incest taboo as well as by the condemnation of homosexuality, lies at the root of the 'normal', heterosexual, anti-homosexual ego, at the root of its ego-ism. The heterosexual male, repressing his gay desire, introjects homosexual 'objects' and sets himself up as the sole 'homosexual object',

28. Freud, 'The Ego and the Id', p. 29.
29. Ibid., p. 30.

transforming homosexuality into autoeroticism and imposing his autoeroticism on women in heterosexual relations. But this is an alienated autoeroticism, based on the renunciation of the father as sexual 'object' and more generally on the repression of the gay desire and the sacrifice of the 'feminine' components that are associated with homosexuality and incompatible with identification with the father and the Norm. It is this alienated male autoeroticism that women increasingly reject; it involves a focussing of male desire for the male, making him into a blind and egoistic condensation of masculinity that seeks to impose itself on women, who embody the femininity that he has negated and is ashamed of in himself. Heterosexual males see in women that portion of themselves which they have been forced from infancy to conceal and repress, and this is why they 'love' women in such a sadly inadequate way.

The 'normal' male ego, then, is largely determined by a series of abandoned homosexual object-cathexes, these being transformed into narcissistic libido and subsequently directed at heterosexual goals. Onto these heterosexual 'objects' the male projects the 'femininity' he has had to repress. The woman, then, is subject to the male in two ways: the man forces on her both his masculinity (a condensation of alienated homosexual desire) and his own 'femininity'. Woman is not recognised as an autonomous being, but comes to be historically defined entirely in relation to the male, on the basis of a complete heteronomy; and heterosexuality, as it presents itself today, is based on this heteronomy and tends to perpetuate it. The Norm maintained by a repressive society marked by male supremacy cannot but be heterosexual.

As an Italian feminist has written:

> Femininity is a drag show, it is the male projection of an idea of woman after he has censored and suffocated her, expelled her and put her in a gynaeceum. This representation is all his work, a whole system of representations, a historical scene that he seeks to direct . . . In all this, there is still no such thing as woman . . . Women, historically, do not yet exist, and the goal of the women's movement is to give women a specific historical reality.[30]

To return, then, to the little boy. Since he has to repress them, his 'feminine' mental traits are *projected*, i.e. transferred, onto a person of

---

30. Anonymously authored, 'Assenti e dappertutto', *L'Erba Voglio* 26, (June–July 1976), p. 7.

female sex, generally the mother. A kind of 'homosexual' intimacy is established between mother and son: the mother is the only one who can understand and intuit her son's need for a 'feminine life', and she can in part satisfy this (among other things, the demand for kindness, tenderness, protection, to be loved, to have his needs catered for). Forced to repress his 'feminine' component in order to identify with the father, the boy is obliged to also repress his own propensity to be giving, tender, sensual, maternal.[31] This particularly leads him to seek tenderness, affection, sensuality, the giving and maternal side in his mother. And this is why, in adulthood, men force women into a corresponding role.

The mother, for her part, 'regards [the child] with feelings that are derived from her own sexual life: she strokes him, kisses him, rocks him and quite clearly treats him as a substitute for a complete sexual object'.[32] And yet the mother is forbidden any overtly sexual love for her child, so that her erotic relationship with her son is expressed in an indirect and alienated form, and the boy really does serve her as a mere substitute. This first suppressed sexual relationship leaves a harmful trace in the erotic life of us all. To quote Myriam Cristallo:

> The mother-child relationship in bourgeois society thus exhibits a double set of contradictions. The first is that education in sexual love is given by the mother, in the privacy of the family milieu . . . thus excluding a wider dialectical relationship with other people. The second, which is closely interwoven with the first, is that this education is vitiated as soon as it is transmitted, since it derives from the concrete experiences of the parents, formed on the alienated terrain of the love market.[33]

In general, it is through his relationship with his mother that the boy forms his first idea of woman. The formation of this idea involves, besides direct contact with the mother, the gradual projection onto her and other women of the boy's own 'feminine' mental component, and the inherited collective image of woman that every man carries within

31. That male persons have desires of motherhood is shown and described by psychoanalysis. See, for example, Georg Groddeck, *The Book of the It*.

32. Freud, 'Three Essays', p. 223.

33. Myriam Cristallo, 'Ma l'amor di madre resta santo', *La politica del corpo* (Rome: 1976), p. 194.

him, the real repository of all the experiences that previous humanity has undergone in regard to woman and *in particular to her oppression.*

Jung gave the name of 'anima' to the image of woman formed in the accumulated male unconscious from the repressed 'feminine' traits and tendencies, and from the presence in the unconscious of an inherited collective image of woman. The anima, then, comes to define the 'feminine' element present in the man, while the 'animus' is the corresponding 'masculine' element in the woman. Though as Jung himself admits: 'If it was no easy task to describe what is meant by the anima, the difficulties become almost insuperable when we set out to describe the psychology of the animus.'[34]

In any event, according to Jung, it is precisely the projection of the anima or animus that respectively orients the boy's sexuality towards the mother, and the girl's towards the father, stimulating the man, in adult life, to seek the woman emotionally and sexually, and vice versa. Heterosexuality dissolves into an interchange of projections: 'A man, in his love-choice, is strongly tempted to win the woman who best corresponds to his own unconscious femininity – a woman, in short, who can unhesitatingly receive the projection of his soul.'[35]

Heterosexuality involves the projection of the other sex that is latent within us onto persons of the 'opposite' sex. It is determined by the repression of both transsexuality, or the original mental hermaphrodism, and of the so-called 'perverse' tendencies, in particular homosexuality.

The young boy desires without differentiation, but he is forced to identify with the father, repressing – as we have already seen – his homoerotic impulses and adapting himself to a heterosexual model. Male heterosexuality, therefore, as it presents itself today, is based on the repression by the man of his 'femininity' and the renunciation of the gay desire, and as such it represents a form of alienated sensuality, *founded on the estrangement of the human being from himself.* Male heterosexuality involves a misconception of self, and hence also a misconception of the other. By projecting his 'femininity' onto the woman, the man 'no longer recognises' either the woman or his own 'femininity'. His exclusive heterosexual desire is an aspiration to *totality* through the misconception both of the woman within himself and of woman as she really is.

The liberation of Eros and the achievement of communism pass necessarily via the (re)conquest of transsexuality and the overcoming of

34. Jung, 'Relations Between the Ego and the Unconscious', p. 204.
35. Ibid., p. 187.

heterosexuality as it presents itself today. The struggle to (re)conquer life is equally, and above all, a struggle for the liberation of the homoerotic desire. The gay movement is fighting to negate the negation of homosexuality, because the diffusion of homoeroticism will qualitatively change our existence and transform mere survival into life. With reference to the concluding essay in the *Grande Encyclopedie des Homosexualites*,[36] Luciano Parinetto maintains:

> If we accept the fundamental male-female bipolarity in human sex, and if at the same time we recognise the capitalist and Oedipal repression of the feminine in the male, then, because something is only repressed if it proves too attractive, we must say to 'normal' people: 'You are the homosexuals' [...] The homosexual and feminist challenge, like the atheist challenge to God, does not just seek to put a positive valuation on something that has emerged under capitalism in a marginalised form. If it does not want to confirm sexual roles in the very act of negating those on which it is itself based, it must present itself as a step towards transsexuality, i.e. something totally different, both from so-called 'normality' and from the dialectical opposite of this.[37]

Parinetto is undoubtedly right. But I must add that the achievement of transsexuality can only follow from the work of the women's movement and the complete liberation of homoeroticism, as well as the other components of human erotic polymorphism; nor must the *utopian* ideal of transsexuality, if it is to serve as a 'concrete utopia', be divorced from the *concrete* dialectic presently under way between the sexes and between different sexual tendencies (in particular heterosexuality and homosexuality). Only the struggle of those who are the historical subjects of the basic antithesis to the male heterosexual Norm can lead to overcoming the present opposition between the two sexes, and that between genital heterosexuality and homosexuality or other so-called 'perversions'. If transsexuality is the real *telos*, it can only be achieved when women have

36. The special issue of *Recherches* magazine, titled *Grande Encyclopédie des Homosexualités,* under the editorship of a collective including G. Deleuze, M. Foucault, Marie France, J. Genet, F. Guattari, G. Hocquenghem, J.-J. Lebel, J.-P. Sartre, etc., was published in Paris in March 1973, but confiscated by the police on the day of its appearance. See the article 'Paris-Fhar', *Fuori!* 10, (June–July 1973).

37. Luciano Parinetto, 'L'utopia del diavolo: egualitarismo e transessualità', *Utopia,* (December 1973).

defeated the male 'power' grounded in sexual polarity and *homosexuals have abolished the Norm that universally prohibits homosexuality*. Besides, given the very important functional role for the perpetuation of capitalism of the subordination of women and the sublimation of certain 'perverse' erotic tendencies in labour, the (re)conquest of transsexuality will coincide with the fall of capitalism and the rejection of alienated and alienating labour: the struggle of homosexuals and women is essential to the communist revolution.[38]

And if transsexuality is the *telos* of the struggle for the liberation of Eros, it is properly a *telos* in the sense that it is an *internal goal*, at once future, past, and present in the unconscious, a repressed potential that is today beginning to reassert itself against capital and its Norm. You can use your own anima (or animus) to understand this.

Critique of the Concept of Bisexuality. 'Neurosis as the Negative of Perversion'

The original and far-reaching theory of bisexuality or 'ambisexuality' (Ferenczi) does not clarify the causes of so-called 'sexual inversion', but it does justify it. According to Otto Weininger, author of *Sex and Character* (1903) and a keen upholder of the theory of bisexuality, homosexuality is neither a vice nor unnatural, given that any man, being also female, can equally well desire another man (who is himself also a woman), just as any woman, being at the same time male, can equally well desire another woman (who is also a man).

But this justification of homosexuality is not good enough (and in fact falls fully within the essentially reactionary perspective of tolerance). Weininger simply tried to fit homoeroticism into the bipolar pattern of heterosexuality. Homosexuality is explained in terms of heterosexual categories. I believe, rather, that homosexuality contains, among its secrets, the possibility of understanding psycho-biological hermaphrodism not as something *bi*-sexual, but rather as erotic in a new (and also very old) sense, as polysexual, transsexual. The heterosexual categories are based on a rejection of the underlying hermaphrodism, on the submission of the body to the neurotic directives of the censored mind, on an ego-istic vision of the world-of-life as determined by the repression of woman and Eros, by compulsory sexual morality, by the negation of human

38. We shall return to this important argument later on. See Chapter 6, section 4.

community and by individualistic atomisation. It is no good trying to use the bisexual and therefore heterosexual categories of our alienated reason, superimposed on the latent and the repressed, to plumb the depths, for we shall only fail to appreciate the full scope of the repression that chains us to the status quo. We revolutionary gays want rather to raise ourselves to transsexuality, as a concrete process of liberation.

For the time being, I simply want to emphasise once again how even the heterosexual psychiatric and psychoanalytic theories of bisexuality reveal the historical contingency of the concept of erotic 'normality'. But this notwithstanding, psychoanalysis has still studied homosexuality only as a form of 'deviance', and has never questioned those erotic manifestations that are considered 'normal' and their ideological absolutisation. Psychoanalysis, in other words, has not deeply investigated the causes of *heterosexual* inversion, since it is too attached to heterosexual primacy. In this case as in so many others, psychoanalysis proves only too loyal to capitalist ideology and doesn't dare to push its own insights or draw 'extreme' theoretical conclusions (and when these inevitably surface from time to time, it avoids concentrating any real critical attention on them).

Given the reduction of original 'bisexuality' to heterosexual monosexuality, Freud was evidently disinclined to classify heterosexuality as an 'aberration': this would have meant, in fact, eliminating the concept of 'aberration' altogether. On the contrary, he took homosexuality as the very prototype of a 'perversion', thereby prejudging his analysis from the very start. As I see it, however, the concept of 'aberration' should be replaced by that of mutilation, for all the presently existing forms of sexuality, each separate from one another, represent mutilations with respect to the potential polymorphous unfolding of Eros.

If it is true that Freud describes homosexuality as the prototype of perversion, he also holds that only genital heterosexuality is not 'deviant'. Even oral sex between man and woman is classed as a 'deviation in respect of the sexual aim', i.e. a 'perversion'; and this despite his assertion in the same essay that 'no healthy person . . . can fail to make some addition that might be called perverse to the normal sexual aim'.[39]

Sexual activity, in fact, is considered 'normal' or 'perverse' simply as a function of standards that are relative and specific to the historical epoch. As we shall see, at the root of the repression of Eros and the classification of sexual acts and tendencies as 'aberrations' there is also an *economic* cause.

39. Freud, 'Three Essays', p. 160.

Marx endures Niebuhr's hypothesis, according to whom all ancient law-givers 'and Moses above all, founded their success in commanding virtue, integrity and proper custom on landed property, or at least on secured, hereditary possession of land, for the greatest possible number of citizens.'[40]

As Freud himself maintained in a more general reflection:

> We must learn to speak without indignation of what we call the sexual perversions – instances in which the sexual function has extended its limits in respect either to the part of the body concerned or to the sexual object chosen. The uncertainty in regard to the boundaries of what is to be called normal sexual life, when we take different races and different epochs into account, should in itself be enough to cool the zealot's ardour. We surely ought not to forget that the perversion which is the most repellent to us, the sensual love of a man for a man, was not only tolerated by a people so far our superiors in cultivation as were the Greeks, but was actually entrusted by them with important social functions.[41]

But despite this and other similar statements, Freud never asked what were the specific reasons that led Western civilisation over the centuries to transform so radically its attitude towards homosexuality. It was sufficient that, 'the sensual love of a man for a man' was deemed an abomination by his contemporaries for Freud to class it among the 'perversions'.

And yet Freud *still did not consider homosexuality as 'pathological' in and of itself.* On the contrary, in his view:

> It is by no means only at the cost of the so-called *normal* sexual instinct that [psychoneurotic] symptoms originate – at any rate such is not exclusively or mainly the case; they also give expression (by conversion) to instincts which would be described as *perverse* in the widest sense of the word if they could be expressed directly in phantasy and

40. Georg Niebuhr, *Römische Geschichte. Erster Theil. Zweyte, völlig umgearbeitete, Ausgabe* (Berlin: Realschulbuchh, 1827), p. 245. Quoted in Karl Marx, *Grundrisse: Foundations of the Critique of Political Economy (Rough Draft)*, trans. Martin Nicolaus (New York: Penguin, 1973), p. 476.

41. Freud, 'Fragments of an Analysis of a Case of Hysteria' (Dora), *Standard Edition,* Vol. 7 (London: Vintage, 2001), p. 50.

> action without being diverted from consciousness. Thus symptoms are formed in part at the cost of *abnormal* sexuality; *neuroses are, so to say, the negative of perversions.*[42]

Freud refused, then, to view either manifest homosexuality or the other 'perversions' as necessarily pathological. On the contrary, psychoneurosis derives in part precisely from the conversion of so-called 'abnormal' sexuality into pathological symptoms. And the neurosis that afflicts present human society as a whole is caused above all by the repression of Eros, the mutilation of an Eros reduced to monosexuality (almost always heterosexual).

The neurosis of us gay men and women (and there is no reason not to speak of a specific neurosis of homosexuals, given that we are all, gay or straight, more or less neurotic under present conditions), is not a function of our homosexuality, but is rather due to the translation into pathological terms of the heterosexual component and the so-called 'perverse' tendencies – which, as against homosexuality, we have in general repressed or at least 'quasi-repressed', to a greater or lesser extent.

It is readily apparent, too, that the neurosis from which we homosexuals suffer depends also, and above all, on the social persecution inflicted upon us simply because we are gay. In other words, it is the psychoneurosis of 'normal' people (based largely on the pathological conversion of homosexuality and other repressed 'perversions') that condemns the manifest expressions of homoeroticism, this being the main factor involved in the neurosis of homosexuals. The psychoneurosis based on the oppression and repression of homosexual desire is the chief cause of the psychoneurosis of us manifest homosexuals. What is pathological and pathogenic is not homoeroticism, but rather its persecution.

The Psychonazis

Freud's view, according to which homosexuality, while a 'perversion', was precisely *not* a pathological syndrome, is far from shared by all psychoanalysts and psychiatrists. This is shown by the comprehensive denial of the more threatening aspects of Freudian thought by the psychoanalytic schools – a denial taken up even by Wilhelm Reich, particularly on the question of homosexuality.

---

42. Freud, 'Three Essays', p. 165.

Sandor Ferenczi, for instance, took an explicitly contrary view to Freud as far as homoeroticism was concerned. In 1909, he defined homosexuality as a psychoneurosis, also maintaining that he did not believe in any universal and congenital homosexuality.[43] In October 1911, at the third congress of the International Psychoanalytic Association held in Weimar, Ferenczi proposed a distinction between subject- and object-homoeroticism:

> A man who in intercourse with men feels himself to be a woman is inverted in respect to his own ego (homoeroticism through subject-inversion, or, more shortly, 'subject homoeroticism'); he feels himself to be a woman, and this not only in genital intercourse, but in all relations of life.[44]

This latter type of homosexuality, according to Ferenczi, forms 'a true "sexual intermediate stage" (in the sense of Magnus Hirschfeld and his followers), thus a pure developmental anomaly'. (Note the facile simplicity of his definition.)

To the figure of the passive homosexual 'suffering' from this 'subject-homoeroticism', Ferenczi counterposed the 'true active homosexual':

> The true 'active homosexual'... feels himself a man in every respect, is as a rule very energetic, and there is nothing effeminate to be discovered in his bodily or mental organisation. The object of his inclination alone is exchanged, so that one might call him a homoerotic through exchange of the love-object, or, more shortly, an object-homoerotic.

It is this 'object homoeroticism', according to Ferenczi, that constitutes a neurosis – an obsessional neurosis, to be more precise. Describing 'object-homoeroticism' as a pathological syndrome, Ferenczi admitted that he found himself 'in opposition with Freud, who in his "Sexualtheorie" describes homosexuality as a perversion'.[45] It is clear that, while

43. Sandor Ferenczi, 'More About Homosexuality', *Final Contributions to the Problems and Methods of Psycho-Analysis* (London: Hogarth Press, 1955), p. 171.

44. Ferenczi, 'The Nosology of Male Homosexuality (Homo-Eroticism)', *First Contributions to Psycho-Analysis* (London: Hogarth Press, 1952), pp. 299 ff. and 313.

45. In the essay titled 'The Role of Homosexuality in the Pathogeny of Paranoia', for example, Ferenczi affirms that, 'the alcohol played here only the part of an agent destroying sublimation, through the effect of which the man's true sexual constitution, namely the preference for a member of the same sex, became evident' ('On the

the label of 'perversion' that Freud applied to homosexuality shows up the reactionary basis of his position towards gay people (even if it is 'inappropriate . . . to use the word perversion as a term of reproach'), other psychoanalysts, including many who were personally close to Freud, such as Ferenczi, could be more overtly reactionary in defining homosexuality as pathological in itself.

On the other hand, however, Ferenczi's line of argument is full of contradictions. In some of his writings, where he deals with the question of homosexuality less directly, he cannot avoid tacitly accepting the existence of a congenital homosexuality, i.e. the universal presence of the gay desire. But if (as these texts suggest) any human being can be viewed as also homosexual, are we then all affected by obsessional neurosis or a 'pure developmental anomaly'?

No: this could not be the case, because, we've noted, Doctor Ferenczi still distinguishes between 'neurotic' and 'healthy' people. Clearly, from his point of view, homosexuality shows itself to be a psychoneurosis or anomaly only when it is manifest, i.e. when it defeats the resistances and escapes repression.

I believe I speak for many homosexuals if I say that, on the contrary (and here we find ourselves closer to Freud's own line of thought), the general neurosis that affects everyone in our society is largely a function of the social suppression of gay desire, its forced repression and its conversion into pathological symptoms.

Ferenczi, it would seem, was unwilling to draw this conclusion. His privileged condition as a heterosexual male, conforming to the Norm, prevented him from discovering the major role played by the repression of homosexuality in the aetiology of the neurosis that torments our society and *Kultur*.[46] To discover this, he would have had first of all to

---

Part Played by Homosexuality in the Pathogenesis of Paranoia', in *Sex in Psycho-Analysis: Contributions to Psycho-Analysis*, [Boston: Badger, 1916], p. 162). Homosexuality is therefore not, above all, just congenital but really the 'true sexual constitution of the individual'. Other writings of Ferenczi's can also be quoted to show that he remained convinced of the universal presence of gay desire; e.g. 'Transitory Symptom-Constructions during the Analysis', in *First Contributions*. Also, 'L'alcool et les névroses' [Alcohol and the Neuroses] (1911) and 'Un cas de paranoïa déclenchée par une excitation de la zone anale' [Stimulations of the Anal Erotogenic Zone as Precipitating Factors in Paranoia] (1911), in which he speaks of the 'social sublimation of homosexuality.' (There are no extant English translations of these last two essays.) For more on Freud's position in distinction to Ferenczi's, see below, p. 49.

46. [Translator's note: Mieli uses the German, which I have preserved.]

recognise his own 'obsessional neurosis' and the anomalous character of his own development as opposed to a free pansexual 'evolution'. He would then have had to consider how it is possible to be truly well and 'healthy' except by liberating one's own desire for people of the same sex. Manifest homosexuality does not in itself guarantee happiness, but there is no genuine liberation without the liberation of gay desire. In order to heal, you need to gather *les fleurs de mal.*

I have mentioned how the majority of psychiatric studies on (male) homosexuality always tend to separate into rigid compartments the categories of 'masculine' homosexuals (Ferenczi's 'object homoeroticism') and 'feminine' ones ('subject homoeroticism'), according to the traditional counterposed models of heterosexual role ascription and the strict differentiation between the sexes. Those psychiatrists and psychoanalysts who venture into the study of homosexuality find themselves unable to refrain from applying to it categories of interpretation that are completely heterosexual. And the anti-psychiatrists? They're better at making sense of Lacan than they are at understanding homosexuality. ('Would you like some Lacan? It's better than a banana ...')[47]

So it is that, filtered through a psychoanalytic lens, we homosexuals find only a very distorted picture of ourselves; almost invariably, the views of psychoanalysts fully match the stereotyped and fallacious ideas that ignorant heterosexuals have of us. (And as far as homosexuality is concerned, all heterosexuals are more or less ignorant.) Far from starting with the appearance of our 'external' life of marginalisation from society, in order to attain through critical analysis the reality of our condition as homosexuals, psychoanalysis, weighed down with prejudices, applies categories of interpretation taken over from the typical heterosexual view of homosexuality. In other words, it proceeds simply from appearance to appearance, fomenting illusions, erecting obstacles to criticism, and reinforcing the prevailing ideology.

Positions that are essentially equivalent to Ferenzci's are found very often in the history of psychiatry and psychoanalysis. It is all too common for doctors to classify the great majority – if not all – 'cases' of manifest homosexuality as neurotic and psychopathological. In their view, homoeroticism is neurotic as an 'infantile fixation of the libido, in particular a fixation at the sadistic-anal stage'; 'by its failure to dissolve the Oedipus

47. [Translator's note: Mieli writes this in French, hinging on the homophonic pun of *Lacan* and *banane.*]

complex and its persistent narcissism'; 'by its repression of heterosexuality'; or finally, 'because of defective sexual development in earliest childhood, arising from some profound deception in connection with the opposite sex'.[48] These are the themes most commonly encountered.

Then there are those who see the cause of homosexuality as lying in the 'panic fear' experienced towards the mystery of the other sex. 'We consider homosexuality to be a pathological biosocial, psychosexual adaptation, consequent to pervasive fears surrounding the expression of heterosexual impulses.'[49]

Hypotheses of this kind immediately reveal themselves to be uncritical and illusory by the way that they try and understand us on the basis of the prejudice according to which heterosexuality can be taken as 'normal' in some absolute sense. And yet, if we follow the psychoanalytic theories pertaining to the 'pathogenesis' of homosexuality, we cannot avoid considering heterosexuality too, by analogy, as a neurosis – a neurosis for the repression of homosexuality, for example, or a neurosis for the panicked fear of sexual relations with a person of the same sex. Paraphrasing Bieber, we could say: We consider heterosexuality to be a pathological, biological, psychosexual adaptation, resulting from pervasive fears surrounding the expression of homosexual impulses.

It is no fun to play hide-and-seek with psychoanalysts – or better, *psychonazis* – nor is it useful to confront them on their home turf. These doctors are awash with stupidities for which the anti-homosexual taboo in their (un)conscious is responsible, and it is certainly not necessary to take their affirmations seriously. And yet too many people, even today, believe they are right, and find in their prejudices support for their own, so that it is impossible for us to completely avoid dealing with them. We should bear in mind here what Domenico Tallone wrote on the psychiatric equation that homosexuality = sickness: 'I would prefer not to have to embark on arguments on a theme which is so completely imbecilic, were it not that this imbecility is still far too successful at replacing good sense with vacuous results backed by academic titles.'[50]

48. Wilhelm Reich, *The Sexual Struggle of Youth* (London: Socialist Reproduction, 1972), p. 59.

49. Irving Bieber quoted by Dennis Altman in *Homosexual: Oppression and Liberation* (New York: Outerbridge & Dienstrfrey, 1971), p. 4.

50. Domenico Tallone, 'Gli stregoni del capitale', in *La politica del corpo* (Rome: Savelli, 1976), p. 66.

It is clear that, unless we simply take over the current prejudice that considers heterosexuality as ipso facto 'normal' and 'natural' but homosexuality as 'abnormal' and 'unnatural', then to say that the majority of 'cases' of manifest homosexuality are psychopathological, and that homoeroticism is a neurosis, forces the admission that heterosexuality too is psychopathic and a disease. And so we may well ask what point there is, and especially in whose interest it is, to diagnose homosexuals as 'neurotic', and we can see how absurd it is to claim to 'cure' homosexuality as a 'sickness' on the basis of the heterosexual standpoint of the psychonazis, which takes itself to be healthy, but is in reality neurotic.

But why is homoeroticism deemed 'abnormal' and 'unnatural'? If the animal being of man is considered the essential aspect of his 'nature', we see immediately that homosexuality is common among the animals, and in certain species actually more widespread than heterosexuality, and female homosexuality just as much as male.[51] Homosexuality is extremely common among primates, and very many sub-primate mammals are also homosexual, to mention only lions, dolphins, dogs (who hasn't seen two male dogs fucking, or two females, for that matter?), cats, horses, sheep, cows, pigs, rabbits, guinea-pigs, rats, etc. There are also birds that are predominantly gay (ducks, for instance).

And yet this kind of evidence does little to open the eyes of the stubborn. Blinkered heterosexuals use the concept of 'nature', like that of 'against nature', according to their own convenience. We can quote what Eurialo De Michelis has to say, for example, in his essay titled 'Homosexuality Seen by a Moralist': 'What force is there in the irresistible argument that "unnatural" love is also found in the animal world? It may be something innocent in beasts, but not so in man, given that human life is particularly made up of that which distinguishes man from the animal world.'[52]

Let's leave the animals alone, then, having seen that they too can love 'against nature', and that human life involves something else (so says De Michelis). Out of some seventy-six differing forms of human society studied by the anthropologists Clellan Ford and Frank Beach, homosexuality was disapproved of and more or less suppressed in only

51. C. F. Ford and F. A. Beach, *Patterns of Sexual Behaviour* (London: Methuen, 1970).
52. Eurialo De Michelis, 'L'omosessualità vista da un moralista', *Ulisse* xviii, (1953), p. 733.

twenty-seven (just over a third). The anti-homosexual taboo that characterises our Western civilisation is thus not a structural element of 'human nature', but rather has a definite, albeit mysterious, historical origin: Sodom and Gomorrah weren't destroyed for nothing.[53]

Finally, we have already seen how psychoanalysis itself, in the words of Freud, declared the universal presence of the homoerotic desire in human beings. I would deduce from all this that heterosexuality, in so far as it bases its own alleged primacy on the completely false assertion that homosexuality is 'unnatural', 'abnormal' or 'pathological', ultimately demonstrates that it is itself *pathological.* More precisely: if love for a human being of the 'opposite' sex is not in fact in an absolute sense pathological, then heterosexuality as it presents itself today, i.e. as the Norm, is pathological, since it derives its primacy from ruling like a despot over the oppression of Eros' other tendencies. This heterosexual tyranny is one of the factors determining the modem neurosis, and – dialectically – it is also one of the most serious symptoms of this neurosis.

In their delirium, many psychiatrists and psychoanalysts, those cops for heterosexual capitalist authority, distinguish various types of homosexuality from the medical and psychological standpoint: according to them, we should speak not of homosexuality but rather of homosexualities. In the same vein, then, we might speak of heterosexualities instead of simply of heterosexuality.

There are doctors who differentiate the various types of homosexuality according to the age of the love 'object': paedophilia or pederasty, if this is a child or adolescent, gerontophilia if the person is old. But what if the sexual 'object' is somewhere in between?

At least as far as paedophilia is concerned, the Greek etymology makes no distinction of sex: παῖς, παιδος (*pais*, *paidos*) can refer equally to a young boy or girl. Should we then distinguish paedophile heterosexuality from other forms of heterosexuality? In fact, when so-called 'normal' people disparage the 'perversion' of paedophilia in relations between people of different sex, they certainly don't refer to it as heterosexuality – since this is their synonym for 'normality' – nor even as paedophilia (given that their ignorance leads them to consider this term as simply synonymous with male homosexuality). They prefer to speak just of 'perversion' period, or, still worse, of 'bestial crime'. For 'normal' people, the man who has sex with a little girl is not a heterosexual but a

53. See Chapter 2, section 2.

monster. And yet *Lolita* sells very well. You can find it in the bookshelves, fantasies, and secrets of the best families.

There are even those doctors who make a show of distinguishing homosexualities according to the supposed modality of sexual 'technique' (sodomy, buggery, etc.). But once again, what is the sense of this distinction if one individual can exhibit several 'homosexualities'? Does he go in for anal sex, sucking cock, kissing, cuddling and masturbation in turns, or even at one and the same time, is he active or passive with his partners, or active and passive with two partners simultaneously? But from the point of view of 'technique', one and the same person can equally exhibit several heterosexualities: anal sex, for example (even if *Last Tango* was banned in Italy), as well as the most traditional genital/frontal heterosexuality.

Finally, what would these confusion-mongering doctors[54] say of those who enjoy at one and the same time various forms of both heterosexuality and homosexuality? What of a person, for example, who having his sister's fist up his ass, himself fucks the sister's boyfriend while masturbating the boyfriend's little sister and sucking off his father-in-law. (And whose father-in-law?)

With all their distinctions, as useless as they are highfalutin, our doctors only model themselves after the uncle (to keep it in the family) in the poem by Catullus:

> Gellius, hearing his uncle anathematise the mere mention
> as well as the performance of love and love's ways
> determined to take full advantage of the situation
> by promptly assaulting his aunt. Uncle
> was discreetly unable even to refer to the event.
> Gellius could do as he wished.
> If he buggered the old man himself
> Uncle would not utter a word.[55]

Still more ridiculous is the distinction made by certain psychonazis according to the characteristics of the homosexual connection: 'relations

---

54. [Translator's note: In the original, Mieli refers specifically to Dr. Azzeccagarbugli, the corrupt lawyer from Alessandro Manzoni's massively influential 1827 novel *I promessi sposi* [The Betrothed].]
55. *The Poems of Catullus*, (Harmondsworth: Penguin, 1966), p. 186.

at a purely instinctual level, or of a more complex erotic love' (Tullio Bazzi). And yet it is precisely this kind of differentiation that today enables the Church to deem homosexual relations as more or less sinful according to their character. (More or less, since they are still sins as far as Catholic morality is concerned.)

Finally, doctors often distinguish forms of 'true' homosexuality from other forms of 'spurious' or 'pseudo' homosexuality (Bergler, Schneider, Servadio, among other champions of this view).

1) 'True homosexuality' is found only when 'a man with feminine impulses is attracted to a man with masculine impulses and a masculine body'.[56] Only in this case, according to the doctors, is there a 'psychosexual inversion of the subject'.

2) It is not however a case of 'true sexual inversion' when a man with 'masculine impulses' is attracted to a man with a 'feminoid' body but 'masculine impulses'. In this case, they would say, the 'object' is unable to love the 'subject'. But why not? Might not the homosexual component that has previously been latent in him now surface, despite his 'masculine impulses' (which the doctors evidently equate with heterosexual desire)? We queens know perfectly well that there is no such thing as an incorrigible heterosexual. You need only catch him at the right moment (and it changes nothing if his body is 'feminoid' or 'masculine'). 'A homosexually experienced male could undoubtedly find a larger number of sexual partners among males than a heterosexually experienced male could find among females.'[57] There is nothing more gay than fucking with a guy who was previously convinced that he didn't feel any sexual attraction for other men, and who then, thanks to your artistry in seduction, suddenly starts to burn with desire in your arms. The medical differentiation between 'true' and 'pseudo' homosexuality is a castle in the air. Homosexuality is always true, and it truly exists even when it is not apparent, i.e. when it is still latent.

3) But the doctors evidently haven't read Hegel, even if they do their damnedest to pass their wicked 'philosophy' off as science. According to some of these doctors, it is impossible to speak of 'true' homosexuality in the case where 'a man with masculine impulses', is attracted to a man

56. Tullio Bazzi, 'L'omosessualità e la psicoterapia', *Ulisse* xviii, (1953), p. 648.

57. Alfred C. Kinsey, Wardell B. Pomeroy and Clyde E. Martin, 'Homosexual Outlet', *The Homosexual Dialectic* (Englewood Cliffs, NJ: Prentice Hall, 1972), p. 15.

with a feminoid body and feminine impulses',[58] even if in this situation – they have to admit it – good for them! – 'it is possible for a reciprocal tie to be formed'.

According to the psychonazis, in fact, as long as a man's 'impulses' remain masculine, it is impossible to speak of genuine psychosexual inversion of the 'subject' or 'true homosexuality'. And here we see how the doctors, bound as they are to the notion of the 'psychosexual inversion of the subject' as a sine qua non for 'true homosexuality', and to the illusory dichotomy of 'subject' and 'object' (even if any subject is always also an object and vice versa), take no account of this third 'case'. They consider it as an expression of 'spurious' homosexuality, though as far as the 'impulses' are concerned, it is in fact symmetrical to the first 'case', which in their view is the sole form of 'true homosexuality'. In this way, by negating the aspect of reciprocity in the concept of 'true' homosexuality, *they negate the possibility of a genuine homosexual relationship*, and reduce 'true' homosexuality simply to an attribute of a certain type of 'subject'.

To sum up: for many psychonazis, homosexuality is true only when accompanied by what they define as a 'psychosexual inversion of the subject', since in this case 'the subject possesses a feminine psychosexuality and it is understandable that he should feel attracted to men'.[59] Only the perfect 'uranian' – 'the mind of a woman in the body of a man' (Ulrichs) – would therefore be truly queer. All others are simply pseudo-queer. Why on earth, then, do people generally lump together all men who want to make love with other men? Perhaps ordinary common sense knows better than the doctors?

It is not hard to see that these doctors, for all their sophisms and fine definitions, flatly reiterate the commonplaces that apply 'interpretative' labels of a heterosexual stamp to homosexuality. According to them, you have to possess feminine psychosexual 'impulses' in order to desire a man. If you don't, then your homosexuality is simply 'pseudo-homosexuality'. It is clear, however, that the type of homosexual situation they define as 'true' homosexuality is that which most closely resembles heterosexuality. They are completely unable to see male homosexuality, for instance, as a relation between men, and reduce it essentially to a certain type of 'invert' with 'feminine' desires directed towards the male: the anti-gay

58. Bazzi, L'omosessualità e la psicoterapia', p. 649.
59. Ibid.

taboo prevents them from understanding that homoeroticism is not just a parody of heterosexuality, but rather something quite different, and this leads them to spew out clouds of bullshit.

We, on the other hand (and even without having read Hegel), consider as truly homosexual any kind of desire, act or relation between people of the same sex. Obvious enough? Of course it is, but when it comes to homosexuality, ignorant heterosexuals know decidedly less than La Palisse.[60]

Included in this definition of what is truly homosexual, then, is the occasional erotic contact that a woman who in general only has relations with men might have with another woman (no matter whether she sees it like this or not); and similarly homosexual is the occasional contact that a man who generally has relations only with women might occasionally have with another man (whether or not he admits it).

According to Kinsey et al, instead of using the terms 'heterosexual' or 'homosexual' as 'substantives which stand for persons, or even as adjectives to describe persons, they may be better used to describe the nature of the overt sexual relations, or of the stimuli to which an individual erotically responds'.[61] They are basically quite correct here, even if their proposal is, in its details, rather abstract and ignores the present situation; for, given the very real historical opposition between individuals who recognise their homoerotic desires and those who desperately deny these, it is impossible today to avoid distinguishing between manifest homosexuals and heterosexuals (including definitively repressed queers). In other words, it would be a dangerous and illusory terminological concealment of the real contradiction that exists between heterosexuality and homosexuality; in this night, not all cows are gay.[62]

To return then to the views of straight psychologists. Many claim that at certain times, due to the effect of certain environmental factors,

---

60. [Translator's note: Mieli's reference is to Jacques de La Palice, a French nobleman whose infamous epitaph – '*Ci-gît le Seigneur de La Palice: s'il n'était pas mort, il ferait encore envie*' [Here lies the Seigneur de La Palice: If he weren't dead, he would still be envied] – was misread to mean "he would still be alive" and gave rise to the notion of the *Lapalissade*, a truism so obvious as to be comic.]

61. Kinsey et al, p.6.

62. [Translator's note: Mieli is making a philosophical joke of sorts (and slyly poking fun at his earlier assertion of having not read Hegel), because the pun concerns Hegel's infamous denunciation of F. W. J. von Schelling's concept of the Absolute. For Hegel, Schelling's Absolute was so indeterminate as to become meaningless: it was, he claimed, the 'night in which all cows are black'.]

homosexual behaviour develops as a purely instinctual and palliative satisfaction. This is sometimes referred to as 'emergency' homosexuality, and is particularly to be found amongst members of an all-male 'community' who are deprived of contact with women, and vice versa. (Prisons, concentration camps, colleges, convents, ships, barracks, etc.) In actual fact, it is quite false even in these cases to speak of 'pseudo' or 'emergency' homosexuality. We have rather to recognise, here too, manifest expressions of a homoerotic desire, which while previously latent, now comes to the surface, given the particular environmental conditions, in a more or less alienated fashion (particularly due to the restrictive and inhuman conditions here).

There are even doctors who refuse to consider male prostitutes as 'true homosexuals', and would rather class these as 'amoral psychopaths' (Tullio Bazzi). But in this case, males who prostitute themselves to women could similarly not be considered true heterosexuals. Are they too, then, to be classed as 'amoral psychopaths'?

In any case, we see hustlers of this kind as homosexuals who, because of the oppression of homoeroticism and the poverty in which they are forced to live, are only able to give expression to their homoerotic impulses when they can justify this, to themselves and to others, by the need to make money (however much of a pretext this might be).[63]

In conclusion, we should note the view of those who only consider homosexuality as a 'psychoneurosis' of people who, instead of being proud of their condition, are ashamed of it, who fear it and try to escape from it. But then it would follow that we could also define as psychoneurotic those heterosexuals who so desperately seek to deny that they have homosexual impulses, since it is precisely this intransigent denial that reveals their fear of recognising homosexuality in themselves, which they cannot accept; what is neurotic about them is that they are closet queens. Those homosexuals who are afraid of being so are neurotic, but so is the heterosexual society which rejects homoeroticism, deeming it shameful and abject, condemning it to latency or marginalisation. Those homosexuals who would prefer to be straight are the mirror image of a society that represses homoeroticism.

But when a gay person does accept himself, then psychotherapy has to recognise that 'the results are virtually zero with those rare subjects who are prepared for such a cure'.[64] Some people might ask how it is

---

63. See Chapter 4, section 3.
64. Bazzi, 'L'omosessualità e la psicoterapia', p. 654.

possible for a homosexual to accept his condition, and at the same time undergo therapy designed to change this. Evidently it is sufficient for the doctors that a gay person is not freaking out day and night because of his homosexuality, to define him as 'self-accepting' and to proceed frequently to try and 'cure' him. But a gay person who really does accept himself, who loves himself for what he is and what he does, and who loves other gay people, would never consent to any kind of 'cure' that sought to transform him into a heterosexual (not even if Delphine Seyrig[65] was to be the nurse).

In any case: Even the orthodox psychoanalysts, generally so optimistic as to the possibilities of their method, are fairly sceptical in this regard. Stekel held that he had 'never seen a homosexual cured by psychoanalysis', and Nacht (1950) conceded that this condition 'is inaccessible to any kind of psychotherapy'.[66]

Clearly, you can't be cured of a disease that you haven't got.

So-Called 'Therapy'

We have still to deal with the view of those who hazard a correlation between homosexual behaviour and hormonal balance, though as Dennis Altman points out, 'a correlation is far from being a cause'.[67] I have already noted how a so-called hormonal 'imbalance' can be found equally among heterosexuals as homosexuals. And as Dr Dreyfus reluctantly concedes, 'the doses of successive hormones systematically given to inverts have in no way enabled us to establish a specific hormonal formula for homosexuality'.[68]

Yet this has not prevented such doctors, more frequently than might be thought, from dabbling Nazi-style in experiments of hormonal 'therapy' for homosexuality. And yet the same Dr Dreyfus is forced to admit: 'Unfortunately I have not seen a case of male homosexuality, whatever might be its biological substrate, cured by the influence of hormonal treatment alone, however vigorously this is pursued'.[69]

---

65. [Translator's note: Seyrig was the Lebanese-French actor and director famous not only for her roles in *Last Year at Marienbad* and *Jeanne Dielman, 23 quai du Commerce, 1080 Bruxelles*, but also for her feminist documentaries and organising work.]
66. Ibid.
67. Altman, *Homosexual: Oppression and Liberation*, p. 5.
68. Dreyfus, 'L'omosessualità vista da un medico', *Ulisse* xviii, (1953), p. 654.
69. Ibid.

A lot of these doctors are not only criminals but imbeciles as well. Many frequently tend to confuse homosexuality with 'masculinity' in women and 'effeminacy' in men. And this despite the fact that Freud, as we have seen, already concluded that 'the degree of physical hermaphrodism is to a great extent independent of psychical hermaphrodism'.[70] Thus we end up with confessions such as that of Robert Stoller, a Los Angeles psychiatrist, who wrote: 'Masculine homosexual men are an exception I cannot discuss since I do not yet understand them'.[71] Exception after exception! But 'masculine' homosexual men, particularly in the USA, are just as common as 'effeminate' ones, even if the latter, naturally enough, are more readily observed.

It is clear that whenever a psychoanalyst departs from Freud and views homosexuality as pathological in and of itself, he develops a propensity to view 'therapy' as both possible and desirable. He sees 'a widespread error of pessimism among analysts about the possibility of therapeutic intervention in the case of homosexuality' (Gian Franco Tedeschi).

Freud, however, refusing to view homosexuality as a pathological syndrome, underscored how, in the psychotherapists's office, to bring about the 'repression of genital inversion, or homosexuality, is no simple thing.' He writes:

> I have found success possible only in specially favourable circumstances, and even then the success essentially consisted in making access to the opposite sex (which had hitherto been barred) possible to a person restricted to homosexuality, thus restoring his full bisexual functions. After that it lay within him to choose whether he wished to abandon the path that is banned by society and in some cases he has done so. One must remember that normal sexuality too depends upon a restriction in the choice of object. In general, to undertake to convert a fully developed homosexual into a heterosexual does not offer much more prospect of success than the reverse, except that for good practical reasons the latter is never attempted.[72]

After this candid admission, Freud concludes:

> As a rule the homosexual is not able to give up the object which provides him with pleasure, and one cannot convince him that if he

---

70. Freud, 'The Psychogenesis of a Case of Homosexuality in a Woman', p. 154.
71. Quoted in Altman, *Homosexual: Oppression and Liberation*, p. 5.
72. Altman, *Homosexual: Oppression and Liberation*, p. 151.

> made the change he would rediscover in the other object the pleasure that he has renounced. If he comes to be treated at all, it is mostly through the pressure of external motives, such as the social disadvantages and dangers attaching to his choice of object, and such components of the instinct of self-preservation prove themselves too weak in the struggle against the sexual impulsions.[73]

Elsewhere, writing to the mother of one of his American 'patients', Freud stressed:

> In a certain number of cases we succeed in developing the blighted germs of heterosexual tendencies which are present in every homosexual, in the majority of cases it is no more possible . . . What analysis can do for your son runs in a different line. If he is unhappy, neurotic, torn by conflicts, inhibited in his social life, analysis may bring him harmony, peace of mind, full efficiency . . .[74]

This letter is perhaps the least reactionary of the positions taken by Freud on the subject of homosexuality. But psychonazis such as Ferenczi, Ernest Jones, G. B. Hadden, Irving Bieber, Enninio Gius, etc. all distanced themselves from Freud's own tolerance. Freud sat cowardly on the fence and never washed his hands of them.

A few years later, Wilhelm Reich threw the Freudian view completely overboard, maintaining that 'any homosexual may cease to feel his inclinations under a very exact psychological treatment, whereas a normally developed individual never becomes homosexual under the same treatment'.[75] On the whole Angelo Pezzana is right to conclude that 'what Reich wrote on homosexuality rivals the keenest of our contemporary sexual fascists'.[76]

And yet despite Reich and his followers, a growing number of young people of both sexes, previously exclusively heterosexual, have moved in the other direction with the development of the feminist and gay movements: in other words, ever more people are ceasing to repress their homosexual desires. The 'good practical reasons' for which Freud did not

---

73. Ibid.
74. Freud, 'Letter to an American Mother', *American Journal of Psychiatry* 108, (1951), p. 252.
75. Reich, *The Sexual Struggle of Youth,* p. 50.
76. Angelo Pezzana, 'Contro Reich', *La politica del corpo,* p. 75.

deem it suitable to lead a heterosexual to homosexuality, are collapsing. Homoeroticism is eroding the barriers of repression and spilling out. Thanks to the struggle of gay people, the whole world is becoming a bit more gay. Many young heterosexuals are finding that letting themselves be the object of homosexual 'contagion' is the most helpful therapy to solving many of their problems. 'Gay is healthy' was one of the first slogans of the American Gay Liberation Front.

But the executioners are not giving in. Many contemporary psychiatrists persist in dedicating themselves to 'curing' people 'affected' with homosexuality, having recourse not just to hormone treatment, but also to psychotropic drugs and psychotherapy, electric shock and (why not?) aversion therapy.[77] Their crimes are severe indeed, and capital permits

77. See Don Jackson, 'Dachau for Queers', *The Gay Liberation Book*, ed. L. Richmond and G. Noguera (San Francisco: Ramparts Press, 1973), pp. 42–9, on the unbelievable tortures inflicted on homosexuals in American clinics. Aversion therapy – remember *Clockwork Orange*? – consists in showing the 'patient' pornographic images of a homosexual type, while submitting them to electric shock – through a mechanism attached to the penis – every time they get an erection. One can imagine (or nearly) the deleterious consequences. I would gladly strangle with my own hands all the doctors who practice aversion therapy.

In the Soviet Union, where aversion therapy for homosexuals is equally widespread, the most fashionable form at present involves the injection of apomorphine. See for example the article 'Rapporto sui comportamenti sessuali in Urss: deviazionista!', *Espresso,* 30 May 1976, which is based largely on *Female Sexual Pathology* by A.M. Sviadosch, head of the sexual pathology laboratory in Leningrad: 'A 1 per cent solution of apomorphine hydrochloride is used. Five minutes after the injection, the drug produces a feeling of nausea, accompanied by heart palpitations and a certain lack of breath and vomiting. The patient is not informed as to the effects of the apomorphine, but believes they are due to a medicine given to him to combat his homosexual tendencies. All ideas and images bearing on the object of his homosexual attachment and acts are consequently rejected as unpleasant. At the start of the treatment, one or two-tenths of a milligram of apomorphine in a 1 per cent solution are injected. Three or four minutes after the injection, indifference towards the partner and homosexual acts sets in. He is then told to look at a photograph of his partner or else to imagine homosexual relations with him. The feeling of nausea and vomiting caused by the apomorphine is thus associated with the homosexual relationship, which acquires a negative connotation . . . The apomorphine therapy should be combined with suggestions and advice, firstly to convince the patient that he is indifferent towards his partner and homosexual acts, later that he feels disgusted by them. This method has been successfully used to eliminate homosexuality in active male subjects.'

As one might note, the Soviet psychonazis nonchalantly use the word 'sick' to define the homosexual; and the editors of *L'Espresso* behave themselves, as is their habit, in a reactionary fashion, limiting themselves to reporting – without adding critical comments – extracts of the Soviet text, translated with the usual disgusting

them to act with impunity, just as only yesterday capital promoted the monstrous medical experiments of the SS.

At the same time, what is labelled 'perverse' still appears absolutely and shamefully aberrant in the eyes of the great majority, and as such susceptible to (im)moral and (un)civil condemnation. Public opinion, slave that it is to the ideology of the epoch, is unable to see the historically relative character of definitions of 'perversion'. In this case, as elsewhere, 'the natural normativity of society is ideology, in so far as it comes to be hypostasized as a natural and immodifiable given' (Adorno).

Those who invoke harsh penal sanctions against homosexuality today are no doubt unaware that until a few decades ago, the legislation of many industrialised countries condemned certain sexual acts such as masturbation, fellatio and cunnilingus, which are today considered quite 'normal'.[78] But people who disparage homosexuals as 'inverts' are evidently untroubled as to the supposedly absolute value of their own prejudices. The great mass of people, in fact, think in this way, and the opinion of the majority of 'child-men' and 'child philosophers' (Herman Hesse) pass itself off as a valid and therefore absolute judgment. Capitalist ideology is decidedly anti-homosexual: psychiatry and psychoanalysis, which have asserted and developed themselves through channels of bourgeois culture, almost invariably repeat its commonplaces. The natural character of the social and sexual status quo, as upheld by the dominant ideology, is not really put in question in scientific research. It is true that there does exist today an anti-psychiatry and an anti-psychoanalyis. But these have themselves essentially retreated into the one-dimensionality of contemporary scientific thinking, which the homosexual liberation movement is helping to criticise. They have simply passed back into the chameleon-like flatness that marks the real domination of capital.[79]

---

laughter. Evidently the 'progressive' Italian homophobe will take pleasure in reading this: in Russia, at least, they treat the queers as they should!

Therefore, I'd also like to strangle the soviet doctors (and the editors of *L'Espresso*). But I haven't got enough hands: our homegrown Maoists would go to pieces if they considered how in China homosexuals are shot if they are caught *in flagrante* after a period of several years of forced 'reeducation', a punishment carried out even when Saint Mao was himself living.

78. See for example Nell Kimball, *Her Life* as *an American Madam* (New York: Granada, 1971).

79. [Translator's note: See my preface for a discussion of his particular use of this figure of the 'flat' and 'chameleon-like' – i.e. the capacity for variable adaption to

The Dogma of Procreation

In *Three Essays on the Theory of Sexuality* (1905), Freud comes to the conclusion that, 'psycho-analysis has not yet produced a complete explanation of the origin of inversion.'[80] Yet to me it appears no less contradictory to investigate the origin of homosexuality when he had by then discovered that homosexuality is congenital. Only in a later work will Freud come to admit that, 'Such an achievement – the removal of genital inversion or homosexuality – is in my experience never an easy matter.'[81]

On the other hand, it's without doubt that we homosexuals don't suffer from 'inversion' but from the social persecution perpetrated against us: 'The homosexual suffer from oppression, not from his homosexuality!' (Domenico Tallone).

It's evident, therefore, that far more than the 'origin' of our homosexuality, we are concerned to investigate and shed light on the motives for its persecution, with a view to making clearer and more effective the battle we are waging against this. If people try and develop an aetiology of homosexual behaviour, why don't they also investigate the reasons for the fixation of desire, on the part of the majority, on 'objects' of the 'opposite' sex? The two questions are complementary, and neither can be resolved without the other. Indeed, an all-round aetiological research, which would also take the second question into account, instead of avoiding dealing with it on the pretext that it concerns an erotic disposition and behaviour that are defined as 'normal', could well make a valid contribution to discovering the reasons that lie behind the persecution of homosexuality. As René Schérer said, we need not ask why a human being can become homosexual, but rather 'why education has led him to establish a difference between the sexes in their capacity to provide pleasure, such that an exclusive heterosexuality can develop out of the absolute ambivalence of infancy?'[82] The usual way in which heterosexuality is presented as 'normal' is through the equation of *love = procreation*. Nothing could be more fallacious; erotic desire and reproduction of the species in no way coincide. To consider sexuality as having procreation

changing conditions yet without substantive/'deep' transformations – as a way to understand the process and phase of 'real domination'.]

80. Freud, 'Three Essays', p. 144, n. 1.

81. Freud, 'The Psychogenesis of a Case of Female Homosexuality', p. 151.

82. René Schérer, *Emilio pervertito* (Milan: Emme edizioni, 1976), p. 74.

as its goal is to apply a teleological-heterosexual – and thus inadequate – schema of interpretation to the complex multiplicity of the erotic function in human existence. As Georg Groddeck wrote:

> For the attempt to refer all erotic phenomena to the instinct of reproduction is one of the greatest stupidities of our time. Every bough of apple blossom, every flower and every work of man is evidence against so narrow an interpretation of the purposes of Nature. Of the twenty-thousand ova capable of being fertilized which are born with the girl child, only a few hundred are left by the time she has reached puberty, and of these, to take a high figure, a dozen come to fruition; and of the many millions of the man's spermatozoa, countless troops perish without even reaching a woman's body. People babble a great deal of nonsense.[83]

Procreation proceeds from a sexual act that is far from exhausting the entire vast range of desire, the full scope of its gradations. It was central to Gide's argument in his *Corydon* that, 'the sensual pleasure, which the act of impregnation brings to each sex, is not, as you know, necessarily and exclusively linked with that act . . . It is not fertilisation that animals seek, but simply sensual pleasure. They seek pleasure, and achieve fertilisation by a fluke'.[84]

Just as with the animals, so to consider procreation as the goal of human sexuality is to mystify heterosexual intercourse, attributing to it a 'metaphysical purpose'. It means misconstruing a pleasure which is in the first place an end in itself, or rather, the end of which is the satisfaction of the sexual impulse. It is an act of hypocrisy.

In nature, sex is not exclusively directed to reproduction. Among very many species of animals, for example, while females come on heat only for short periods of the year (oestrus cycle), males do not undergo such pauses. And then, precisely when they are on heat, many female animals frequently develop homosexual relations. The sow acts the boar, the mare acts the stallion, the cow acts the bull, etc., mounting other females, and frequently even males.[85]

83. Groddeck, *The Book of the It*, p. 108.
84. André Gide, *Corydon* (London: Secker & Warburg, 1952), p. 47.
85. See Enrico Fulchignoni, 'L'omosessualitil nelle donne', *Ulisse* xviii, (1953), p. 709.

Many people see in sexuality an *end* (that of procreation), but they refuse to recognise how this teleology is a *form* within their own judgement. And misunderstanding it in this way, they tend to absolutise it, imputing to nature a historically determined peculiarity of human thinking, a specific form of judgment at work precisely in that moment where, conversely, we need to suspend judgement in order to understand what really lies in Eros, beyond all prejudices, with a view to being able to live and enjoy this in freedom.

The persecution of homosexuality is situated within the wider frame of sexual repression in general. The dogma of procreation, seen as the one true goal of sexuality, historically arose as the crowning ideological achievement of the effective reduction of Eros to monogamous heterosexuality, and at the same time, as a justification for the condemnation delivered by society against all other libidinal tendencies, so that they come to be sublimated in the economic sphere. If it became necessary to explicitly stress that the purpose of sexuality was *reproduction,* this was in order to conceal the true purpose of sexual repression: the exploitation of women and men in *production.* We shall return to this fundamental argument later on.[86]

In any case, we can see how absurd it is today to continue rejecting homosexuality as alien to procreation, when our planet is suffering among other things from overpopulation. Overpopulation is determined above all by the oppressive persistence of the anti-gay taboo.

The procreation dogma also forms part of patriarchal religion and culture. It is the expression of a male society, in which women, who are the real subjects of procreation (*men do not generate, just fuck*), are oppressively bound to a subordinate role.

Adriana Guardigli has drawn my attention to the fact that only women can really understand and know what procreation involves, and how reproduction is linked with sexuality. By oppressing women and sexuality, society represses the procreative instinct that forms part of Eros, and the female Eros in particular. Perhaps the present ambivalent (love and hate) relations between parents and children are equally bound up with the repression of this instinct.

The dogma of procreation, therefore, doesn't only express the repression of sexuality in general. It marks also – and in particular – the alienation of the instinct towards procreation, which has been repressed

86. In Chapter 6, section 4.

by the species and emerges only in the form of extraordinary 'reminiscences' of the experiences of maternity.

Oedipus or The Other

> Work in this field is pioneer work. I have often made mistakes and had many times to forget what I had learned. But I know, and am content to know that as surely as light comes out of darkness, so truth is born of error. – Jung[87]

Ultimately, no one has yet succeeded in working out why some people become gay and others straight. Yet it is not difficult to see why the majority of people are straight, and only relatively few gay. This, as I have shown, is a function of the social oppression which tends to reduce the original polymorphous richness of Eros (transsexuality) to a rigid heterosexuality. But why some individuals still become gay, despite the very strong condemnation of homosexual tendencies, is something that we do not as yet understand. Just as all the various hypotheses so far formulated as to the historical origin of the anti-homosexual taboo still do not give us an exhaustive and certain explanation, so too it is very difficult to establish what induces us gays not to identify with the Norm and to recognise our desire in homosexuality.

Homosexuality is as old as the species, in fact even older, and yet ever renewed, even if today we are still just taking the first steps towards understanding it. And since the voices of gay people have generally been condemned to silence, only very few speak to us out of the past. We could make a comprehensive review here of the various opinions of psychoanalysts/psychonazis as to the reasons leading to the prevalent assertion of homosexual desire. But this has already been done by others,[88] and with little to show in the way of results. In general, they draw on psychoanalysis in an attempt to give a 'scientific basis',

---

87. Carl G. Jung, 'Psychology of the Unconscious', *Collected Works,* Vol. 7 (London: Routledge, 1953), p. 116.

88. See for example Erminio Gius, *Una messa a punto dell'omosessualità* (Turin: Marietti, 1972). This is one of the most reactionary works on homoeroticism published in Italy in recent years. The author is a priest (more or less), teaching in the psychology faculty at the university of Padua. Among other 'scientific' views that he quotes is that of Gino Olivari,* for example, a quack who has spent years engaged on the most absurd experiments in 'therapy' for homosexuality.

somehow or other, for their more or less contradictory judgements on homosexuality. I prefer, rather, to shed a critical light on this argument in the practical perspective of liberation, and will therefore restrict myself to considering two or three of these theories involving the relationship between homosexuality and the Oedipus complex; theories which, for one reason or another, I find particularly interesting.

There are those who consider heterosexuality as the 'normal' solution to the Oedipus complex, and homosexuality simply as an 'inverted' solution. In this sense, homosexual men would have experienced a particular exasperation, deep torment and the feeling of being irredeemably betrayed by their mothers, leading them to drastically distance themselves from the female 'object'. Given that the mother whom they love belongs exclusively to the hatred rival, the father, they would then renounce not only her but also any other woman, directing their desire solely towards the male. Freud offers us a similar interpretation, *mutatis mutandis*, in a 'case' of female homosexuality.[89]

But what specific factors determine such a distancing from the sex of the loved parent, instead of a concentration of desire on him or her? In other words, what, from the Oedipal standpoint, is the original differentiation between gays and straights? For on the basis of the classical conception of the Oedipus complex in its 'normal' or 'positive' form, even those who become heterosexual feel themselves exasperated, betrayed, and tormented by the evident superiority and exclusiveness of the parental relationship, which prevents the realisation of the desired love relation between daughter and father, or son and mother. And yet, if they are male, they do not renounce the female sex in general as they have had to renounce the mother. On the contrary, it is on women that they fix the 'object' of their sexual impulse, while, if they are female, they focus their desire on the male sex, instead of withdrawing from it. Freud suspected the existence 'of some special factor which definitely favours one side or

---

* [Editor's note from original volume: Gino Olivari (1899–1988) was a singular figure, a scholar and missionary dedicated to the cause of helping homosexuals. From the start of the 1950s, he worked to 'cure' homosexuals of their condition and to publish studies that argued, like many 'therapists' of those years, that the best way to make a homosexual heterosexual was to make them go to bed with a woman. At the same time, he fought against repressive laws and against the demonisation of homosexuals, facing a trial as a result. From the start of the 1960s, his encounter with the gay movement contributed to his partially modifying his antiquated theories.]

89. Freud, 'The Psychogenesis of a Case of Homosexuality in a Woman', pp. 156–8.

the other [i.e. heterosexuality or homosexuality], and which perhaps has only waited for the appropriate moment in order to turn the choice of object in its direction'.[90] But he did not even try to give evidence of this.

According to many psychoanalysts, the entry into the Oedipal phase, the characteristics of the complex and its dissolution, are determined by the way that the oral and anal phases have been traversed. The English school of psychoanalysis stresses the importance of infantile oral aggression, its 'projections' and the function of these in the assertion of homosexuality. In his 1910 essay on Leonardo da Vinci, Freud viewed the oral 'fixation' on the penis as a direct displacement of the primary attachment to the breast. Homosexuality would then derive from a 'fixation of the erotic needs on the mother'.[91]

In 1921, Freud came to the following conclusion:

> The genesis of male homosexuality in a large class of cases is as follows. A young man has been unusually long and intensely fixated upon his mother in the sense of the Oedipus complex. But at last, after the end of puberty, the time comes for exchanging his mother for some other

90. Ibid., p. 158.

91. Freud, 'Leonardo da Vinci and a Memory of His Childhood', *Standard Edition,* Vol. 11 (London: Vintage, 2001), p. 99, note. In his 'Analysis of a Phobia in a Five-Year-Old Boy' (the case of 'little Hans'), Freud put forward the following hypothesis: 'In those who later become homosexuals we meet with the same predominance in infancy of the genital zone (and especially of the penis) as in normal persons. Indeed it is the high esteem felt by the homosexual for the male organ which decides his fate. In his childhood he chooses women as his sexual object, so long as he assumes that they too possess what in his eyes is an indispensable part of the body; when he becomes convinced that women have deceived him in this particular, they cease to be acceptable to him as a sexual object. He cannot forego a penis in any one who is to attract him to sexual intercourse; and if circumstances are favourable he will fix his libido upon the "woman with a penis", a youth of feminine appearance. Homosexuals, then, are persons who, owing to the erotogenic importance of their own genitals, cannot do without a similar feature in their sexual object' (*Standard Edition,* Vol. 10 [London: Vintage, 2001], p. 109). Freud's error here lies in the extension of the above hypothesis to apply, quite falsely, to all 'cases' of homosexuality, though this does not mean that it is necessarily invalid in some. In many of his works, Freud tends to offer the most 'definitive' possible interpretation of the homosexual phenomenon, and yet these interpretations show a wide variation. And none can be considered The Truth simply because it was put forward by the father of psychoanalysis. They should be viewed rather as hypotheses, sometimes in fact as mere opinions. We can only use psychoanalysis as an instrument for shedding light on the homosexual question if we compare the different hypotheses and attempt a synthesis guided by the critical revolutionary spirit.

> sexual object. Things take a sudden turn: the young man does not abandon his mother, but identifies himself with her; he transforms himself into her, and now looks about for objects which can replace his ego for him, and on which he can bestow such love and care as he has experienced from his mother. This is a frequent process, which can be confirmed as often as one likes, and which is naturally quite independent of any hypothesis that may be made as to the organic driving force and the motives of the sudden transformation.[92]

Once again, then, Freud does not even touch on what is of particular interest to us here, i.e. the specific causes and mechanisms of this transformation that leads to identification with the mother and the assertion of homosexuality at puberty. I will return later, and in a more substantial manner, to these Freudian hypotheses, when I take up the ideological character of Franco Fornari's adherence to them.[93] For the moment I would only like to stress again the discrepancy in Freud's thinking. His theory of sexuality upholds the existence in each person of homoerotic tendencies, particularly so in children ('polymorphous and perverse'), and thus recognises a congenital homosexuality; and yet Freud then goes on, as in the text just quoted, to inquire as to the genesis of homosexuality. But if homosexuality is congenital in us all, there is clearly no sense in investigating its genesis. What is necessary, rather, is to investigate what it is that determines the repression of homosexual desire in most people, and makes possible its assertion in the minority.

Identification with the mother, it is true, is something of which many male homosexuals are consciously aware, alongside their identification with the father (whereas heterosexual men are generally only conscious of their identification with the same-sex parent). This emphasises the transsexual ambiguity of our being in-becoming, closer to the underlying transsexuality than is the rigid monosexuality of straight people; our ambiguity is closer to the child's way of being.

It is not for nothing that we are gay, that we are crazy queers, and for a better world, I truly think that the 'education' of young people should be entrusted to gay men and women: *let the little children come to us!*[94]

---

92. Sigmund Freud, 'Group Psychology and the Analysis of the Ego', *Standard Edition,* Vol. 18 (London: Vintage, 2001), p. 108.
93. See Chapter 6, section 5.
94. [Translator's note: Mieli's reference is to Christ's words in Matthew 19:14: 'Let the little children come to me, and do not hinder them, for the kingdom of heaven belongs to such as these.']

I should also say that, while reading a poem by Pasolini, I was reminded of the Freudian interpretation that I have detailed here (though neither seeing nor searching for precise associations between Freud's interpretation and this poem: the association is one that came from myself, immediately linking, in my memory, the one with the other.) Certainly this poem reflects a single case, one in which not all – and perhaps very few – homosexuals will recognise themselves, but its beauty is such as to contain within itself a profound truth (and one that at least for me, in a certain sense, worthwhile). For this reason, I'd like to transcribe it in its entirety. It is titled 'Plea to my Mother'.

It's hard to express in the words of a son
what, at heart, I'm not really like.

You alone in all the world know what love
has always come first in my heart.

This is why there's something terrible you should know:
it's from your grace that springs my sorrow.

You are irreplaceable. This is why the life you blessed
me with will always be condemned to loneliness.

And I don't want to be alone. I have an infinite
thirst for love, for bodies pure and soulless.

For the soul is in you, it is you, but you are
my mother, and in your love are my fetters.

I went through childhood enslaved to a sentiment,
lofty and incurable, of overwhelming commitment.

It was the only way to feel alive, the only color,
the only form, and now it's over.

Still, we survive—in the confusion
of a life reborn outside of reason.

I beg you, oh, I beg you: don't wish for death.
I'm here, alone, with you, in an April to come.[95]

95. 'Plea to my Mother', trans. Stephen Sartarelli in *The Selected Poetry of Pier Paolo Pasolini: A Bilingual Edition* (Chicago: University of Chicago Press, 2014), pp. 315–17.

I do not believe in the exclusive identification by homosexual men with their mothers (nor in the theory according to which gays are supposed to seek in their partner the substitute for their own ego). I believe, rather, as I have already said, that we are aware more than straight people of the identification with both parents, of the existence within us of both sexes. One thing, however, is certain: true love for his mother does prevent a man from accepting the heterosexual Norm that insults, objectifies and oppresses women. But this does not prevent us from loving other women, and I believe that the more homosexuality is liberated, the more it will be us gays who enjoy love and erotic intensity with women. Genuine love for the other sex cannot but be accompanied by the full desire, auto- and allo-erotic, for one's own sex.[96]

It is also true, moreover, that historical and social factors place us gays far closer to the condition of women than are male heterosexuals, even if we still enjoy, to a variable extent, certain privileges and gratifications that are decidedly male, at the social, psychological and even sexual levels, notwithstanding all the harshness of the persecution and marginalisation we face from society – and which, obviously, male homosexuals face because they are homosexual, not because they are male.

But in a society where the subordination of the female sex is closely bound up with the erotic desire of the woman for the man (the greater part of women being heterosexual), and with male supremacy in the heterosexual relation, couldn't we put forward the hypothesis that those men who generally abstain from sexual relations with women and do not treat them as sexual objects, experiencing instead desire for the male, stand to a certain degree closer to the condition of women, at least in some of its aspects? A gay man knows very well what it's like to go to bed with a straight man, someone who generally fucks women and from time to time goes with a queer just to 'prove his very normal potency' (or so he says). He knows what it means to be treated as a convenient hole, a sexual object on which the male, convinced of his own 'superiority', inflicts a mediocre, neurotic and egoistic desire. Many gay men, moreover, understand what it is to go around dressed 'as a woman', i.e. they know what it means to be considered as a second-class human being, as the second sex.

The precise extent to which homosexual men live situations similar to those experienced by women is impossible to establish. These situations, moreover, vary from case to case, and among gay men themselves,

96. See Chapter 5, section 4.

the more 'effeminate', i.e. the queens, often suffer humiliation and violence that the most 'virile' gays who pass as straight can only imagine with horror. I am quite content, however, to be an obvious, 'feminine' queen: and the suffering that, in this society, comes with this forms the measure, or if you prefer the mirror, of the hard yet fragile and precious beauty of my life. It is a great destiny to possess and seek to live with clear awareness what the regular mass of people, in their accustomed idiocy, disparage and try to strangle. As a comrade from the French gay movement wrote: 'We demand our "femininity", the same thing that women reject, and at the same time we declare that these roles are devoid of sense'.[97] And Daniele Morini admitted:

> It has been hard for me to recognise my desire as a queer for what it is. And even after breaking through two barriers ('I can't because I'm *not* homosexual' / 'I can't because I'm too politicised to have an alienated desire'), I now face a further fear: that of discovering myself a woman with a desire explicitly tied to the male. The refusal to live an alienated role hides a fear of what might be revealed by living it to the full. Or perhaps the fear of being male?[98]

In trying to grasp what it is that enables some people to strongly assert their homosexual desire, despite the social condemnation of homoeroticism, I believe that we have to take into consideration the complete Oedipus complex, i.e. both its so-called 'normal' or 'positive' and its 'negative' or 'inverted' aspects. We need, that is, to take account of the 'triangular character of the Oedipus situation and the constitutional bisexuality of each individual' (Freud) – or, as I would rather frame it, the constitutional *transsexuality* of the individual. To quote Freud again:

> Closer study usually discloses the more complete Oedipus complex, which is twofold, positive and negative, and is due to the bisexuality originally present in children: that is to say, a boy has not merely an ambivalent attitude towards his father and an affectionate object-choice towards his mother, but at the same time he also behaves like

97. *Où est passé mon chromosome?*', FHAR, *Rapport contre la normalité* (Paris: Editions Champ Libre, 1971), p. 66.
98. Daniele Morini, 'La Bella e la Bestia', Il *Vespasiano degli omosessuali,* published by the Collettivi omosessuali milanesi, (June 1976), p. 16.

> a girl and displays an affectionate feminine attitude to his father and a corresponding jealousy and hostility towards his mother. It is this complicating element introduced by bisexuality that makes it so difficult to obtain a clear view of the facts in connection with the earliest object-choices and identifications, and still more difficult to describe them intelligibly.[99]

In order to form a full idea of the Oedipus complex, therefore, we need to bear in mind both the child's hetero- and homoerotic tendencies. If only the 'positive' aspect is taken into account, then infancy (and also puberty, which frequently involves a revival of the complex) will be interpreted in categories that are exclusively heterosexual. It is then impossible to grasp the full complexity of the Oedipal situation, given that infancy is 'polymorphously perverse', and not just heterosexual, or to understand the complexity of the pubertal stage, given that puberty, as is well known, displays a rich resurgence of gay desires, frequently more numerous and intense than heterosexual, in the context of the intensification of Eros that characterises this stage of development. For what reasons, then, need the young boy, given his 'undifferentiated' polymorphous disposition, be jealous of the mother and feel rivalry with the father, rather than the other way round as well? And why is the little girl jealous of her father instead of her mother? Psychoanalysis itself – as we shall see later on[100] – sees jealousy among heterosexual adults as a veiled expression of homoerotic desire. (In the case of a man, for example, jealousy over a loved woman who is involved with someone else indicates that it is unconsciously he who desires this other man.) But childhood is far less disguised. Homosexuality is not yet repressed, and in the boy's 'positive' Oedipal jealousy over the mother we must also recognise his desire for the father; the so-called 'positive' and 'negative' aspects of the complex are intertwined.

Freud goes on to say:

> Analytic experience then shows that in a number of cases one or the other constituent disappears, except for barely distinguishable traces; so that the result is a series with the normal positive Oedipus complex at one end and the inverted negative one at the other, while

99. Freud, 'The Ego and the Id', pp. 31 and 33.
100. See Chapter 3, section 4.

> its intermediate members exhibit the complete form with one or other of its two components preponderating. At the dissolution of the Oedipus complex the four trends of which it consists will group themselves in such a way as to produce a father identification and a mother-identification. The father identification will preserve the object-relation to the mother which belonged to the positive complex and will at the same time replace the object-relation to the father which belonged to the inverted complex: and the same will be true, mutatis mutandis, of the mother-identification. The relative intensity of the two identifications in any individual will reflect the preponderance in him of one or other of the two sexual dispositions.[101]

I do not believe that the different patterns assumed by the two identifications depends simply on the greater or lesser weight of the two sexual dispositions (homo- and heterosexual). I am sure that it also depends on educastration, or the social and family repression that forcibly leads the boy to identify with the father and renounce the male 'object', and the girl to identify with the mother and renounce the female 'object'.

We can put forward the hypothesis, then, that those who become homosexual, thanks to the particular richness of their predisposition to homoeroticism, fail to renounce the male (father) object, if they are themselves male, or the female (mother) object, if they are female. And that the strength of the congenital homosexual disposition is reinforced by a certain tendency (whether conscious or not) on the part of the parent of the same sex to establish a homoerotic relation with the child, a special emotional bond.

In general, because of the anti-homosexual taboo (and the taboo on incest), the object-choice that the son makes for the father is castrated, negated, by the father himself; and similarly with the girl and her mother. This 'normally' leads to the predominant identification of the boy with the father and the girl with the mother. As Freud explains it, identification serves as a substitute for the forbidden 'object' – and the 'object' most strictly forbidden is that of the 'inverted' Oedipus complex. Prevalent identification of this kind with the same-sex parent leads to maintaining only the heterosexual type of object-choice, because this is based above all on the repression of homoerotic desire and because the parent introjected by way of identification is heterosexual. This

101. Freud, 'The Ego and the Id', p. 34.

would then explain the repression of homosexuality in so-called 'normal' individuals.

It would follow, then, that homosexual desire is not repressed in those who find a certain response to their homoerotic object cathexis in the same sex parent: those in whose infancy, therefore, the 'negative' or 'inverted' Oedipal tendency is not suddenly and brutally repressed, but finds a certain channel of expression in the dialectic of family relations. The renunciation of 'objects' of the 'opposite' sex would follow from a lack of need to identify with the same-sex parent, and hence with his heterosexual behaviour, as well as from the sense of guilt, or the internalisation of the social condemnation, which befalls those who do not completely identify in this way with the prescribed patriarchal model of male or female, i.e. who do not fit the Norm. The sense of guilt leads to a feeling of inferiority vis-a-vis 'normal' people, those who are endowed with an object-choice that society deems higher, positive, 'normal', etc. We can thus put forward the hypothesis that the repression of desire for the other sex in homosexuals is actually due to the social condemnation of homosexuality, which leads the homosexual to feel guilty and hence unworthy of the choice defined as 'normal', i.e. an impossible candidate to please people of the other sex. Oppression, moreover, forces the homosexual to wage a constant struggle against both his external persecutors and his induced sense of guilt, the persecutor within, with a view to defending (alone against all) his 'anomalous' choice, his homoerotic desire, concentrating all his libidinal energy into this. The liberation of homosexuality in society and the extirpation of the sense of guilt (of false guilt) will therefore lead – I am convinced – to the rediscovery, on the part of gay people, of their erotic desire for people of the other sex, and the discovery of the particular attraction that persons of the other sex feel towards them.

I would have preferred not to force the reader to follow me through this complex and hypothetical argument, which at some points is certainly obtuse. But as I said, this field is difficult to explore, and only a few people have taken the trouble to do so. As for hypotheses, I could advance a few more, but none of these, I believe, are sufficiently interesting to reproduce here. I think that practical liberation, above all, will foster further analysis: only the general emancipation of homosexuality will shed real light on the history of its oppression and its ever-new resurgence, despite persecution, over the centuries.

The women's movement has discovered the importance of the love relation between every woman and her mother, i.e. the 'inverted' Oedipus complex. In a text written in 1974, a Milan feminist group explain how 'homosexuality in the broad sense, as a relationship with the mother, is the primary and basic relation for all women'. Melanie Klein 'stresses the Oedipal tendencies that "naturally" press the little girl towards her father, but this does not succeed in explaining why the father is always internalised as a sadistic father, if not by reference to the frustrated relation with the mother'.[102] Rivalry with the male sex, however, is for women a consequence of this fundamental homosexual relation with the mother.

In fact,

> the mother disappoints the little girl, not because she 'incorporates the father's penis' but rather because she is *possessed* by the law of the father. Through the desire of the mother, the 'penis' acquires great prestige in the eyes of the little girl, and becomes the object of admiration and desire [. . .] Only possession of the 'penis' guarantees omnipotence and hence power over the mother (power to possess and destroy her). *Identification/assimilation with the male*, as a gesture of penis envy, thus *precedes* love for the male [. . .] In the little girl, sadistic impulses rapidly mingle with the fantasy of possessing a destructive 'penis', while the object of desire and aggression generally still *remains the mother*. With the man, she establishes instead a kind of 'paedophile complicity', or herself assumes masculine characteristics, or else repeats, through seduction and the sexual act, the symbolic introjection of the penis. Heterosexual love, therefore, is generally, for the woman, the reconfirmation of the masculine position. We would then be able to modify the customary assertion that the woman seeks the mother in the man, and say rather that through love for the man – the repeated reappropriation of the penis – the woman actually seeks to possess the mother.[103]

From the gay standpoint, as from the feminist one, it is impossible to refer to the Oedipus complex without a complete recasting of the theories that bear on it, and without effectively taking into account the complex

102. [Translator's note: Mieli does not provide a source for this quotation.]
103. Alcune Femministe Milanesi, 'Pratica dell'inconscio e movimento delle donne', *L'Erba Voglio* 18-19, (Oct. 1974–Jan. 1975), pp. 12–23.

in its full extension. According to Deleuze, no one should 'believe that homosexuality is sufficient to escape from the classical categories of psychoanalysis: Oedipus – castration – death drive.'[104] But even recognising that homosexuality, in the same way as heterosexuality, is based on a conception rooted in the difference of the sexes which finds its grounding in the Oedipal triangle and which is challenged by our underlying transsexuality, we gays do not recognise ourselves in the classical Oedipal categories, because homosexuality, in a certain sense, negates Oedipus. Homosexual desire threatens the Oedipal reproduction. In Hocquenghem's words: 'The direct manifestation of homosexual desire stands in contrast to the relations of identity, the necessary roles imposed by the Oedipus complex in order to ensure the reproduction of society. Reproductive sexuality is also the reproduction of the Oedipus complex; family heterosexuality guarantees not only the production of children but also (and chiefly) Oedipal reproduction, with its differentiation between parents and children.'[105] Homoerotic desire threatens Oedipal reproduction: 'Homosexual desire is the ungenerating-ungenerated terror of the family, because it produces itself without reproducing.'[106]

In dealing with the assertion of heterosexuality, we have seen how its supremacy, determined by way of the Oedipal phase, is based on the repression of homoerotic tendencies. The revolutionary homosexual struggle is thus waged against a form of oppression that is prior to Oedipus. Oedipus is negated by negating its premises. Deleuze, again, with a benevolent impulse, admits:

> There is of course a revolutionary potential in certain homosexual groups. I believe this is not just because they are homosexual, it is rather that their homosexuality has allowed them to question the differences between the sexes. And through this questioning, they become able, in their marginal position, to tackle the problem of sexual desire as well.[107]

---

104. Gilles Deleuze, in a contribution to the workshop held on 8–9 May 1973 in Milan by the collective of *Semeiotica e Psicanalisi; Psicanalisi e politica* (Milan, 1973), p. 45.
105. Guy Hocquenghem, *Homosexual Desire* (Durham, NC: Duke University Press, 1993), p. 106.
106. Ibid., p. 107.
107. Deleuze, *Semeiotica e Psicanalisi*, p. 45.

Well, thank you very much.

We revolutionary queers see in the child not so much Oedipus, or the future Oedipus, as *the potentially free human being*. We do indeed love children. We are able to desire them erotically, in response to their own erotic wishes, and we can openly and with open arms grasp the rush of sensuality that they pour out and make love with them.

That is why paedophilia is so strictly condemned. It sends messages of love to the child, whom society, through the family, seeks to traumatise, educastrate, and negate, imposing on the child's eroticism the Oedipal grid. The oppressive heterosexual society forces the child into a period of latency; but this is nothing but the deadly introduction to the prison of a latent 'life'. Paedophilia, on the other hand, 'is an arrow of libido directed at the foetus' (Francesco Ascoli).

2

Fire and Brimstone, or How Homosexuals Became Gay

The Homosexual Antithesis and the Norm. The Staging of 'Love'

It can be said that there is a real relation of opposition between heterosexuality and homosexuality, in society as in every individual existence. Just as there is a dialectic between the sexes, so there is also a dialectic between sexual tendencies and forms of behaviour. The antithetical relation that exists between heterosexuality and homosexuality must be deeply analysed: in fact, the direct path to the overcoming of monosexuality and the affirmation of the female sex and of transsexuality necessarily passes straight through the development of this contradiction between hetero- and homoeroticism.

Save for some rare exceptions, which only confirm the rule, heterosexuality and homosexuality are mutually exclusive. These exceptions are the 'cases' of, strictly speaking, bisexuality (i.e. of 'amphigenic inversion'[1]), 'cases' in fact of people who experience conscious sexual attraction towards both sexes, and 'freely' indulge their bisexual desire. (Today, however, the fact of feeling attracted to both sexes is not in itself sufficient for overcoming the *bi*polar contradiction between the sexes, for overcoming bi-sexuality.) These bisexuals, however, are almost all either predominantly heterosexual or predominantly homosexual. The former usually behave in a way that essentially conforms to the Norm (they are exceptions, we can say, who only confirm the Norm), while the latter, as a general rule, can be more easily identified with 'homosexuals of strict observance' (as Francesco Pertegato calls them) than with the predominantly heterosexual bisexuals.

1. [Translator's note: The term appears early in Freud's 'Three Essays': 'They may be *amphigenic* inverts, that is psychosexual hermaphrodites. In that case their sexual objects may equally well be of their own or of the opposite sex. This kind of inversion thus lacks the characteristic of exclusiveness.' Freud, 'Three Essays', p. 136.]

Bisexuality may be viewed as a compromise, often a rather poor one, between the repressive Norm and transsexuality. But you don't make a revolution through compromises. A revolutionary homosexual today, who might well have sexual relations with women, will certainly not define himself as bisexual, among other reasons because, if by bisexuality is meant the sum of heterosexuality and homosexuality, he will refuse to define his relations with women as heterosexual. He will rather say that his encounters with women are unfortunately still tainted in large part by heterosexual conditioning, a conditioning that he seeks to combat and overcome. Heterosexuality, in fact, is the Norm based on the repression of Eros, and a gay revolutionary who does not accept the Norm will certainly not conduct his erotic relations with women in the heterosexual, and hence 'normal', sense. He will far prefer to eliminate the heavy residues of heterosexuality that still encumber these. We shall take up this line of argument again below.[2]

In any case, among the majority of people today, manifest heterosexual desire rules out homosexual desire, and vice versa. And yet the specific predominance of the one does not exist without the simultaneous and antithetical latent presence of the other. Heterosexuality cannot be considered socially 'normal' if homosexuality is not judged a 'perversion'. The condition of homosexuals is the mirror image of a society that sees itself as heterosexual.

On the one hand, it is heterosexuality that holds 'power', we might say; heterosexuality is the Norm which the system upholds. Homosexuality, on the other hand, plays the role of the negative, the antithesis with respect to this institutionalised normality. As Andre Morali-Daninos wrote in a popular work:

> Were homosexuality to receive, even in theory, a show of approval, were it allowed to break away even partially from the framework of pathology, we would soon arrive at the abolition of the heterosexual couple and of the family, which are the foundations of the Western society in which we live.[3]

Given that the parental couple on which the family is based is a heterosexual relation, the education of children and young people is

2. See Chapter 5, section 4.

3. André Morali-Daninos, *Sociologie des relations sexuelles;* quoted in FHAR, *Rapport contre la normalité*, p. 70.

necessarily stamped in a heterosexual mould. The goal of educastration is the formation of a new heterosexual bond; every human being is constricted and mutilated by the dictatorship of heterosexual genitality. (And genitality, in the language of the sexophobe-sexologists, properly designates the penetration of the female sex organ by the male, with the purpose of procreation.)

The ideology of heterosexual primacy affects the minds of very many so-called 'revolutionaries'. It is sufficient to read a book like *The Grammar of Living*, for example, to see how people like David Cooper are still tied to a conception of heterosexuality as the principal expression of Eros. Heterosexual ideology also structured the thinking of Wilhelm Reich, convinced as he was of the need for an 'evolution' that would abolish the earlier stages (pregenital, anal and homosexual) in order to attain the perfect heterosexual genital orgasm. Schérer wrote about Reich that, 'in spite of the breadth of his body of work, his theory remains illuminated by, and obstinately committed to, frontal sexuality'.[4] Too many people claim to 'liberate sexuality' without putting the ideology of heterosexual primacy in question. The anus, in particular, remains proscribed. (The male anus, that is.)

Religion consecrates in matrimony the same heterosexual relationship that the state institutionalises. In this society, the conception of 'love' that is so heavily propagated is purely heterosexual in character. Erotic 'romanticism' – in the broad sense – is almost always heterosexual: *Death in Venice* is a rare exception, and even today, *Ernesto*[5] is seen as scandalous. And if homoeroticism is banned from society, or at best merely tolerated, then the ideal of heterosexual 'love' is broadcast in every possible way. Yet this much trumpeted 'love' is not love at all. Capital propagates the alienation of love; the so-called 'normal' couple is based on an alienated amorous bond, since the objectified and stereotyped woman is not woman but rather the negation of woman, and the phallic and deficient male is not man but the negation of both man and woman. The spectacle of heterosexuality cannot be identified with any deep amorous desire. Heterosexuality as it presents itself today is nothing but the dominant 'normal' form of a mutilated Eros. As well

4. Schérer, *Emilio pervertito*, p. 60.

5. [Translator's note: *Ernesto* is Umberto Saba's unfinished novel from 1953, published posthumously in 1975, a queer *Bildungsroman* that focuses on the early affairs of Ernesto, a 16-year-old boy from Trieste.]

as the negation of homoeroticism, it is above all the negation of love between persons of different sex.

The capitalist spectacle represents the maximum estrangement reached by the human species in the stage of its prehistory. And yet it is precisely the general spectacle character of contemporary society that leads those who reject it to recognise the hallmarks of a stage production in all the absolutisation of present and past: to understand how ideology passes off heterosexuality as the sole, 'natural' and eternal form of Eros. The revolutionary critique of the *society of the spectacle* will unmask the ideology of heterosexual primacy.

A deep and loving desire moves, and can be glimpsed, beneath, through, and beyond the present contradictory expressions of 'love'. Perhaps love is the tendency towards overcoming the individualist, solipsist, idealist and 'normal' delusion; love is the tendency to annihilate the outworn neurotic and ego-istic categories of 'subject' and 'object'. Feuerbach, in his way, had an inkling of this. Marx too.

The spectacular advertisement of alienated heterosexuality cannot but be anti-gay, whether explicitly or implicitly, given that the repression of homosexuality is indispensable to determining this type of heterosexuality. But if press, advertising and the mass media as a whole are constantly celebrating heterosexuality, fashion clearly reflects the homosexual taste that is prostituted to capitalist production and exploited by the system.

The woman-object[6] – sexy, 'captivating', well-dressed, well-made-up, hair styled to perfection, an empty simulacrum that is put on the market as a commodity designed for heterosexual fantasy – is the creation of a male homosexual *aesthetic* fantasy. It is aesthetic in the original Greek sense (*αισθησις*), tailored to the sensual desire for the woman which is almost universally latent in us manifest homosexuals. What excites straight men is the image of an artificial 'woman' springing from the censorship of erotic desire for the female that generally characterises male homosexuals (photographers, fashion designers, hair stylists, make-up artists, film directors). More than a real woman, heterosexual men desire a disguised homosexual fantasy of 'woman', and this is what they masturbate over. Tiziana V. maintains that the woman-object

6. [Translator's note: This is a specific portmanteau Mieli uses: 'donna-ogetto'. It could also be translated as the 'objectified woman', but given his reliance on a loosely Hegelian version of dialectics throughout, the specificity of a subject treated as object is important to underscore.]

created by designers, hairdressers, and others is nothing other than a *phallus* disguised as a woman, or better, a woman disguised as a phallus. If this is true, the heterosexual desire for this woman-object and for this feminine appearance is really a homosexual desire, the desire for cock. Manolo Pellegrini has drawn my attention to the way that the reified woman of pornographic magazines (of the *Playboy* type), photographed and posed as a general rule by gay photographers, is characterised by a stiffness of form (erect breasts, firm and protuding buttocks), whereas women generally tend more than men to a softness of form, a relaxation of bodily tissues. What is the source of this desire by the gay photographer to depict, and by the heterosexual man to desire, a stiff, erect, firm body, such as is rarely met with in reality, if not the secret intention on the gay man's part to display a male body, stiff and hard like an erect penis, and the secret desire for this on the heterosexual's part?

'Heterosexuality', therefore, is further imposed even in its subjection of homosexual taste and fantasy.[7] Heterosexuality is imposed even when its content bears the clear sign of homosexuality. Heterosexuality triumphs.

By contrast, love between people of the same sex represents a taboo. It is not talked about much, not taken into account. If it is mentioned at all, this is almost a slip of the tongue. It is discussed only in terms of disparagement, commiseration, condemnation, disgust (or tolerance), in the way that people speak about a disease, a vice or a noxious social pest. Heterosexual society is marked, in the words of Franceso Saba Sardi, by a profound

> form of 'racism,' when confronted with the homosexual and deviants in general, prescribing the very language that it uses: the signifiers and allusions that are resorted to in denoting the 'queen', the 'dyke', the 'queer', the 'fag', and so on. The abundance of synonyms, and the euphemisms that always accompany them, bear witness to the attraction and the contorted curiosity that the phenomenon generates, not to mention the inevitable tendency to use what the English call 'lavatory humour' in confronting such deviants, a humour that is denigrating and scornful. The same kind of jokes are told about both mad people and homosexuals.[8]

7. See Chapter 6, section 1.
8. Francesco Saba Sardi, 'La società omosessuale', *Venus* 7, (November 1972), p. 37.

In the eyes of the greater part of so-called 'normal' people, heterosexuality goes together with procreation, while homosexuality is associated with vice and prostitution. It is commonplace that a bad woman is both a whore and a lesbian. The scornful conception of transvestism serves as a link between prostitution and homosexuality. And the 'invert' is an evil individual who does dirty things and seduces children in public gardens or third-run cinemas.[9]

When a famous person such as Pasolini, for example, is brutally murdered by a young hustler, society opens its surprised eyes to this contradictory phenomenon hidden with it (and this is the only real connection between homosexuality and prostitution, leaving aside the prostitution which many transvestites are forced into). It finds that there are all these 'delinquent' young boys, who of course are really heterosexual – 'It's obvious that this Pelosi [the killer of Pasolini) can't be a queer; if he did that kind of thing, it was simply because he was hungry ...' – but who sell themselves for a few thousand lire and a plate of spaghetti to homosexuals in search of a bit of friendly company.[10] In reality, of all the present expressions of the homosexual ghetto, none is so profoundly akin, so evidently conforming to the heterosexual society, as this parasitic and violent form of hustling. Perhaps this is why, to the eyes of 'normal' people, these so-called 'heterosexual' male prostitutes are so easily unnoticed. And in this way there passes unnoticed, too, one of the modes of exploitation that the heterosexual society inflicts on us gays.

The Anti-homosexual Taboo. Its Origins

Freud already felt the need to take into account 'the fact that inversion was a frequent phenomenon – one might almost say an institution charged with important functions – among the peoples of antiquity at the height of their civilisation'.[11]

As a result of historical and anthropological investigation, the Danish psychiatrist Thorkil Vangaard came to recognise the universal presence of homoerotic desire. Robert J. Stoller, for his part, writes:

> In other circumstances of time and place, contrary to what happens in our Western society, a homosexual act may be an important assertion

9. When I was a child, I searched in vain for someone who would 'entrap' me.
10. See Chapter 4, section 3.
11. Freud, 'Three Essays on The Theory of Sexuality', p. 139.

> of the individual's male identity, rich in the sentiment of a proud masculinity. Vangaard and Karlen relate cases where the homosexual act is used formally, publicly and in a religious context so as to transmit virility from man to boy and establish bonds of honourable virility between adult lovers.[12]

Géza Róheim described the customs of some Australian tribes among whom initiation rites and circumcision were accompanied by homosexual relationships between adults and young boys.[13]

Clellan Ford and Frank Beach stress the fundamental role that homosexuality plays among several peoples in North Africa, New Guinea and Australia. Marise Querlin has studied homosexual behaviour among certain North American tribes already mentioned earlier by Margaret Mead and Ruth Benedict, and similar behaviour among the indigenous inhabitants of Siberia. Malinowski described the severe repression of homosexuality among the Trobriand people of northeastern New Guinea.[14]

Finally, Freud also noted how, already in his time, the pathological standpoint of homoeroticism had given way, in scientific thought, to the anthropological.[15]

As John Lauritsen has summed up, homosexuality flourished throughout the ancient world: among the Scandinavians, Greeks, Celts, Sumerians, and throughout the 'Cradle of Civilisation', the Tigris-Euphrates Valley, the Nile Valley, and the Mediterranean Basin. The art and literature of these peoples offer testimony to an unhindered acceptance and often exaltation of same-sex love. The anti-homosexual taboo that marks our Western civilisation would appear to be of Hebrew origin. The ancient Hebrews were the first people in history to condemn homosexuality.[16]

---

12. Robert J. Stoller, 'Faits et Hypothèses', *Nouvelle Revue de Psychiatrie*, no. 7, (1973).
13. Géza Róheim, *Héros phalliques et symboles maternels dans la mythologie australienne* (Paris: Gallimard, 1970).
14. Ford and Beach, *Patterns of Sexual Behaviour*; Marise Querlin, *Women Without Men* (London: Mayflower, 1968); Margaret Mead, *Male and Female* (New York: Perennial, 2006); Ruth Benedict, *Patterns of Culture* (London: Routledge, 1980); Bronislaw Malinowski, *Sex and Repression in Savage Society* (London: Routledge, 2015).
15. Freud, 'Three Essays on The Theory of Sexuality', p. 139, note.
16. John Lauritsen, *Religious Roots of the Taboo on Homosexuality: A Materialist View* (New York: Self-Published, 1974), p. 6.

The Bible records two celebrated episodes of mass homosexuality, that of Sodom and Gomorrah (*Genesis* 19–20) and that of the Benjaminites (*Judges* 1 9–20). According to Pietro Agostino d'Avack,

> In both cases, the inhabitants of Sodom, being informed of the arrival of the two angels, and the Benjaminites of Gibeah, apprised of the arrival of the Levite, tried violently to grab these visitors away from those who had extended hospitality to them (Lot in the first episode, the Ephraimite in the second), with a view to satisfying their libidinal desires; and on both occasions the hosts, out of respect for the sacred duties of hospitality, did not just refuse, but actually offered instead their own daughters. In one case as in the other, the Lord's revenge was visited in the most terrible fashion on the impious. Sodom and Gomorrah were completely destroyed by fire and brimstone, while the people of Gibeah and the other Benjaminite tribes who had run to their aid were confronted and annihilated in battle, at the Lord's command, by the other tribes of Israel, their cities and villages all abandoned to the flames, and men and animals put to the sword.[17]

The destruction of Sodom is ascribed by the Bible to Abraham's time, which means approximately 2,000 BC. And yet it seems clear that the anti-homosexual taboo was not imposed on the Hebrew people at so early a date.

An explicit prohibition on homosexuality is contained in the books of Moses. Mosaic law prescribed that men who had sexual relations with one another should be put to death, so that the chosen people should differentiate themselves from the practices of those around them. 'You shall not lie with a man as with a woman: that is an abomination'.[18] In line with the divine punishment for the 'crime' of the people of Sodom, the capital punishment imposed by Hebrew law for this offence was that of burning.

---

17. Pietro Agostino d'Avack, 'L'omosessualità nel diritto canonico', *Ulisse* xviii, 1953, p. 682.

18. *Leviticus* 18, 22; See ibid., 20, 13.
Luciano Parinetto notes: 'As the fact of prostatic orgasm can be demonstrated, it is impossible in fact to "lie with a man as with a woman", except if the imaginary aspect alone is taken into account. But God-father-law is not concerned with the truth, only with duty, and this prescribes role-playing' ('Analreligion e dintorni. Appunti', *L'Erba Voglio* 26, (June–July 1976), p. 20).

It is more than probable, however, that Hebrew legislation against homosexuality did not in fact date back to the time of Moses, the exodus from Egypt and the conquest of Palestine. It seems rather that the legislative portion of the Mosaic books was compiled predominantly during the Babylonian exile (sixth century BC), when the activity of priests and Levites was especially intense.

In his pamphlet *Religious Roots of the Taboo on Homosexuality: A Materialist View*, John Lauritsen explains why he inclines to the opinion of those scholars who see the anti-homosexual taboo among the Hebrews as having been imposed during the Babylonian exile. Earlier, homosexuality was not only accepted, it was actually vested with important religious functions; according to Lauritsen, male prostitutes followed a sacred vocation and practised their art in the Temple.[19]

We still do not know what precise motivations led the ancient Hebrews to condemn homoeroticism. John Lauritsen shows how unconvincing are the various hypotheses that scholars have put forward to explain this. For my part, I believe that only a deeper study of ancient Hebrew history from a homosexual standpoint will enable us to put forward some valid explanatory hypotheses. This work, however, still lies in the future.

What is clear is that there was some kind of connection between the preservation of Hebrew national tradition, particularly that of monotheism, and the rejection of homosexuality. The Hebrews ended up by identifying homosexual 'practices' with the religions and customs of the heathen; the destruction of Sodom and Gomorrah, in their eyes, was provoked by the wrath of Jahweh at an alien people for their alien customs.

Some passages from the Old Testament link homoeroticism with the cult of Ashtoreth (the great female divinity of the northern Semitic peoples, who most probably represented the fertilised soil, and was the patron of sacred prostitution) and her heavenly spouse Baal, a cult which the Hebrews were particularly inclined to 'decline' into, particularly given their common habitation and mingling, in the land of Palestine, with the Canaanites (Solomon, for example, built altars to Ashtoreth, which were subsequently destroyed by the reforming king Josiah). It would seem that the Canaanite cult of Baal was linked with certain 'obscene practices' (*Numbers* XXV). For me, it was also interesting to discover how, among the southern Semites, the corresponding figure to

19. Lauritsen, *Religious Roots of the Taboo on Homosexuality*, p. 6.

Ashtoreth, 'Athar, was a male divinity – a fact which has led some people to hypothesise the remote existence of the cult of an ancient divinity of androgynous character, only later differentiated into a goddess among the northern Semites and a male god among their southern relations. But these are only hypotheses, and there may be others that are more convincing.

What is certain, however, is that by way of Christianity, the Jewish condemnation of homosexuality has been handed down to us.

But in what sense can one speak today of an anti-homosexual taboo?

According to Freud, 'the meaning of "taboo"... diverges in two contrary directions. To us it means, on the one hand, "sacred", "consecrated", and on the other "uncanny", "dangerous", "forbidden", "unclean".'[20] Now in our society homoeroticism is certainly considered uncanny, dangerous, forbidden and unclean, a fact which is not difficult to establish. But can we also say that it is somehow treated as sacred and consecrated, something from which it is necessary to keep a respectful distance?

On the one hand, we have seen how originally, before it was persecuted, male homosexuality was something sacred among the Hebrews, being practised in the Temple in the form of prostitution, also how the Hebrews later came to connect homosexuality with the cult of a divinity worshipped by other peoples. The Judeo-Christian moral and religious tradition has marked Western society down to today. In a certain sense, therefore, we can say that today the anti-homosexual taboo conceals the originally sacred character of its object. Later on, ancient Greek culture also became a profound influence on Western civilisation, and among the Greeks, homosexuality certainly did originally have a sacred character, as well as being both erotic and chivalrous.[21]

Today, on the other hand, even when so many people no longer believe in the devil, homosexuality still keeps its diabolical connotations, as 'vicious', 'perverted', 'dishonourable', 'unclean' and 'revolting'. It remains a 'sin against nature', and as far as the Church is concerned, any sin is inspired by the devil. But the diabolical precisely serves as a medium between the sacred and the 'unclean'. 'It is precisely this neutral and intermediate meaning – 'demonic' or 'what may not be touched' – that is appropriately expressed by the word 'taboo', since it stresses a

20. Sigmund Freud, 'Totem and Taboo', *Standard Edition,* Vol. 13 (London: Vintage, 2001), p. 18.

21. Carlo Diano, 'L'Eros greco', *Ulisse* xviii, (1953), pp. 698–708.

characteristic which remains common for all time both to what is sacred and to what is unclean: the dread of contact with it' (Freud).[22]

In dealing with homosexuality, heterosexual society suffers from what Freud described as a 'taboo sickness', an obsessional neurosis (as society is obsessed with the presence of us gays):

> As in the case of taboo, the principal prohibition, the nucleus of this neurosis, is against touching; and thence it is sometimes known as 'touching phobia' or *'delire de toucher'*. The prohibition does not merely apply to immediate physical contact but has an extent as wide as the metaphorical use of the phrase 'to come into contact with'. Anything that directs the patient's thoughts to the forbidden object, anything that brings him into intellectual contact with it, is just as much prohibited as direct physical contact.[23]

Heterosexual society prohibits or at least rejects gay relations, erotic contact between bodies of the same sex, and in the same way it rejects any contact with open homosexuals, those who have not been forced into hiding, pushed into corners or excluded from society. It condemns, moreover, any idea or fantasy with a clear homoerotic content (so that gay thoughts and fantasies, especially those of heterosexuals, must remain secret). Many heterosexuals have decisively repressed their own homosexual desire, and even when this repression is not completely successful, they at least conceal their gay fantasies from others as something intimate and essentially shameful, which is not to be communicated.

But the anti-homosexual prohibition owes its strength and its constricting character specifically to the relation with its unconscious counterpart, the latent and never eliminated homosexual desire, that deep necessity that cannot be consciously recognised: 'the basis of taboo is a prohibited action, for performing which a strong inclination exists in the unconscious' (Freud).[24]

We shall see later on how homosexual desire continuously shifts around, with a view to overcoming the barrier that forces it to remain unconscious, and seeks surrogates for the forbidden 'object', substitute 'objects' and practices that then also enter into the complex of phenomena

22. Freud, 'Totem and Taboo', p. 25.
23. Ibid., p. 27.
24. Ibid., p. 32.

that can be interpreted by the concept of sublimation of the gay desire (or else its conversion into pathological symptoms).

The anti-homosexual taboo is all the more severe in as much as the prohibition directs energy against a very strong inclination that exists in a latent state: for heterosexuals, homosexuality always represents an 'instinctual temptation'.

The inherent prohibitions on homosexuality are transmitted from generation to generation, by the tradition represented in the authority of society and parents, and despite the fact that every single individual newly experiences, in the course of development, the congenital homosexual impulse in all its potential fullness. The gay desire remains very strong even among those peoples who have respected the anti-homosexual taboo for thousands of years. If this were not so, then the taboo would have no reason to be maintained with such rigour.

The society in which we live displays an ambivalent attitude towards the prohibitions which the anti-gay taboo imposes on it. At the unconscious level, both individual and collective, nothing could be more pleasant than to transgress it – but people are afraid. And fear proves to be more powerful than the impulse to enjoyment. According to Freud, again, 'the desire is unconscious . . . in every individual member of the tribe just as it is in neurotics'.[25] Reversing this statement, we might say that the population is neurotic because the desire to transgress, i.e. in this case to transgress the sexual Norm, is unconscious in each individual. *For liberation, we need to learn to openly enjoy such transgression.*

The manifest homosexual who has transgressed the anti-gay taboo becomes taboo himself, 'because he possesses the dangerous quality of tempting others to follow his example: why should *he* be allowed to do what is forbidden to others? Thus he is truly contagious in that every example encourages imitation, and for that reason he himself must be shunned'.[26] It is out of envy that we gays are pushed aside, insulted, derided and censured. In this way people try to exorcise and push aside the gay desire that our presence makes surface in society, forcing everyone to confront it. If other people did not punish and censure our homosexual transgression, they would end up wanting to do the same things as we, the transgressors, do. And it is true that, if the example of one person who has violated the anti-gay taboo should lead others to follow, then disobedience to the prohibition would spread itself like a 'contagion'.

25. Ibid., p. 31.
26. Ibid., p. 32.

The objective of the revolutionary struggle of homosexuals is not social tolerance for gays, but rather the liberation of homoerotic desire in every human being. If the only result were that so-called 'normal' people should 'accept' homosexuals, then the human race would not have recognised its own deep homosexual desire, it would not have come to terms with the universal presence of this and would go on suffering without remedy from the consequences of this repression that is itself an oppression. We revolutionary homosexuals, today, seduce others to imitate us, to come with us, so that together we can undertake the subversion of the Norm that represses (homo)eroticism.

Today, the persistence of the anti-gay taboo provides a sure and potent weapon in the capitalist arsenal: it serves to stupefy people, to maintain a neurotic and submissive 'calm'. The taboo transforms one of the basic erotic tendencies into a source of horror and guilt, denying every human being the possibility of erotic relations with half the population, dividing people and keeping them apart, preventing love between man and man and woman and woman, and making a fundamental contribution to perpetuating the opposition between the sexes. People 'know very well' (even if they don't have a clear understanding) that they have homosexual impulses. The system can then play on their guilt, severely prohibiting homosexuality, which it stamps with the mark of infamy. 'Normal' people feel guilty because, underneath it all, they know that they are a little queer themselves. But the sense of guilt is the umbilical cord that chains the human species to capital, trying to strangle it. If we want to live, we must sever this monstrous bond once and for all.

Today, the great fear that surrounds homosexuality doesn't live on air alone. Deep down inside, everyone can smell the blood that has been shed over millennia to keep the anti-homosexual taboo respected and feared (through castration, imprisonment, exile, torture and death). When they look into themselves, everybody knows that they are potentially condemned to the flames.

The Persecution of Homosexuals Over the Centuries

The repression of homosexuals today, for all its harshness, is only the echo of a horrendous persecution perpetrated for thousands of years. As we have just indicated, the anti-homosexual condemnation of the Hebrews was spread throughout the West with the rise of Christianity.

Already at the end of the republican era in Rome, a *Lex Scantinia*[27] was issued against 'male abuses' between free citizens, providing for a fine of 10,000 sesterces for the 'guilty' parties.[28] It is clear, therefore, that Christianity already found in Rome an environment that was favourable to the punishment of homosexuality (but for what reason?). In the time of St Paul, this fine was raised to the confiscation of half a man's estate.[29]

During the decline of the empire, legislation developed a severity that was previously unknown. In the 4th century Christianity became the official state religion. Shortly before, in 300, the Council of Elvira had decreed that 'sodomites' were ineligible for the Christian last rites. In 342 a decree of Emperor Constantine imposed the death penalty for the 'crime of sodomy'. A later legal code, that of Theodosius, Valens and Arcadius, condemned homosexuals to be burned alive in the square (390). For centuries, the punishment of burning, explicitly recalling the destruction of Sodom, was the penalty most frequently provided for in legislation.

In 538, Justinian prescribed torture, mutilation and castration for homosexuals; the capital punishment of beheading with a sword, already imposed for adultery, was subsequently extended to 'sodomy' also.[30]

And yet under Justinian, a homosexual, even if he had confessed, was only beheaded if, after already being arrested once, he had shown evidence of persisting in his 'aberrant practices', thus refusing to submit to the rigorous canonical penitence imposed the first time. This apparent 'lenience' was however made up for by the fact that anyone could be accused of 'sodomy'. The most suspect evidence of a child or slave was sufficient to condemn a man to infamy and death, such that 'pederasty became the crime of those to whom no crime could be imputed' (Edward Gibbon).[31] In two successive edicts, Justinian defined homosexuality as a

---

27. [Editor's note from original volume: The Latin sources don't make it possible to establish with precision the date, contents, or even the name of this law. It might be reasonably supposed that it punished, through a fine, the seduction of freeborn minors or *inter ingenuos* relations, i.e. between adult Roman citizens. In the latter case, however, it's likely that the penalty fell solely on the passive partner of a homosexual relation.]

28. d'Avack, 'L'omosessualità nel diritto canonico', p. 682.

29. [Editor's note from original volume: The most recent studies maintain that the hypothesis of increased sanctions against homosexuals at the start of the imperial period was unfounded. See for instance E. Cantarella, *Secondo natura, la bisessualità nel mondo antico* (Milano: Rizzoli, 1995), pp. 182–5).]

30. Ibid., p. 683.

31. Quoted by John Lauritsen, *Religious Roots of the Taboo on Homosexuality*, p. 10.

'diabolical and unlawful lust', warning his subjects to abstain from such 'immoral and disgusting activities, which are not even committed by animals'. Evidently the emperor saw what it suited him to see, or perhaps he really had never seen two male dogs fucking. Justinian saw himself as the instrument of the 'just anger and revenge of God' against those 'guilty of sodomy', who, with their 'crimes', 'have provoked famines, earthquakes and pestilences'...

Equally severe and harshly repressive laws against homosexuality were issued in the following centuries, backed by the full weight of civil and ecclesiastical authority, from the early Middle Ages through to the French Revolution (and even beyond).

The *Lex Visigotha* condemned 'sodomites' to castration, harsh imprisonment, and, if they were married, the immediate confiscation of their goods in favour of their sons or other heirs.

Besides castration, this code also provided for the death penalty. The Danes, for their part, condemned 'sodomites' to be burnt (*Jura Danica*), while the *Capitulari Franchi* of Angesiso and Bendetto Levita called for the death penalty for male homosexuals, as it did for those guilty of incest and having sex with animals (*bestialitas* or *sodomia ratione generis*). A later *Capitulari* issued by Louis the Pious, king of the Franks and emperor (778–840), confirmed the punishment of burning for these 'crimes', drawing on Roman law.

According to these *Capitulari*, homosexuality was at this time most widespread among the Spaniards, Provençals and Burgundians, and this induced the legislators to recommend a rigorous application of the penalties provided for, in order that the 'unnatural vice' should not too gravely contaminate other peoples.

With the passage of time, homosexuals in some cities were no longer burned alive, but rather hanged in the public square and then killed with the sword (this was the case in many Italian cities, including Milan, Bologna, Aviano, Ferrara, Rome, Trieste, Osimo, Collalto, and in Valtellina). The 'crime of sodomy' was included among the list of offences for which torture was permitted during the trial, with a view to extracting a confession from the accused and his 'accomplices'.

Instead of being burned alive or hanged, homosexuals from the nobility were instead generally beheaded, with the loss of all their feudal privileges, which could not be handed down to their heirs. And yet it is a well known fact that many aristocrats or well-off commoners managed to buy their way out by paying large sums of money to potential informers, or to the public authorities, making themselves liable to constant heavy blackmail.

In general, if the accused were less than eighteen years of age and their offence was limited to the 'passive role', then instead of being condemned to death, they were punished with the lash, long terms of harsh imprisonment, branded, or else, as in Spain and Sicily, sent to the galleys either permanently or for a long period.

The statutes of Tarvisius, 'with a spectacular sense of the macabre' (d'Avack), provided that 'a man [guilty of sodomy] is to be stripped of all his clothing in the public street, and impaled to the stake by a nail through his member, and remain there a full day and night; on the next day he is to be burned outside the city. A woman is to be stripped of all clothes and bound to the stake, and remain there a full day and night, on the next day she is to be burned outside the city'.[32]

It is clear, then, that lesbians were no less horrendously persecuted. Even later, the celebrated criminologist Prospero Farinacci (1544–1618) noted how he had seen 'several women who had offended in this way' burned in Rome.

Persons suspected of homosexuality were often punished atrociously even when there was no direct evidence of their 'guilt'. In Venice, one man accused of 'sodomy' in 1282 was condemned to the loss of both eyes, even though the court had not succeeded in extracting a confession.

In Tuscany, where homosexuality was very widespread, persecution was somewhat less harsh, since – in the judgement of certain jurists of the period – if the death penalty were imposed for every 'crime of sodomy', then the whole country would be covered with stakes and gallows. In Lucca, all the same, capital punishment was decreed for 'active sodomy', the 'passive' partner being condemned to a lesser penalty, though in Florence only recidivist homosexuals, caught *in flagrante delicto* for the second or third time, were condemned to the stake.

According to several historians and chroniclers of the time, homosexuality nevertheless became ever more widespread in Italy, particularly after the Black Death of 1348. Perhaps because, between the risk of catching plague and that of ending up burned at the stake, more people were prepared to risk the punishment in order to enjoy themselves before they died. At all events, statutes from around this time multiply and harshen still further the repressive provisions.

32. d'Avack, 'L'omosessualità nel diritto canonico' p. 682. [Translator's note: This passage is provided in Latin by Mieli.]

In Milan, during the 15th century, homosexuals were branded on the forehead. This is why, at a later date, people who wore a fringe that covered their forehead were called '*sodoma*', and the fringe a '*copneulo*' (ass-cover).

In the following centuries, the penal code remained substantially unchanged, 'and it was more or less identical throughout both Italy and the other European states, as can be seen from the statutes of Bologna (1561), Ferrara (1566), Milan, Rome, the Marches, etc. in the seventeenth century, the Florentine *Bandi* of 1542, 1556 and 1669, the Sicilian *Prammatiche* of 1504, the criminal codes of Charles V and Maria Theresa, the Portuguese *Ordinanza Regia,* the Spanish *Nova Recopilation,* etc.'[33]

In the Middle Ages, the persecution of homosexuals stood in close relation to the repression of heresy: 'heresy and homosexuality became one and the same thing' (Szasz).[34] According to Westermarck,

> During the Middle Ages heretics were accused of unnatural vice as a matter of course. Indeed, so closely was sodomy associated with heresy that the same name was applied to both. In 'La Coutume de Touraine Anjou' the word *herite,* which is the ancient form of *heretique,* seems to be used in the sense of 'sodomite'; and the French *bougre* (from the Latin *Buigarus,* Bulgarian), as also its English synonym (bugger), was originally a name given to a sect of heretics who came from Bulgaria in the eleventh century and was afterwards applied to other heretics, but at the same time it became the regular expression for a person guilty of unnatural intercourse. In medieval laws sodomy was also repeatedly mentioned together with heresy, and the punishment was the same for both.[35]

The term 'faggot', still used today in the United States to refer to male homosexuals, and almost always derogatory, derives from such medieval expressions as 'fire and faggot', and 'to fry a faggot', originally referring to the punishment inflicted on heretics and 'sodomites'. Those heretics who recanted, in order to escape the death penalty, were forced to wear

33. Ibid., p. 685.

34. Thomas S. Szasz, *The Manufacture of Madness* (New York: Harper & Row, 1970), p. 164.

35. Edward Westermarck, *The Origin and Development of Moral Ideas,* quoted by Lauritsen, *Religious Roots of the Taboo on Homosexuality,* p. 12.

the emblem of a faggot embroidered on one sleeve. Thus the word ended up as a symbol for the stake, and when heresy was no longer a problem requiring the death penalty, it remained to denote homosexuals. In 1533, during the reign of Henry VIII, the penalty for 'sodomy' in England was changed from burning to hanging. The death penalty itself, however, was only abolished in 1861, and in Scotland not until 1889.

In Spain, during the thirteenth century, homosexuals were condemned to castration and stoning. It remained for Ferdinand and Isabella to introduce the stake, in 1479.[36] In 1541, Nicolas V entrusted the Inquisition with full powers for the repression of homosexuality. In the seventeenth century in Portugal, laws provided for condemnation to the stake, or alternatively the lash and the galleys.

In Amsterdam in 1730 (today the gay capital of Europe!), two hundred men and boys were tried for 'sodomy', with a hundred and seventy condemned to death. Holland at this time saw a real hunt for 'sodomites': the streets were papered with notices inviting the population to denounce to the authorities anyone suspected of being homosexual.

Persecution by the state was backed up by religious morality, both Catholic and Protestant. In some states, as for example in Spain, the public authorities requested the ecclesiastical courts to try cases of 'sodomy'. Even today, the Church is still responsible, either directly or indirectly, for anti-gay repression.

The writings of the Church fathers are replete with references to homosexuality. St Paul gives Christ special merit for saving the Christians from this '*immundita*' (uncleanness), the source of horrendous contamination and dishonour of body and spirit, and yet so widely diffused among the heathen (e.g. *Romans* 1, 26–27).

> An ancient Christian tradition, moreover, recorded by St Jerome and reiterated in successive centuries of ecclesiastical writings as a definite historical fact, actually held that the birth of the Saviour, the 'redeemer of the natural order', brought the sudden death of all sodomites 'living against nature', among them the poet Virgil.[37]

But given the tremendous spread of homoeroticism in this period, it is clear that if this had actually happened, there would have been 'such a

36. Szasz, *The Manufacture of Madness*, p. 164
37. d'Avack, 'L'omosessualità nel diritto canonico', p. 681.

general decease that the Roman empire would have collapsed straight away'.[38]

St Augustine, 'who by his youthful libertine experience remains, of all the Church fathers, the expert on the sins of the flesh',[39] considered homosexuality a worse and more abominable vice than adultery and even incest. And according to Thomas Aquinas, later on, homosexuality was a shameful sin with which a person 'debased his own sex' and to which only bestiality, an even worse vice, was inferior, 'debasing the species'. On the other hand, St Thomas considered masturbation a far worse sin than the rape of a woman, since 'just reason declares that the purpose prescribed for the sexual act is procreation'. That said, it's clear that while a rape can lead to the birth of a son, jerking off can't lead to the birth of a dick.

There is little point is tracing all the diverse positions taken on homosexuality by the theologians and canon lawyers throughout the centuries, nor in going into either the full range of punishments provided (including terms of imprisonment that were generally from ten years up to life), or again the various papal bulls against '*sodomia*', 'that horrendous wickedness', as Pius V defined it (1558). Homosexuality, by tradition *peccatum illud horribile inter Christianos non nominandum* ['that horrible sin not to be mentioned among Christians'], was now defined by the canon lawyers of the sixteenth century, with baroque pomposity, as 'something filthy, detestable, extremely grave, evil, disgusting, horrendous, immense and abominable', as well as 'a most loathsome, serious, foul, abominable and devouring sin'.

Finally, we are unable to follow in all its details the curious (alas! sadly curious!) dispute among canon lawyers on the subject of *coitus interruptus* between men. The Church tried long and hard to establish whether a man who fucks another but does not come into his ass - *immissio veretri in vase praepostreo* without *effusio seminis* – should be considered less guilty than those who have ejaculated within. Nor can we follow the debates that surrounded female homosexuality; for having established that an 'unnatural' coitus with *immissio veretri* was indispensable for the 'crime of sodomy', the theologians were unclear as to in what sense it was possible to speak of genuine 'sodomy' in a relationship between women, given the absence of *immissio veretri*. Believe it or not, they ended up

38. Ibid.
39. Ibid.

taking as the significant criterion the lesser or greater development of the clitoris of the woman on top. If a 'gynaecological' examination had established that the clitoris, by virtue of its singular development, could have served as a penis, then the court proceeded without further ado to torture, with a view to extracting confessions and 'imposing on both parties the appropriate penal sanctions'.[40]

Meanwhile, though the anti-homosexual taboo claimed countless thousands of victims in Europe, homoeroticism continued to prosper in those lands outside the influence of Judea-Christianity. The anti-gay taboo was unknown in China, Japan, India, the Arab world, Africa, Australia, Siberia or pre-Columbian America.[41]

Contemporary Legislation and the Homosexual Rights Movement

In his 'philosophical novel' *Aline et Valcour,* the Marquis de Sade presents a visit to France by Zamé, the idealised legislator of an unknown Pacific island. In the course of his stay, the host accompanies him to the law courts, as busy as ever in their grotesque and summary sentencing. Zamé is here the narrator.

> —What crime has that unhappy man committed, I asked.
> —He is a homosexual, I was told. You can well see that his is a terrible crime, it stops the growth of population, even destroys it, so that this scoundrel well deserves to be destroyed himself.
> —Well argued, I replied to my philosophical friend, your reasoning is indeed that of a genius.

Zamé and his guide then immediately proceed to visit a monastery, where a young girl is taking her vows.

> —What is this girl doing, my friend?
> —She is a saint, I was told. She is giving up the world, and is going to bury in the depths of a nunnery the seed of twenty children that she would otherwise have borne for the state to play with.
> —What a sacrifice.
> —Oh indeed, sir, she is an angel, she has a place already in heaven.

---

40. Ibid., p. 697.
41. Lauritsen, *Religious Roots of the Taboo on Homosexuality*, p. 12.

> —Quite outraged, and unable to bear such inconsistency, I turned to my friend and said: Sir, on the one hand you bum to death a man whose crime, you say, is that of restraining the population, while on the other hand, you now celebrate a young girl who is committing the same crime. You Frenchmen should bring your affairs into a logical order, otherwise it is quite understandable that any rational foreigner who visits your country should take it as the very centre of madness and absurdity.[42]

This was written by the Marquis de Sade, that outrageous libertine, in the Bastille, the year before the outbreak of the French Revolution. In the name of reason, 'his work discloses the mythological character of the principles which religion says are the foundations of civilisation: the Decalogue, paternal authority, property'.[43]

In 1791, in the same spirit of the Enlightenment (Diderot had seen in homosexuality a natural remedy against both overpopulation and syphillis!), the French Constituent Assembly abolished the death penalty for the 'crime of sodomy'.

In 1810, accepting a new draft legal code from his minister Cambacérès, himself gay, Napoleon finally legalised homosexuality; homosexual relations in private between consenting parties were no longer considered an offence in the countries where the Napoleonic code was enforced, among them Italy.

With the fall of Napoleon, Italian legislation partly reasserted its former persecutory character. In the Sardinian code of 1859, article 425 treated homosexuality as a crime, if associated with violence or scandal. Yet when the Sardinian code was extended to the Southern provinces in 1861, article 425 was abolished.[44]

Under fascism, although specific anti-homosexual legislation was not introduced, the island of Ventotene was set aside, among other purposes, as a place of confinement for gays.[45] At the end of 1941, moreover, the old

42. Donatien Alphonse François de Sade, *Aline et Valcour* (Brussels: J. J. Gay, 1883), Vol 2, pp. 206–7.

43. Max Horkheimer and Theodor Adorno, *Dialectic of Enlightenment* (London: Allen Lane, 1973), p. 115.

44. Marc Daniel and André Baudry, *Gli omosessuali* (Florence: Valecchi, 1974). See also Lauritsen, *Religious Roots of the Taboo on Homosexuality.*

45. [Editor's note from original volume: Homosexuals were confined on other islands as well, in particular the Tremiti. After 1985, thanks to the availability of new documentation, several historical studies have reconstructed a framework that reveals

1869 penal code for the army and navy was reintroduced, this providing particular 'disciplinary' sanctions (up to ten years forced labour) for 'crimes of unnatural passion'.

Present Italian legislation does not treat homosexual relations as a special type of offence. In fact, according to the ministerial statement on a new draft penal code:

> This filthy vice . . . is not so widespread in Italy as to require the intervention of the criminal law. This should be standardised according to the principle of absolute necessity, and there is no justification for creating new offences unless the legislators should find forms of immorality that disrupt social life in an alarming way. This is happily not the case in Italy for the vice under consideration here. These reasons against the criminalisation of homosexuality have convinced me . . .[46]

So if homosexuality is not in itself a crime in Italy today, this depends on the statistical information available to our legislators. If these gentlemen should however realise that acknowledged homosexuals in Italy make up at least 4.5 per cent of the population, and so-called 'bisexuals' far more, it would then follow that homosexuality should perhaps be criminalised after all.[47]

In any case, as we can see from the ministerial statement on the diffusion of this 'filthy vice' in Italy, present legislation

> leans against homosexuality in *indirect* ways, in the sense that the condemnation of homosexuality can be taken into account when this comes up against certain other interests that are different from the interest involved in the struggle against homosexuality itself. Thus

---

the repressive measures against homosexuality in the fascist period. In particular, see *Nel nome della razza: Il razzismo nella storia d'Italia 1870–1965*, ed. Alberto Burgio (Bologna: Il Mulino, 1999).]

46. This ministerial report is quoted by Salvatore Messina in 'L'omosessualità nel diritto penale', *Ulisse* xviii, (1953), p. 675.

47. The World Health Organisation estimates that the number of 'true' homosexuals in Italy (in this psychonazi distinction between 'true' and 'pseudo' homosexuality) comes to some 2,475,000, i.e. about 4.5 per cent of the entire population, male and female. And on top of the 1,120,000 'true' male homosexuals, I would assume at least some 5 million bisexual males in Italy, i.e. men who have sexual relations with both women and other men.

> homosexuality can be punished when it is accompanied by extremes of carnal violence (or violent acts of desire), or when the obscene act is performed in a place exposed to the public; here is also the crime of 'corruption of minors'.[48]

The accusation of *plagio*, moreover, can always be injected to liven up the charges against someone like Braibanti.[49]

But if present Italian legislation is relatively permissive as far as homosexuality is concerned, repression by the police is severe indeed. Moreover, if the law only indirectly threatens to punish, moral norms proclaim the conscious internalisation of a far more severe law.

In the course of the last thirty years, there have been various attempts to introduce specific anti-gay penalties. On 5 April 1972, for example, the Italian Centre of Sexology[50] organised the first international festival of sexology at San Remo, at which certain people declared their 'intention to collect . . . information to support a legislative proposal by the Social-Democrat party which would put homosexuality outside the law'.[51]

---

48. Messina, 'L'omosessualità nel diritto penale', p. 473.
49. [Translator's note: Aldo Braibanti was a remarkable figure in Italian postwar culture, an anti-fascist partisan, poet, experimental theater director, expert on ants, and polymath intellectual who, amongst many other activities, made anti-Stalinist interventions within the PCI (before breaking with them) and worked with Carmelo Bene. In 1968, he was sentenced to nine years in prison (subsequently reduced in part for his past as a partisan fighter) on the obscure charge of 'plagiary' (*plagio*), a sort of spiritual kidnapping or psychic 'plagiarism'. According to the charges, he allegedly seduced two young men successively to leave their families and live with him in a homosexual relationship, during which he psychically controlled them (the implication being that they would not have engaged in homosexual activities without his Mabuse-like influence). Braibanti was the first and only person to be tried and convicted under the *plagio* charge, which had been reintroduced by the fascists, and his farcical trial led to an outpouring of support from figures such as Pasolini, Bene, Umberto Eco, and others.]
50. [Editor's note from original volume: It isn't certain if the intentions of the Italian Center of Sexology, a Catholic-oriented organisation, were really that of promoting a law to make homosexuality legally punishable. The stated aim of the meeting at San Remo was to focus on the most modern therapies for sexual deviance, which included the most humiliating and violent psychiatric treatments. It was on this occasion that the Italian gay movement organised its first public initiative, strongly contesting the meeting and gaining attention from mass media. As for laws against homosexuals, all the same, there was no more talk of it.]
51. Alfredo Cohen, Introduction to *La politica del corpo*, p. 18.

A similar situation obtains in France. For a whole century, until the Vichy regime, there seem to have been no condemnations expressly for homosexuality. On 6 August 1942, however, Marshal Pétain published an anti-gay decree. Guy Hocquenghem has shown how the new French penal code drawn up after the Liberation contained an article that reproduced the fascist decree almost word for word. Article 331 of this code, adopted on 8 February 1945, punishes with 'a term of imprisonment from six months to three years . . . whosoever will have committed an indecent or unnatural act with a person of the same sex, under the age of twenty-one'. A second law on homosexuality, this time phrased in terms of 'public indecency', was voted in 1960 after the return of De Gaulle. Up till then, the penal code had not distinguished between homosexual and heterosexual 'indecency'. Article 330, paragraph 2 of the law of 25 November 1960, however, prescribes that: 'When the public indecency consists of an unnatural act with an individual of the same sex, the penalty will be a term of imprisonment from six months to three years and a fine of 1,000 to 15,000 francs'. As Hocquenghem points out, heterosexual indecency is cheaper: a 500 to 4,500 francs fine only.[52]

In 1964, the French courts condemned 331 people for 'unnatural' acts, rising to 424 in 1966. A bitter police persecution continued to be waged against what deputy Paul Mirguet classed alongside tuberculosis and alcoholism as one of the most dangerous 'social diseases' (18 July 1961). The Front Homosexuel d'Action Révolutionnaire later adopted this phrase as the title of their first newspaper, *'Le Fléau Social'*.

In the Federal Republic of Germany, it was only recently (in 1969, and again in 1973) that the Bundestag modified paragraph 175 of the penal code that had made homosexual relations between males a criminal offence, although lesbian relations were not included.

Yet Germany was the country that had seen the first formation, anywhere in the world, of a gay liberation movement, at the end of the nineteenth century – even if this did have a 'petty-bourgeois democratic character', as Thorsten Graf and Mimi Steglitz put it.[53] In 1897, two years after the death of Karl Heinrich Ulrichs, the great pioneer in the struggle for homosexual liberation in Germany, the first official

52. Guy Hocquenghem, *Homosexual Desire*, p. 65.

53. Thorsten Graf and Mimi Steglitz, 'La repressione degli omosessuali nella società borghese', *Gay gay: storia e conscienza omosessuale* (Milan: La Salamandra, 1975), p. 118.

organisation seeking equal rights for gays, the Scientific Humanitarian Committee, was founded in Berlin.[54] This committee was set up and led for thirty-five years by Magnus Hirschfeld, author, among other works, of a kind of encyclopedia of homosexuality titled, *Male and Female Homosexuality*.[55] The main activity of this organisation, for three decades, was a petition against paragraph 175 of the Prussian legal code. The signatories of this petition were not only homosexuals. It was signed by some six thousand 'personalities' of the day, half of these being doctors. On 13 January 1898 the Social-Democrat leader August Bebel took the floor in the Reichstag to support the petition, which Kautsky and Bernstein had also signed.

During the Weimar period in Berlin, the homosexual question became highly topical, and it seems to have been discussed on all sides.[56] In December 1922, the Reichstag voted to draw the petition to the attention of the government, but the government rejected it, and for several years nothing more was done. Finally, 'on 16 October 1929 the Reichstag commission on criminal law decided that, "immoral acts between males" should not be included in the new penal code. The provisions of paragraph 175 . . . were abrogated, with the support of both Communist and Social Democrat deputies'.[57]

At the same time, the Scientific Humanitarian Committee sponsored a World League for Sexual Reform. In this cause, Hirschfeld and other fellow workers travelled across the globe, especially in the United States, but also to the Far East and even China, everywhere holding meetings on the theme of homosexual emancipation. At the time of its greatest expansion (in the late 1920s), some 130,000 people belonged to organisations affiliated to the World League for Sexual Reform.

The triumph of fascism in 1933 prevented the abrogation of paragraph 175 from coming into force. Between 1933 and 1935, the gay movement was brutally smashed by the Nazis, and in 1935 the laws against homosexuality were not only reintroduced, but actually strengthened. The

54. Lauritsen and Thorstad, *The Early Homosexual Rights Movement (1864–1935)*, p. 9.

55. Magnus Hirschfeld, *Die Homosexualität des Mannes und des Weibes* (Berlin: Louis Marcus, 1920). See also *Sexualpathologie. Ein Lehrbuch für Ärzte und Studierende* (Bonn: Marcus and Weber, 1922).

56. Ivan Goll, *Sodoma e Berlino* (Milan: Il formichiere, 1975).

57. Thorsten Graf and Mimi Steglitz, 'La repressione degli omosessuali nella società borghese', p. 92.

penal sanctions of paragraph 175 were extended to include the 'crimes' of homosexual kissing, embracing, and even fantasy.

The last of a series of bulletins from the Scientific Humanitarian Committee was published in February 1933 by Kurt Hiller.[58] Magnus Hirschfeld emigrated to France, where he died a short time later. In 1933, a Nazi attack wrecked the Berlin Institute for Sexual Science, where both the Scientific Humanitarian Committee and the World League for Sexual Reform had their offices. More than ten thousand books in the Institute's library were destroyed. A bust of Hirschfeld was carried in a torchlight procession and thrown onto the flames.

In June 1934 Hitler decreed the purging of the SA, Ernst Röhm's 'brown-shirts'. In the 'night of the long knives', Röhm was caught by the SS in bed with a young man, and executed in the Munich plison of Stadelheim. The greater part of the SA leadership, who were holding a jamboree at Weissee, in Bavaria, were murdered on the spot. The yellow press organised 'the stupid staging of "moral crimes" which had long been common knowledge' (Thomas Mann).

From then on, the concentration camps began to swell with homosexuals, their uniforms bearing on the chest and right trouser leg a pink triangle some seven centimetres high, to distinguish them from the Jews, Gypsies, political detainees, etc. Later, homosexuals from other countries occupied by the Nazis were sent to concentration camps in Germany and Austria.[59] These 'inverts' were often castrated by doctors officially entrusted with this task; many died as a result of forced labour or disease, others ending up in the gas chambers. Today, the homosexual liberation groups in West Germany have adopted the pink triangle as their badge.

We do not know exactly how many gay men and women were exterminated in the camps, though the homosexual victims of Nazism must have totalled some hundreds of thousands. 'An exact estimate is impossible', write John Lauritsen and David Thorstad, 'because homosexuals, especially those in the military, were routinely shot without trial. The concentration camp records, which would have provided information, were systematically destroyed when the German defeat became apparent'.[60]

58. Kurt Hiller, one of the most prominent exponents of the homosexual equal rights movement, died in 1972 at the age of 87.

59. John Lauritsen and David Thorstad, *The Early Homosexual Rights Movement (1864–1935)*, p. 44.

60. Ibid., pp. 44–5.

We do know, however, that between 1937 and 1939 alone, some 24,450 men were condemned to imprisonment in Germany for 'unnatural acts'.[61]

In England, as mentioned above, the death penalty for the 'crime of sodomy' was abolished only in 1861 – and in Scotland not until 1889. In the late nineteenth century, an influential campaign for homosexual liberation was waged in Great Britain by the socialist writer Edward Carpenter, destined to occupy a leading place in the gay pantheon. His works were known in many countries, being translated into German, Italian, Norwegian, Dutch, Bulgarian, Russian and Japanese. The anti-homosexual hysteria that broke out in England after the Oscar Wilde trial prevented the publication in some countries of Carpenter's masterwork *Love's Coming of Age*. But several decades before, the appearance of *Leaves of Grass* by Walt Whitman, whom Carpenter had twice met and highly esteemed, had already exerted a notable emancipating influence among Anglo-Saxon homosexuals.[62]

The trial of Oscar Wilde, accused of 'gross indecency' for his homosexual relationships, took place in London in 1895:

> The Wilde affair was a turning-point in the literary and social life of England, as the Dreyfus affair had been in France. Certainly England was not divided politically and there was not the slightest doubt about the guilt of the culprit, but in both cases the conservative elements felt themselves threatened.[63]

It is said that trains leaving for the Continent were packed with anxious gays. And the Irish, too, began to stir, spreading the view that Wilde had been slandered by the 'abominable English judges'. The same protests were issued in 1916, when one of the greatest Irish patriots, Sir Roger Casement, was charged with secret dealings with the German enemy. In order to prejudice the jury, the police issued to them Casement's homosexual diary. The judges succeeded in antagonising his own supporters, both in Ireland and the United States, who publicly denounced his homosexuality. Still today, many Irish nationalists continue to maintain that the Casement diaries are not genuine, but were rather fabricated

---

61. 'Lo sterminio degli omosessuali nel Terzo Reich', *Fuori!* 12, (Spring 1974).
62. John Lauritsen and David Thorstad, *The Early Homosexual Rights Movement (1864–1935)*, pp. 32ff.
63. Philippe Jullian, *Oscar Wilde* (London: Paladin, 1971), p. 271.

by the police and courts in order to slander and turn public opinion against him. In their eyes, it seems, homosexuality is incompatible with greatness of spirit and heroism.

It was only in 1967 that homosexuality was legalised in England and Wales. Paradoxically, the anti-gay statute is still in force in Scotland and Northern Ireland, so that a homosexual who is a 'free' citizen in London and Cardiff, becomes a criminal if he moves to Edinburgh or Belfast! Nor does the legalisation of homoeroticism apply to the armed forces or merchant navy.

Swiss laws permit 'unnatural' relations between adults, but 'protect' young people under twenty and punish 'abuses' of their 'inexperience' ... gays can thus be condemned for making love with minors, even when these consent.

Legislation in Denmark, Sweden and Holland is more permissive. These states contain the best-organised homosexual ghettoes in Europe, and within certain limits the police protect the good functioning of the 'perverts'' activities. Far smaller ghettoes have also grown up in France and West Germany. In England, on the other hand, a more overt repression is directed against the ghetto meeting places: there do not exist, at the present time, safe gay baths or orgy rooms in bars and dance halls. Each day, magistrates condemn dozens of homosexuals arrested on cruising grounds the night before.

In Belgium, it was only in *1965* that a specific law on homosexuality was voted. Under the rubric of the 'protection of youth', this made a criminal offence of 'indecent assault' committed without violence against a youth of less than eighteen. And a certain Captain Tilmant of the Belgian police wrote in the *Revue de la gendarmerie belge* (1969, iv):

> For the purposes of adequate prevention and firm repression, the police force must endeavour to have a thorough knowledge of that secret world [of the homosexual] where, we understand, witnesses are rare and informants reticent . . . In the case of homosexuality more than in any other, the old adage 'the police are only as good as their files' takes on its full meaning.[64]

In Austria, homosexuality was legalised only recently (1971). Even so, gay people are not allowed to form organisations of an explicitly homosexual character. The gay community in Vienna is one of the most constricted in Western Europe.

---

64. Quoted by Guy Hocquenghem, *Homosexual Desire*, p. 66.

In Japan, however, one need only reach the age of thirteen to be officially authorised to dispose of one's body in gay relations; no other country in the world has such a low age of consent. Japan, in fact, still preserves a historic, if contradictory, tradition of tolerance towards homoeroticism.[65]

In the USA, with the exception of Illinois, Connecticut, Hawaii, Oregon, Delaware, Texas, and (since 1975) North Dakota and California, *homoeroticism is still considered a crime in its own right.* (It was only recently that the Californian legislature repealed a law which had been on the statute books for more than a century, and punished homosexuality with penal servitude and castration.) The penalty provided for varies from State to State, but around ten years' imprisonment is often prescribed. 'Not only are these laws ineffective in preventing millions of Americans from engaging in the "crime" of homosexual love, they actually *encourage other real crimes*, like the blackmail of gays'.[66]

Besides police violence and corruption, and the severe legal repression which American homosexuals face in all those states where homosexuality is still not legalised, the very existence of anti-gay laws poses a constant threat, and at times even strengthens the forms of open discrimination that gay people must confront every day. In some States, it is difficult for gays to find work; they must carefully conceal their sexual inclinations if they are to be accepted, and they are forced to live in constant fear of being discovered or sacked, with very little chance of finding new employment, given the cause of their dismissal. Besides, the majority of landlords are not prepared to rent housing to gay people; it is very difficult to find accommodation, except for those able to pay highly inflated rents. Even in the privacy of their own homes, homosexuals have to be extremely careful: there's sure to be trouble if their neighbours find out that they are gay. They will very likely be denounced and evicted. And in schools, hospitals, prisons and barracks, if a homosexual is discovered, or someone is even suspected of homosexuality, he finds himself isolated, mocked, segregated and even beaten up by both his 'superiors' and his 'comrades'.[67]

---

65. See S. Jwaya, 'Nan sho k' ('Homosexuality in Japan'), *Jahrbuch für sexuelle Zwischenstufen* 4, (1902).

66. Kipp Dawson, *Gay Liberation: A Socialist Perspective* (New York: Pathfinder Press, 1975), p. 6.

67. Up until September 1975, there was an unwritten rule in the USA that the armed forces did not recruit homosexuals, and dismissed any soldiers who came out

But it is in no way as if the USA was particularly backward. We have to admit, in fact, that on the whole America today is the most gay of the countries under the real domination of capital. Even in countries where homosexuality is not considered a crime in itself, such as Italy for example, similar forms of discrimination are an everyday fact. We shall see shortly how the legalisation of homosexuality does not in fact bring full rehabilitation of homosexuals in the eyes of public opinion, nor does it do much to lighten the burden of repression that weighs on their shoulders.

In very many other countries, homosexuality is still completely outlawed. This is the case, for example, in Spain,[68] Portugal, Greece, and Israel,[69] not to mention the 'socialist' or Third World countries. It is worth mentioning the official reply of the German Democratic Republic to a letter from the international liaison group of London GLF in February 1972, which reveals how 'socialist' East Germany deals with the problem of homosexuality. According to that country's official representative, the problem does not exist there, as there are no homosexuals.[70] No comment.[71]

---

or gave themselves away. It was a real 'proclamation', then, when Leonard Matlovich, an air force captain, wrote to his commanding officer on 6 March 1975 stating that he was homosexual and had no intention of leaving the force. The result of the ensuing scandal was that Matlovich was successful. As from September 1975, in principle, the Pentagon decreed the abolition of the regulation providing for automatic expulsion of gays. But the abolition of this rule only confirmed what had long been tacitly acknowledged, i.e. that there are a high percentage of gays in the American armed forces. In many barracks, homosexuality is an everyday fact. Despite this, however, Oliver Sipple, the ex-marine famous for his action on 22 September 1975, when he deflected the gun that Sarah Jane Moore was pointing at President Ford, brought legal action for damages against several newspapers and magazines for claiming he was homosexual.

68. See Enrico Airone, 'Spagna: fascismo!', *Fuori!* 1, (June 1972). Even in Spain, however, homosexual liberation groups have more recently emerged.

69. In both 1955 and 1971, attempts were made by the socialist and liberal parties in Israel to legalise homosexuality. Both times, the initiative failed. Kurt Hiller wrote: 'That representatives of an ethnic minority that has been horribly persecuted should themselves persecute an equally harmless and guiltless biological *(sic!)* minority – what sentiment could arise in a thinking person other than boundless contempt!' (Quoted by John Lauritsen, *Religious Roots of the Taboo on Homosexuality*, p. 15).

70. See Mario Rossi, 'Berlino: l'omosessualità scavalca il muro', *Fuori!* 11, (Winter 1973). A description of the extremely hard conditions in which gay people live in East Germany and the Soviet Union can be found in an article by Thomas Reeves, 'Red and Gay, Oppression East and West', *Fag Rag* 6, (Autumn 1973).

71. [Translator's note: Mieli writes this in English in the original.]

As far as the USSR is concerned, the tsarist legislation against homosexuality was repealed in December 1917. This testifies to a certain relaxation towards homoeroticism on the part of the proletarian state power at the time of its birth (and this in a country that had passed suddenly from feudal to socialist legislation). In a pamphlet titled *The Sexual Revolution in Russia* (1923), Dr Grigorii Batkis, director of the Institute of Social Hygiene in Moscow, wrote:

> Concerning homosexuality, sodomy, and various other forms of sexual gratification, which are set down in European legislation as offences against public morality – Soviet legislation treats these exactly the same as so-called 'natural' intercourse. All forms of sexual intercourse are private matters. Only when there's use of force or duress, as in general when there's an injury or encroachment upon the rights of another person, is there a question of criminal prosecution.[72]

When the Soviet Union sent delegates to the first international congress of the World League for Sexual Reform held in Berlin in 1921, an increasingly clear counter-revolutionary tendency had started to proliferate in Russia. The defeat of the revolution in central Europe dealt the Soviet Union a blow that led to the establishment of a bureaucratic capitalism.[73] But the USSR continued to send delegates to successive international congresses of the League (held in Copenhagen in 1928, London in 1929, and Vienna in 1930; a fifth congress, originally due to be held in Moscow on the theme of 'Marxism and Sexual Problems', was in the event held in Brno, Czechoslovakia, in 1932).

The *Great Soviet Encyclopedia*, published in 1930, showed how the USSR, while now entering into the years of full counter-revolution, still maintained at this time an attitude of 'toleration' towards homoeroticism:

> In the advanced capitalist countries, the struggle for the abolition of these hypocritical laws is at present far from over. In Germany, for example, Magnus Hirschfeld is leading an especially fierce and not

72. Quoted in John Lauritsen and David Thorstad, *The Early Homosexual Rights Movement (1864–1935)*, p. 64.

73. See Amadeo Bordiga, *Strutture economiche* e *sociali della Russia d'oggi* (Milan: Editoriale Contra, 1966); and *Russia e rivoluzione nella teoria marxista* (Milan: Il formichiere, 1975).

> unsuccessful struggle to abolish the law against homosexuality . . . it is already obvious that the Soviet evaluation of the features and characteristics of homosexuals is completely different from the West's evaluation. While understanding the wrongness of the development of homosexuality, society does not place and cannot place blame for it on those who exhibit it. This breaks down to a significant degree the wall which actually arises between the homosexual and society and forces the former to delve deeply into himself.[74]

But, suddenly, the full weight of the counter-revolution came down upon Soviet gays. In March 1934, a law was introduced in the Russian Federal Republic providing up to eight years' imprisonment for homosexual acts. This law was the result of Stalin's personal intervention. Its definition of homosexuality was confined to males. The non-Russian republics were subsequently requested to inscribe this statute in their own legal codes without modification. The Soviet press launched a vicious campaign against homosexuality, now defined as a symptom of the 'degeneration of the fascist bourgeoisie'. In both tone and content, this attack was virtually identical to the anti-gay campaign waged at the same time by the German Nazis. And as in Germany, so in the Soviet Union too, the persecution went unheard. Those arrested included a large number of writers, musicians and other artists; they were condemned to various terms of imprisonment or deported to Siberia. These mass arrests led to panic among Soviet homosexuals, and were also followed by a large number of suicides in the Red Army. For any itching of the ass, Stalin prescribed extermination: capital can be sneaky, after all ...

Today, Soviet doctors are not even aware of the etymological roots of the term 'homosexuality'. Thus according to the third (1971) edition of the *Great Soviet Encyclopedia:*

> Homosexuality (from the Latin *homo* and *sexus*) – a sexual perversion consisting in unnatural attraction to persons of the same sex. The penal statutes of the USSR, the socialist countries, and even some bourgeois states, provide for the punishment of homosexuality (*muzhelozhestvo* – sodomy between males).[75]

---

74. Lauritsen and Thorstad, *The Early Homosexual Rights Movement (1864–1935)*, pp. 64–5.
75. Ibid., p. 65.

There can be no doubt that persecution is far sharper today in the Soviet Union, Cuba[76] or Poland than in England, France or Italy. We have seen how, in almost all the countries dominated by capital, more tolerant legislation has been introduced: and yet all the same, tolerance is still the negation of liberty. Tolerance is repressive. Capital offers 'the spectacle of a life which is free, but which revokes its freedom by law, hence declaring it to be an appearance, and on the other hand contradicting its free laws by its action' (Bruno Bauer).[77]

In actual fact, the 'freedom' that is guaranteed homosexuals by the law is reducible to the freedom to be the excluded, the oppressed, and the exploited, to be the objects of moral and often physical violence, and to be isolated in a ghetto that is generally dangerous and almost always blatantly squalid. As Francesco Saba Sardi writes:

> Late capitalist society, while it may extend to homosexuality the legal sanction of tolerance, still imposes on homosexuals a mark of infamy, ridicule or compassion, confining them to a more or less gilded ghetto in which the homosexual is induced to act out his role in a caricatured way. Just as the Jew, in the ghetto or concentration camp, became the Jew of the anti-Semitic and Nazi campaign, so this smarmy and cunning Jew, the masochistic Jew, has his counterpart today, at least in certain respects, in the 'queen'.[78]

In one of the European countries where homosexuals have attained the highest degree of political emancipation, Holland, they still remain marginalised, relegated to a functional ghetto, and imprisoned in the gilded cage that is gay Amsterdam. (Even if, we must add, you can enjoy yourself far better and more relaxedly in the Amsterdam saunas than in the toilets of the Piazza del Duomo in Milan …)[79]

---

76. See the drastically anti-homosexual declaration from *Granma,* the official newspaper of the Cuban Communist Party, 9 May 1971, and the reply of the New York Gay Revolution Party, both printed in *Come Out,* Spring–Summer 1971.

77. [Translator's note: Mieli does not provide a source for his citation, but the passage is drawn from *The Jewish Question*, Bauer's 1843 book most famous for the response ('On the Jewish Question') that Marx publishes the following year (and where he cites this very passage). Later in this volume (footnote 100), Mieli returns to 'On the Jewish Question' to mark it as the source of his distinction between 'political emancipation' and 'human emancipation'.]

78. Francesco Saba Sardi, 'La socièta omosessuale', *Venus* 7, (November 1972), p. 36.

79. One of the most famous international gay guides, published in Amsterdam, is the *Incognito Guide.* Its title tells all, being the very motto of the ghetto into which

Besides, and this should always be stressed, repression in the countries of capitalist domination remains very severe, despite the official legalisation of homosexuality:

> In cases of indecency, action may be taken against someone who does not repel an indecent caress quickly enough . . . one simply needs to stay too long in a street urinal to be convicted of indecency . . . [and] policemen may go as far as incitement (in Turkish baths, for instance) in order to provoke the offence. Repression does not merely delight in poking into people's underpants, it seeks the outrage, it provokes it in order to condemn it (such police behaviour is frequent in the USA).[80]

Agents provocateurs of this kind also infest the gay community in England, Germany, France and Italy, almost everywhere in fact. On one occasion in London, I was all but seduced by a very attractive policeman who came into the toilet at Shepherd's Bush dressed in black leather and started masturbating, his handcuffs at the ready to catch the queens.

The Church: From Obscurantist to 'Progressive'

Despite the massive anti-erotic campaign waged by the system, despite the obtuse despotism of the heterosexual Norm, the countries dominated by capital have seen in the last few years the first stirrings of a very slow maturing, on the part of many people, around the homosexual question. This is true even if, in the same measure that people start to speak of homosexuality, the ashamed ignorance and the mass of reactionary prejudice that characterise the general approach of 'normal' people towards those who are 'different' also come to light, and the distance between those who openly reject homoeroticism and those who are more tolerant and 'progressive' in reality proves to be very small.

The Catholic Church, for centuries the harsh judge of 'sodomites', has decisively confirmed its backward positions. The Sacred Congregation for the Doctrine of the Faith, in its *Declaration on Certain Questions of*

---

one opens more or less hidden doors in almost all countries of the world. Where the ghetto is not organised by the ruling system, clandestine ghettoes exist. The *Incognito Guide* lists the public toilets where you can meet other homosexuals in Moscow, for example, and the most frequented parks and bars in Madrid.

80. Guy Hocquenghem, *Homosexual Desire*, p. 65. [Translator's note from original translation: Translation modified.]

Sexual Ethics (January 1976), took pains to distinguish between 'homosexuals whose inclination, deriving from bad education, lack of normal sexual development, contracted habit, bad example or other similar cause, is transitory or at least not incurable, and those homosexuals who are definitively such by virtue of a kind of innate instinct or pathological constitution judged incurable'.[81]

As can be seen here, the Church still uses the psychonazi distinction between 'spurious homosexuality' or 'pseudo homosexuality' and 'true homosexuality'.[82] It is not by chance that Father Roberto Tucci, director of Radio Vatican, 'recognised in the *Declaration*, with reference to homosexuality, a greater attention to certain scientific findings'.[83]

The *Declaration* fails to mention again the 'first kind' of homosexuals (those whose 'aberrations' are 'transitory or at least not incurable'), perhaps because they are unwilling to give aid and succour to all the pseudo 'pseudo-homosexuals' among the clergy, and even ensconced on its leading bodies.

As far as the second category are concerned, i.e. the incurable 'true homosexuals', the Sacred Congregation recommends that 'in pastoral activity' they should be

> received with understanding and sustained in the hope of overcoming their personal difficulty and social disadvantage. Their guilt is to be judged with caution; but no pastoral method should be used which ... accords them a moral justification. According to the objective moral order, homosexual relations are acts lacking the essential and indispensable moral criterion.
>
> Homosexual acts are intrinsically disordered, and they can in no case receive any kind of approval.

Reactionary judgements of this kind, however, actually promote the homosexual liberation movement. For if on the one hand they perpetuate the guilt of the Catholic homosexual who sticks obstinately to his faith, on the other hand they lead a growing number of Catholic gays to abandon the Church, break with a religious tradition that is sullenly repressive and adopt a view of the world and of life that is different, less

81. *Avvenire*, (16 January 1976).
82. See Chapter 1, section 5.
83. *Avvenire*, (16 January 1976).

conformist, and hence potentially more disposed towards a revolutionary awareness.

But for quite a few years now, the Church (or capital) has been inventing structures of recuperation, even in dealing with gays who are less subdued by religious morality. Today, the Church is also the Church of dissent. Thus some members of the clergy are beginning to take up positions in favour of an 'emancipation' of homosexuals, opposing the stigma of an 'unnatural' sin that is traditionally imposed on gays by the Church.

Among the Franciscans, there is the case of Father Vittorino Joannes.[84] Father Marco Bisceglia,[85] a priest in Lavello (near Potenza), whom the local bishop deprived of his parish, maintains that it is not homosexuals 'who are destined for Hell, but rather those who exclude, insult, deride them and drive them to despair and suicide'.[86] The former nun Marisa Galli, known already for the dissent she expressed on the question of divorce, candidly stated:

> As an Italian Catholic believer, I feel guilty for the evil we have inflicted on so many homosexual brothers with our attitude, in such contradiction to the message of the gospel. They really have the right to denounce us for our slanders. The treasures of the Vatican would not be enough to compensate those whom we have injured with our prejudices, our sexual illiteracy and our ignorant and conscious cruelty.[87]

No, the treasures of the Vatican would not be enough. Too many 'sodomites' have died over the centuries on the fires of the Holy Inquisition; and too many homosexuals believe, still today, because of what the Church assures them, that they are 'sick people who therefore need to be cured; and that anyone who speaks in favour of homosexuality, even if

84. Another Jesuit, Father Arturo Dalla Vedova, was arrested in Rome on 6 November 1975 for having written 'pig' and other derogatory expressions on posters put up in memory of Pasolini.
85. This priest was, after this, the founder of the first society of Arcigay (in Palermo in 1980) and the first coordinator of the network of societies that from 1985 gave life to the Arcigay national network. At the end of this work, Father Bisceglia returned to the Church.
86. *Corriere della Sera*, (17 May 1975).
87. Ibid.

this is his own reality, commits a sin against God by going against nature' (Ornella Dragoni).[88]

Outside Italy, and particularly in Holland, noted independent Catholic theologians, such as Pfeurten, Oraison, Biet, Gottschalk, and the least obnoxious of them, van de Spijker,[89] have re-examined the entire Church attitude towards homoeroticism from a 'progressive' standpoint. For his part, Monsignor L'Heureux, the bishop of Perpignan, declared in a radio broadcast on 18 October 1974:

> It is absolutely necessary to reach a clear definition on this question, in order to make possible a pastoral activity that can aid homosexuals to attain the sacraments more readily, to fill themselves more deeply with the word of God, to meet collectively; whether among themselves or with others, in order to reflect on the necessities of the Christian life, and finally not to blame themselves for acts they might be led to commit, and which might seem abnormal in relation to the Christian tradition.[90]

We should note how, for the first time here, by using the conditional 'might seem' (*paraître*), a Catholic bishop has opened the possibility of a new reflection on homosexuality in moral theology. But this paternalistic attitude is a false facade. Above all, Monsignor L'Heureux is concerned to aid homosexuals 'not to blame themselves', even though it is clear that it is not in fact homosexuals who blame themselves, but rather that they are blamed by society in general and the Church in particular. Self-reproach, when it is present, simply reflects the condemnation inflicted by external persecution.

More precisely, Monsignor L'Heureux says that homosexuals should be helped 'not to blame themselves for acts they might be led to commit'. Why 'might be' and not 'are'? And 'led' by whom or what? Taken as a whole, in fact, this sentence has a decidedly ambiguous ring to it. And when read in the context of the entire declaration, it can well be interpreted as an invitation to gays to extirpate the roots of their guilt by renouncing homosexual 'practices' ('not to blame themselves for acts').

88. Omelia Dragoni, 'Una testimonianza', *Fuori!* 12, (Spring 1974), p. 22.

89. See Paola Elio, 'Omosessualità e religione', ibid., pp. 13–16.

90. Monsignor Henri L'Heureux's statement was reported on 6 January 1975 in the bulletin *David et Jonathan*, organ of the French Christian homophile movement.

What the bishop of Perpignan grants with one hand, he withdraws with the other, just like a magic trick. And what he pushes for above all is simply the integration of homosexuals into ecclesiastical structures.

The Protestant denominations have recently adopted still less conformist attitudes, in the same operation of recuperating homosexuality once it surfaces. For some two years, for example, the general meetings of the London Gay Liberation Front were regularly held at Notting Hill Gate in the All Saints church hall, and the meetings of the transvestites and transsexuals group actually in the sacristy. There are also churches that organise religious services expressly for gays, above all in the USA.

On the other hand, those churches that do not insist on ecclesiastical celibacy are generally more disposed to admit more or less openly the homosexuality of many priests – and this with less hypocrisy than the Catholic Church. In the USA there are more than twenty branches of the Universal Fellowship of Metropolitan Community Churches, a special church for homosexuals, led by Rev. Troy Perry. Troy Perry has also celebrated a good number of gay marriages.[91]

The prospect of marriage between homosexuals is of still greater interest to the system than to even the gay reformists. In the USA, the press, which passed over almost in silence the massacre of thirty-one homosexuals in New Orleans in 1973 (one of so many slaughters by the hetero-state), published several articles in the course of that year celebrating marriage between two women or two men.[92] In Sweden and Norway, the press and TV discuss the right of homosexuals to marry, while the moderate gay organisations confine their demands to complete acceptance on the part of society. The heterosexual status quo, by way of its 'progressive' wing, is working for a total integration of homosexuality, its re-entry into the structure of the family – by the back door, of course.

Repressive Desublimation, Protection, Exploitation, False Guilt, and Reformism

It is impossible to avoid bringing to light this implicit, or even explicit, intention to recuperate homosexuals that lies behind the new 'progressive'

91. See Ronald M. Enroth and Gerald E. Jamison, *The Gay Church* (Grand Rapids: Eermann, 1974); also Kay Tobin and Randy Wicker, *The Gay Crusaders* (New York: Arno Press, 1972).

92. See Charles Shively, 'Wallflower at the Revolution', *Fag Rag* 6, Boston, (Autumn 1973).

attitude of certain churches and states. It is necessary also to stress how the slow evolution of religious morality and of certain strata of public opinion towards more understanding and tolerant positions tends toward the partial substitution of the traditional form of aggression towards us gays for one of protection. But if aggression is phallocratic and protection paternalist, phallocracy and paternalism are just two sides of the same patriarchal coin. As Oscar Wilde said during his trial: 'The one disgraceful, unpardonable and to all time contemptible action of my life was my allowing myself to be forced into appealing to Society for help and protection . . .'[93]

The protection of homosexuals, 'permissive' morality, tolerance and political emancipation obtained within certain limits in the countries of capital's real domination: all this reveals itself in substance to be functional within the programme of homosexuality's commercialisation and exploitation by capitalist enterprise. The commercialisation of the ghetto pays well: bars, clubs, hotels, discos, saunas, cinemas and pornography provide important footholds for those seeking to exploit the 'third sex'. Capital carries out a repressive desublimation of homosexuality. 'Sexuality is liberated (or rather liberalised) in socially constructive forms. This notion implies that there are repressive modes of desublimation'.[94]

The system deploys the same manoeuvre with respect to other so-called 'perversions'. Voyeurism, for example, is one of the most profitable 'perversions' for capital (cinema, pornography, etc.), while remaining in reality repressive. People go to the cinema to see a commodity make love, and this involves a repressive desublimation of the voyeuristic component of our desire, instead of us watching one another make love, enjoying and understanding ourselves and fusing voyeurism with other forms of pleasure. Repressive desublimation and commercial exploitation are inseparable; Eros remains focussed on work and the production of alienating commodities, to the extent that its repressive desublimation provides a market for these.[95]

Tolerance, on the other hand – 'repressive tolerance', as Marcuse calls it – only confirms our marginalisation. In fact, to tolerate the homosexual

---

93. Philippe Jullian, *Oscar Wilde*, p. 264.
94. Herbert Marcuse, *One-Dimensional Man: Studies in the Ideology of Advanced Industrial Society* (London: Routledge, 2002), p. 75.
95. See Chapter 6, section 4.

minority, without the majority questioning the repression of their own homoerotic desire, means recognising the right of those who are 'deviant' to live on the basis of their 'deviance' and hence to be marginalised. And this favours the highly increased exploitation of homosexuals on the part of the system that marginalises them.

In the Italian cities, in Spain, Greece, Portugal and other countries noted for their generally backward customs, a semi clandestine industry of the 'third sex' flourishes, based on ties of strict convenience between entrepreneurs, the police and organised crime. In the United States, too, the great majority of bars where gay people meet are controlled by the Mafia. Paradoxically, the laws of the State of New York still consider homosexuality as such a crime, though New York City, along with Tokyo and San Francisco, contains what is undoubtedly one of the most extensive, most magnetic and best organised of homosexual ghettoes in the world (including its nearby outcrops of Fire Island and Provincetown). Further evidence of the 'rational character of capitalist irrationality' (Marcuse) is given by the link that exists between economic organisations revolving around the exploitation of homoeroticism, and the judicial system. What is prohibited can be sold at a higher price.

What we need to bear in mind, above all, is the effective linkage, in society under the real domination of capital, between aggression and protection, as two sides of the same relationship to us gays. Between violence and protection, there is no middle zone. In the last instance, the homosexual must be the object of aggression, so that he can then be protected and effectively exploited. On the other hand, protection and integration provide gays with palliative gratifications as well as inuring them to submission and weakening the force of their protest (and apparently, its very motivations). It is clear that neither aggressors nor protectors are aware of the mechanisms that exist between violence and protection, nor are they concerned to become so. Protection constitutes the medium that links aggression to exploitation, a fact which only revolutionary gays have properly understood.

Unfortunately, even today the majority of homosexuals remain trapped in illusions of political emancipation within the existing capitalist and inhuman structures of the establishment. Far from being surprising, this must be viewed as the product of thousands of years of habituation to the Norm (both 'normal' and normative), which induces homosexuals, the transgressors, to feel guilty. In the hope of integration, many gays indulge the fantasy of having the father system forgive sins that they have not in fact committed. But the sense of guilt is essentially functional to perpetuating capital's domination ('Don't travel without a ticket …'), and liberalisation and tolerance themselves provide footholds for the guilty feeling of those who are content merely to be tolerated, the better to be exploited. A homosexual has to feel in a certain sense guilty, in order to put up with the anguish and anxiety of the ghetto, and to renounce any genuine freedom. Capital, on the other hand, cannot forgive any sin. First and foremost, since there are no sinners, and secondly, because capital is seventy times seven[96] an industry of sin.

The ideal of political emancipation does not involve any qualitative leap vis-à-vis the conditions of marginalisation and exploitation in which homosexuals are presently placed, nor a repudiation of the sense of guilt which would shed light on those really responsible for homosexual suffering. It is time for homosexuals to regain the energies that this guilt has confiscated, and channel them into a genuinely emancipatory struggle, both pleasurable and subversive.

The sense of guilt that the system induces in us is a false guilt, but at the same time it is the most intransigent enemy to homosexual liberation. We have to root it out, and to do this we must recognise it in its many and varied habitual disguises. To be aware of it is already to confront it, instead of continuing to be blindly dominated by it.

This false guilt is the hitman of the system within us, the agent of death that torments us incessantly. As Corrado Levi has written: 'Our sickness is not that of being homosexual, but of having the sense of guilt. This has been induced and maintained in us by the father, and by those heterosexuals afraid of their own homosexuality'.[97]

The homosexual has been forced to internalise the social condemnation of homoeroticism, a condemnation that might any day strike at him. 'Normal' people, however, have adapted to the anti-gay taboo – internalising this condemnation in the most drastic fashion, and personifying the heterosexual Norm. They cannot refrain from ascribing guilt to anyone who transgresses the Norm, since such a person lives what they have

96. [Translator's note: Mieli's reference here, used to signify an endlessly repeated tendency, is once again Biblical: in this case, Matthew 18:12, where Jesus responds to Peter's question about how many times he should forgive a brother who sinned against him: 'I do not say to you, up to seven times, but up to seventy times seven.']

97. Corrado Levi, 'Il Lavoro di presa di coscienza. Problematiche e contributi dal lavoro di presa di coscienza del collettivo *Fuori!* di Milano, 1973', *Fuori!* 12, (Spring 1974).

repressed, and so by repression, discrimination and violence, they induce the homosexual to believe himself guilty. It is heteros who foment the sense of guilt in gays.

Corrado Levi shows how the feeling of guilt that often afflicts the gay person 'has repercussions in a kind of inhibition in his behaviour in general'. In the course of consciousness-raising meetings held in Milan,

> the connections between homosexuality and self-punishment became clear . . . and how this was stirred up by the police, the father, etc. The detailed analysis of the sense of guilt led to identifying and thus isolating our internalisation of the prevailing morality and values, which we can therefore proceed to repudiate together with the sense of guilt.

A gradual elimination of false guilt

> is a result proceeding in parallel with the analysis and overcoming of the prevailing values, norms and behaviours. The sense of guilt is tied up with transgressions of the aims towards which the repression of homosexuality, which we are subjected to from childhood, is designed, and which in adulthood then becomes self-repression (with the compulsion to repeat), in the context of the present deformation of the individual by Oedipal-patriarchal education. And it is reinforced by the guilt that is imposed on sex and the body by the Judeo-Christian culture. It is symptomatic, to take only one effect of this sense of guilt, to note how many times, discovering themselves different from certain prevailing values and behaviours, the sense of guilt leads people to adopt other prevailing values and behaviours in a very rigid form, as a compensation for these transgression.[98]

We can thus understand how a homosexual, led by the system to feel guilt because he transgresses the anti-gay taboo, often tries in some form or other to vindicate himself in the eyes of society, to adapt to all its rules and become conservative and reactionary, repressive and death-dealing in his turn. The homosexual can thus be transformed into an instrument of capital. 'We know very well', observes Angelo Pezzana, 'that those homosexuals who have positions of power are precisely the people who combat homosexual liberation'.[99]

---

98. 'Dibattito', ibid.
99. Ibid.

Apropos the 'discreet face of the *pédés*', some comrades in the French Groupe de Libération Homosexuel wrote:

> Just as the black American movement had to struggle against the black bourgeoisie, which was violently opposed to the ghetto revolts and which mimicked the racist white society, in the same way we cannot say that any homosexual whatsover is *a priori* on our side, 'even if …' Because if every homosexual experiences sexual repression, this comes about in different ways according to his social position, his conditioning, and his ideas. What does he do at work? What does he do in his daily life? France under Giscard permits its homosexuals to live and survive with dignity, with *Arcadie*, in hypocrisy and disguise. This type of established homosexual is among the first to oppose our revolt. He is generally one of our enemies.[100]

The burden of condemnation that is internalised, and the conditions of unfreedom and desperation in which we live, still induce too many homosexuals to content themselves with one form of adaptation or another, to cultivate the fascist dress, home and smile of *L'Uomo Vogue* (which at one time I myself tried to adopt and identify with), and/or to aspire to the attainment of further civil rights. The system only profits from this: 'The system is the Leopard inciting us to try and change everything in such a way that it all remains the same'.[101]

Even those gays involved in the liberation movement are not all fully aware of the need to wage the struggle in a totalising and revolutionary perspective, towards *human emancipation* instead of just *political emancipation*;[102] relatively few are aware as yet of the revolutionary disruption potentially contained in their condition, and of what they must do to translate this into deeds.

---

100. Nicholas B. and Jean L., *Homosexualité et militantisme: quelques réflexions de base* (leaflet produced for the theoretical weekend held 13–14 September 1975). *Arcadie* is the name of the French integrationist homosexual movement.

101. Collettivo Redazionale di *Fuori!*, 'Gli omosessuali e l' utopia', *Almanacco Bompiani* (1974). [Translator's note: 'The Leopard' is a reference to the novel of that title by G. de Lampedusa and its hero, the aristocrat who skillfully prepares to adjust to the rise of the Italian bourgeoisie.]

102. Throughout this book, I use the terms 'political emancipation' and 'human emancipation' in the sense given them by Karl Marx in *The Jewish Question* . 'Political emancipation' means integration into the system, while 'human emancipation' means genuine liberation, revolution and communism.

At the present time, the movement is made up of both revolutionary and integrationist homosexuals; the activities of the groups, moreover, often conflict with one another. But it is through such difficulties and contrasts that the movement dialectically grows and is transformed. Beyond the formal political distinctions between one organisation and another, one collective and the next, beyond the differences of interpretation and content, the gay movement as a whole is the historical movement for the liberation of homosexuality, even if it cannot but reflect, for the time being, the contradictions and limitations of the general social situation, which is predominantly counter-revolutionary.

The organisational structure of the gay groups themselves, while more elastic and gay, and less authoritarian, than the traditional or ultra-left political rackets, often remains, all the same, substantially hierarchical (even if the collectives scarcely ever recognise official hierarchy of any type). The effective homosexual leaders often tend – and sometimes unconsciously – to lead 'their' groups like little gangs to be more or less kept to heel, and on which they base their own prestige and personal power. Still essentially *political* figures, they are as such patriarchal and reactionary, beneath all the feathers and glitter.

Besides, a certain inertia and the insufficient level of gay subversive consciousness on the part of many members of the group, tends to assign 'leader' roles to a few people, and to confirm them in these roles, for all the discussions against authoritarianism and charismatic leaders that are held within the collectives, discussions which often boil down to dialectical clashes that are in actual fact a power play between rival leaders.

It is also the case that many homosexuals, consumed and obscured by the induced sense of guilt, the internalisation of the social condemnation, when they meet for the first time in liberation groups are suddenly assailed with remorse, often unconsciously, by the internal superego, which condemns them for having dared to disobey the social superego that has established their marginalisation and is opposed to a revolutionary awareness. Like the sons of Freud's mystical primitive father, who after uniting in a homosexual bond find the strength to kill him, but are then overtaken by remorse and establish in memory and substitution for the father the totem, the phallic fetish, so the homosexuals who meet in liberation groups are largely powerless against the attack from the superego that immediately assails them, and find themselves forced to establish in their midst leaders, phallic and charismatic figures who 'command' them, personifying the authority of the superego that binds every individual member of the group with the sense of guilt.

On the one hand, we must not apologise for all the existing homosexual organisations. Only a critical attitude to their history, their formation and development, can shed light both on the importance of the gay-communist perspective, and on the revolutionary that is present, potentially or in actual fact, inside them.

On the other hand, even if not all of us gays are for the revolution, it is impossible to understand the homosexual question without making constant reference to the concrete individuals who set this in motion by their struggle and research. They provide us with keys for a revolutionary reading of the historical and social problematics that bear on homosexuality, of the ideological (and) psychoanalytic disquisitions on the 'perversions', even when they are themselves far from revolutionary. No one can better interpret the Freudian analysis of the Schreber case,[103] for example, than someone who has himself tried to establish what it means to be a crazy queen, to be condemned as such, to revolt against repression and the internalised form of the condemnation. And a queen may be reformist, but he's always still a queen.

Oscar Wilde has been labelled both a camp conservative and a decadent socialist, but from the standpoint of homosexual liberation he was, willing or not, a revolutionary. It is true that today the system is infinitely better prepared to recuperate the moderate expressions of homosexual struggle than it was a century ago. Thus the sense of guilt that shows clearly through in the works of Wilde, and at times even dominates these, is less serious than the present sense of guilt that leads many gays into reformism, if we consider the present self-interested propensity that capital displays towards tolerance, compared with the very severe persecution of homoeroticism in nineteenth-century England.

The most radical expression of the homosexual liberation movement, both practical and theoretical, took place in the wake of the workers' and students' struggles of 1968 and 1969 in Europe, and in the USA of the deep revolt stamped on American society, and particularly on the minds of young Americans, by the insurrections of black ghettoes and the temporary revolutionary assertion of the black movement.[104] At the

103. Freud, 'Psycho-Analytic Notes on an Autobiographical Account of a Case of Paranoia', *Standard Edition*, Vol. 12 (London: Vintage, 2001).

104. In 1970, Huey Newton, Minister of Defense of the Black Panther Party, wrote: 'There is nothing to say that a homosexual cannot also be a revolutionary. And maybe I'm now injecting some of my prejudice by saying "even a homosexual can be a revolutionary". Quite the contrary; maybe a homosexual could be the most

same time, moreover, both in America and Europe the formation of gay groups was deeply influenced by the radicalisation and expansion of the feminist movement to be seen in the late 1960s. The subsequent reflux of these struggles, the counter-revolutionary stabilisation of capitalist power and the stagnation of social and existential discontent, have all notably contributed to a fragmentation of the gay movement.

In France, it became clear in 1974 that the Front Homosexuel d'Action Révolutionnaire, known as the most extreme of the European groups, had to all intents dissolved. This did not mean that the homosexual movement in France was dead. It was rather transformed and divided into smaller groups (the most important of which is presently the Groupe de Libération Homosexuel), which, from differing positions and without any pretence at uniformity for the sake of formal unity, are waging a struggle around objectives that are largely shared.

In Britain, the Gay Liberation Front, which had its heyday in 1971–2, gradually adapted itself to the confines of a para-reformist struggle, bringing it closer to the politics of the Campaign for Homosexual Equality, the British integrationist organisation. But this does not mean that there are not still revolutionary collectives existing in England.

In the USA, the leading role that was once held by the GLF is now occupied by more moderate groups such as the National Gay Task Force, particularly strong in New York, and the Gay Activists Alliance, an organisation that broke away from the GLF as early as 1969. This first split was provoked by disagreements within GLF between the more radical elements, who openly supported the Black Panthers and favoured an intensification of struggle, and the reformists, disposed to a politics that was showy but cautious, and who were against the gay movement giving support to other liberation struggles. In America, too, however, there are still various revolutionary homosexual collectives who do not form official organisations, but are the most advanced expressions of the real movement.

In Italy, the federation of *Fuori!* with the Radical Party[105] clearly indicates the assertion of a counter-revolutionary, reformist political line

---

revolutionary'; 'A Letter from Huey', Len Richmond and Gary Noguera (eds), *The Gay Liberation Book*, p. 142. See also Francesco Santini, 'Sgombrar la strada', *Comune futura* 2 (November 1976).

105. [Translator's note: Contrary to their name, the Radical Party (Partito Radicale, or PR) was a largely reformist center-left party with libertarian overtones. Emerging in 1955, the PR lasted until 1989 but never received significant vote tallies.]

in the homosexual movement. Symptomatic of this was the participation of *Fuori!*, which presented its own candidates on the Radical list, in the elections of June 1976, and the pathetic tone of the electoral campaign. In Italy, however, revolutionary homosexual groups have emerged in various cities, among them the Milan Homosexual Collective and the autonomous collectives in Florence, Pavia, Venice, Padua, Naples, Catania, Cagliari, etc.

We may say, then, that if reformist homosexuals aspire to parliament, revolutionaries do not accept compromises with the political racketeers of the system, whether parliamentary or ultra-left. They continue to struggle for themselves as revolutionaries (and) homosexuals, knowing that only the firmest intransigence, the closest solidarity and the rejection of all politicking and casuistic manoeuvres can keep them free from capitalist recuperation, and actually promote the achievement of liberation.

Ideology. The Homosexual Revolutionary Project

Revolutionary criticism has shown how the ideology based on the capitalist mode of production, on the alienation of labour and the reification of the human subject, involves the absurd absolutisation of contingent historical values and the hypostasis of opinions (scientific, ethico-moral, socio-political, psychological) that are in reality relative and transitory. This ideology upholds the 'naturalness' of the present system and mode of production: it absolutises it in an ahistorical manner, thereby concealing its underlying transience. What is hypostatised here by ideology as 'normal' and normative is nothing but the visible version of what in reality changes, transforms, and develops together with the development of the means and mode of production, with the dynamic of the contradiction between capital and the human species, with the entire movement of society. But much as capital has so far withstood the revolutionary movement, and managed to repress it, so too its ideology has survived the upsurge and progressive spread of the theory of the proletariat, with respect to which it has sought – and often partially managed – a recuperation, without ever grasping the essence of it.

At 120 years' distance from the *Communist Manifesto*, people's heads are still filled with ideological absurdity. The ideology of wage-labour still marks the *Weltanschauung* of *one-dimensional man*,[106] even though capital has reached the stage of real domination, in which,

106. [Translator's note: Mieli writes *Weltanschauung* in German in the original, placing both it and 'one-dimensional man' in italics, which serves in part to mark

> Thus it is no longer merely labour, a defined and particular moment of human, activity, that is subsumed and incorporated into capital, but the whole lifeprocess of man. Capital's process of incarnation [*Einverleibung*] which began in the West about five centuries ago, is now complete. Capital is now the common being [*Gemeinwesen*], oppressor of man [...] Capital incorporates the human brain, appropriates it to itself, with the development of cybernetics; with computing, it creates its own language, on which human language must model itself etc. Now it is not only the proletarians – those who produce surplus-value – who are subsumed under capital, but all men, the greater part of whom is proletarianized. It is the real domination over society, a domination in which all men becomes the slaves of capital [.][107]

For its part, the bourgeoisie is 'demonstrated to be a superfluous class' because nearly all 'its social functions are now performed by salaried employees' (Engels).[108] This real domination is characterised by the immanent tendency towards socialisation which transforms capitalism into state capitalism, while the state, as a 'committee for running the common affairs of the bourgeoisie', itself becomes a capitalist enterprise. This general slavery tends to present itself as (participation in) the management of production by the workers: the waged are transformed into automatons who manage and administer the very system that enslaves them. Meanwhile, the substitution of living labour by science and technology 'becomes the universal form of material production ... [and] circumscribes an entire culture; it projects a historical totality – a "world".'[109]

> The increase of the productive force of labour and the greatest possible negation of necessary labour is the necessary tendency of capital [...] The transformation of the means of labour into machinery is the realization of this tendency. In machinery, objectified labour materially

---

them as specific terms in the history of Marxism, the latter more recently current at the time of his writing, given the ubiquitous influence of Marcuse's *One-Dimensional Man* throughout the European New Left.]

107. Jacques Camatte, from 'Note on the formal domination and real domination of capital' (1972), included in *Capital and Community*, pp. 72–3.

108. Friedrich Engels, *Socialism: Utopian and Scientific*, https://www.marxists.org/archive/marx/works/1880/soc-utop/

109. Marcuse, *One-Dimensional Man*, p. 158.

> confronts living labour as a ruling power and as an active subsumption of the latter under itself, not only by appropriating it, but in the real production process itself; the relation of capital as value which appropriates value-creating activity is, in fixed capital existing as machinery, posited at the same time as the relation of the use value of capital to the use value of labour capacity; further, the value objectified in machinery appears as a presupposition against which the value-creating power of the individual labour capacity is an infinitesimal, vanishing magnitude[.][110]

The necessary economic premises for the creation of communism are thus completely developed (and overdeveloped): capitalism itself has reduced necessary labour to a minimum. But people continue to work for capital (which now takes charge of all the activity that the proletariat performs in the factory), they continue to survive for capital's sake. This real domination so much subsumes human life into itself, and determines people's thinking to such an extent, that even now – when it would be enough to stop the system's machinery for the species to be able to rediscover itself, its own biological salvation and communist freedom – the revolution is still held back from asserting itself.

Ideology leads people to think according to the inhuman criteria of capital and puts the brakes on the growth of a universal and communist human consciousness that would oppose once and for all the cancerous domination of this 'automated monster'.

The struggle of women and the theoretical expressions of their movement have made it clear how ideology is phallocentric, hinging as much on the subjugation of the female sex to the male as on the capitalist mode of production. And as dominant ideology is specifically white and Eurocentric, it has been literally set aflame by the struggles of black people: rising up in the ghettoes of America in the 1960s and destroying the cities of capital, they have reopened for the species the prospect of communist revolution, the perspective of human emancipation.

Lastly, that ideology is heterosexual is something that we homosexuals have shown for the first time, in a disruptive way, over the course of the last few years, from the founding of the New York Gay Liberation Front in summer 1969 through to today.

But through all its specific and persisting characteristics (bourgeois, male, Eurocentric, heterosexual), what we must recognise in this ideology

110. Karl Marx, *Grundrisse*, p. 693–4.

above all today is capital itself, its real domination. Today, ideology is unitary and strikes all differently in the same mode. We have to get rid of it, in order to give life and thought back their free and human 'form' and 'essence', at present reified in the deadly cogs of the capital-machine. The 'privileges' that society cherishes today are revealed in substance as exclusively functional to the perpetuation of the system; the bourgeois, white, heterosexual male is also almost always an obtuse and unfortunate solipsist, the most despicable puppet of the status quo, which negates in him the woman, the black, the queer, and the human being.

If ideology is unitary and anthropomorphic, the (in)human mask of capital, we, on the other hand, are today far too divided, and above all divided from one another, despite all being in the same underlying situation, suffocated by the weight of the system. We are divided, but it is capital that pits us against each other and divides us.

By cultivating the deep specificities of each individual case of personal oppression, we can advance to the revolutionary consciousness that grasps in my specific case of oppression also yours (because you, too, hetero, are a negated gay), and in your specific case, also mine (because I, too, am a negated woman), so as to recognise in us all the negated human species, beyond all historically determinate separation and autonomy. Revolution can only form this recognition of our common repressed being, reflected today in separate forms in society, in those who live, in their daily life, through and against the suppression of a particular aspect of human 'nature'[III] (being a woman, homoerotic desire, etc.) that the system negates.

The proletariat itself, and the struggle of women, blacks and us gays, have all indicated the fundamental importance, in the perspective of human emancipation, of everyone who – in relation to the absolutised values of ideology – is considered marginal, secondary, anomalous, or downright absurd. The life of the species resides there. If the ideology of power is absurd, the reality this veils can be discerned only by living what this ideology negates and relegates to a corner deemed absurd. Schizophrenia is a gate of access to revolutionary knowledge; and only loving a

---

III By human 'nature' I don't mean something determinate, stable, unchanging, absolute or hidden. I have no exact idea of what precisely lies underneath and is natural, and would view human 'nature' rather in the materialistic sense as a becoming, i.e. in relation to the historical period and social context, thus together with the economic and sexual dialectic.

black person, knowing black people can truly lead to understanding why communism will be black, of all colours.

A critical theory, growing as a function of a gay revolutionary project, cannot but take into account everything that is eccentric to the narrow confines of what the dominant subculture considers 'normal', permissible, rational. For us homosexuals, there is a clear alternative. Either to adapt to the established universe, and hence to marginalisation, to the ghetto and derision, adopting as our own values the hypocritical morality of heterosexual idiocy which the system requires (albeit with the inevitable variants, seeing as it's hard to give up a cock in the ass), and hence to opt for a heteronomy. Or else to oppose ourselves to the Norm, and the society of which this is the reflection, and to overturn the entire imposed morality, specifying the particular character of our existential objectives from our own standpoint of marginalisation, from our 'different' being, as lesbian, bum-boy, gay, in open contrast to the one-dimensional rule of hetero monosexuality. In other words, to opt for our 'homonomy'. As Sartre wrote about Gide:

> In the fundamental conflict between sexual anomaly and accepted normality, he took sides with the former against the latter, and has gradually eaten away the rigorous principles which impeded him like an acid. In spite of a thousand relapses, he has moved forward towards *his* morality; he has done his utmost to invent a new Table of the Law
>
> . . . he wanted to free himself from other peoples' Good; he refused from the first to allow himself to be treated like a black sheep.[112]

Gide's position is not essentially different from that of all of us other homosexuals: it is a question of opposing the 'normal' morality and of choosing what is good and what is bad from our own marginalised point of view. If we aspire to liberation, we must reject the existing standards. It is a question of making a choice that rejects the Norm. But a gay moralisation of life, which combats misery, egoism, hypocrisy, and the repressive character and immorality of customary morality, cannot take place unless we uproot the sense of guilt, that false guilt which still ties so many of us to the status quo, to its ideology and its deathly principles, preventing us from moving with gay seriousness in the direction of a totalising revolutionary project.

---

112. Jean-Paul Sartre, *Baudelaire* (London: Horizon, 1949), pp. 48–9.

We know that the discovery of what is hidden by the label of 'anomalous', with which dominant ideology covers up so many expressions of life, helps to demonstrate the absurdity of this ideology. But the gradual accumulation of evidence against the alleged absolute value of capitalist science and morality is only a secondary result of the analysis of those questions and arguments which public opinion considers more or less taboo. Above all, it is a question of discovering what these questions disclose about our own underlying 'nature'.

A direct approach to the homosexual question shows the basic importance of the homoerotic impulse in any human being, and makes a contribution to tracing the issues inherent to its repression and its disguise. We know, in the words of Norman O. Brown, that 'it is in our unconscious repressed desires that we shall find the essence of our being, the clue to our neurosis (as long as reality is repressive), and the clue to what we might become if reality ceased to repress'.[113]

Homosexuality contains, and sometimes conceals, a mystery. One might say that this mystery is the man-woman, but this is unfortunately not enough to either describe or understand it. Our mystery, as much as we can know and intuit it, is far more than *bi*-sexual. And the world-of-life is the *tonalli* and the *nagual*: beyond totality lies everything else.[114]

The revolutionary gay movement (con)tends to (re)conquer our deep mysterious being.[115] Revealing the historical-existential secret that has up till now been gleaned and preserved in our marginal position, forced as we have been for millennia and for all the most oppressed years of our individual lives to remain secret, we homosexuals, with our voice and all the expressions of our presence, are beginning to reveal what is without doubt one of the fundamental mysteries of the world. Perhaps homosex-

113. Norman O. Brown, *Life Against Death: the Psychoanalytical Meaning of History* (Middletown, CT: Wesleyan University Press, 1988), p. 23.

114. [Translator's note: Mieli's reference, of the *tonalli* and the *nagual*, are to concepts within indigenous Mesoamerican cultures: to the Nahuatl words, respectively, for the 'daysign' (i.e. marking the mystical significance of one's day of birth but also, in Mieli's context, a tight spiritual bond with a specific animal) and for a human with the magical capacity to shapeshift into animal form.]

115. [Translator's note: Mieli uses here again that pun whose meaning is inevitably lost in translation. In Italian, the phrase is *Il movimento gay rivoluzionario (com)batte per la (ri)conquista del nostro essere misterioso profondo*, and as the verb *battere* means not only to strike but also to go out cruising for sex and to make oneself available, the sense here is of a double struggle, one that remains equally erotic and political, and always collective. See Footnote 4.]

uality is indeed the key to transsexuality; perhaps it does point towards that something which for thousands of years the repressive requirements of *Kultur* have struck down.

The repression of homosexuality stands in direct proportion to its importance in human life and for human emancipation. If we want to look upon the massacre that has decimated us in the past, it is to better understand the ancient burden of condemnation that still hangs heavily inside each of us even today, to better understand the spectacular and ambiguous way in which this massacre is perpetuated in 'our' times: and in so doing, to reach a better awareness of the revolutionary force that is in us, in our desire.

With its real domination, capital seeks to take possession of even the unconscious, that 'human essence' whose manifest expressions could not but be condemned to death by the systems of repression that preceded it. It may be successful, either because it is more difficult today for the unconscious to explode in an uncontrolled fashion, given the efficiency of conditioning, or because, by way of repressive desublimation, capital enables the unconscious to 'emerge' in alienated forms, in order to subsume it, to deprive men and women of it, and to deprive women and men of themselves. The logic of money and profit that determines the liberalisation of the so-called 'perversions' is not simply an economic fact: it promotes the submission to capital of the whole of human life.

This demonstrates the arduous complexity of our revolutionary project, to recognise and express a humanity that transcends capital, without offering ourselves up to be devoured by it. In fact, if this should happen, then capital would simply puke us back up in its own forms, so that we may be nourished on this vomit to reproduce a new 'humanity', ever more digestible because it has already been digested.

This is why we have to take extreme positions, not yielding a single inch on the things that really matter, nor abandoning the intransigent struggle for the liberation and conquest of every aspect of our being-in-becoming.

It is due to the awareness of this that a number of homosexuals have stressed, in the last few years, the need to forge instruments for an autonomous ('homonomous') struggle of our own, working out our own theory and deepening the critique of capitalist liberalisation. The situation of those gays who see themselves taking part in a movement (historical, rather than simply formal) differs from that of André Gide in its collective character, in that the 'system' of homosexuality provides a belonging-together[116] in which more and more people feel involved. For us, it is no longer a question of delineating an individual project antithetical to the prevailing morality, but rather of an intersubjective project conscious of our own gay responsibilities and goals, facing outwards to involve the whole of humanity. We homosexuals must liberate ourselves from the feeling of guilt (and this is one of the immediate goals of our struggle), so that homoeroticism spreads and is 'contagious'. We have to make the water gush from the rock: to induce 'absolute' heterosexuals to discover their own homosexuality, and to contribute, through the confrontation and dialectical clash between the sexual tendency of the minority and that of the majority, to the attainment of a transsexuality, towards which the underlying polysexual 'nature' of desire itself points. If the prevailing form of monosexuality is heterosexuality, then a liberation of homoeroticism, this Cinderella of desire, forms an indispensable staging-post on the road to the liberation of Eros. The objective, once again, is not to obtain a greater acceptance of homoeroticisicm by the hetero-capitalist status quo, but rather to transform monosexuality into an Eros that is genuinely polymorphous and multiple; to translate into deeds and into enjoyment that transsexual polymorphism which exists in each one of us in a potential but as yet repressed form.

To conduct our struggle in a truly 'homonomous', original, and originally subversive way, we lesbians and gay men have to suspend judgement on everything (the ideals, theories, analyses, compartmentalised models, etc.) that has up till now at once dragged us in and excluded us, insofar as it is a product of the heterosexual majority. We have the gay task of reinterpreting everything from our own vantage point, with a view to enriching and transforming the revolutionary conception of history, society and existence.

We are sick to death of treading those ready-made trails that do not take us into account, of adhering to moral and theoretical systems which base their assumed reliability largely on our exclusion, on the banishment of homoeroticism (and we alone can clarify the way this happens and why). We are tired of simply fusing our forces with those who struggle for an ideal of the future which, even if utopian, appears to us as still too dangerously similar to this disgraceful present, since it does not take into

116. [Translator's note: Mieli uses the hybrid word *co-inereza*, which would literally translate to *co-inherence* or *inherence-with*.]

account the homosexual question and its crucial bearing on the goal of complete human emancipation.

Only we gays can understand that within what has been silenced in our history, in the terrible and sublime secrets of public toilets, under the weight of the chains with which the heterosexual society has bound and subdued us, there lies concealed the uniqueness of our (potential) contribution to revolution and to the creation of communism.

3
Heterosexual Men, or Rather Closet Queens

Sport

If heterosexual society and homosexuality are in conflict, even when this is legally disguised, as in the more permissive and democratic countries, and a peaceful coexistence is proclaimed, the contradiction is still reflected in the existential universe of each individual. If One-Dimensional Man is a divided self, then the present incompatibility between heterosexual and homoerotic desire makes a major contribution towards widening this split.

Given our original and underlying transsexuality, and recognising the polymorphous and 'perverse' disposition of the child to an eroticism that makes no exclusive distinction as to the sex of the 'object' of its libidinal impulse, it is clear that each one of us has a hidden erotic attraction towards the sex that is not (or is scarcely) the focus of our conscious desire. We do not intend to discuss here the extent to which the repression of a given component of desire can be stable and definitive: rather, we will take a look at some of the results of the sublimation of homosexuality and/or its conversion into 'pathological syndromes'.

It is worth repeating: anyone who holds him- or herself to be 100 per cent heterosexual is hiding a big 'percentage' of censored gay desire. 'The increasing number of obsessional homoerotics in modern society would then be the symptom of the partial failure of repression and "return" of the repressed material'.[1] But a 'failure' for what? Clearly for the absolute heterosexual Norm and its paladins, among whom we must count Ferenczi himself.

We homosexuals, on the other hand, save for some very rare exceptions, are always at least somewhat aware of the persistence in us of an

1. Sandor Ferenczi, 'The Nosology of Male Homosexuality (Homo Eroticism)', p. 317.

erotic desire for persons of the other sex. The standpoint of marginalisation or 'deviance' once again proves a 'privileged' one with respect to the comprehension of the 'reality' of things, of that reality which lies behind the appearance that the prevailing ideology proffers as ontological.[2]

It's through the idea of a sublimation of homoerotic desire that many social and individual phenomena can actually be interpreted and understood. Sport, for example, isn't just a peaceful extroversion of the death instinct, or as Konrad Lorenz has it, 'a cathartic discharge of aggressive urge'.[3] It is also a masked expression of homoerotic tendencies, often permitting physical contact between members of the same sex; and it translates the unconscious positive feeling of mutual attraction into a negative mode of antagonism and competition. In his film *Women in Love*, Ken Russell illustrated the mechanism of this conversion very well, along with its broad emotional scope, in the scene where the two male heroes wrestle naked in front of the fire.

Converted expressions of homosexual desire can be similarly recognised in the mania for sport and the worship of sporting stars: what lies behind and inside the myth of Rivera or Monzón?[4]

Proust asked himself, 'why, when we admire in the face of this person a delicacy that touches our hearts, a grace, a natural gentleness such as men do not possess, should we be dismayed to learn that this young man runs after boxers?'[5] But it is really no surprise that a tender and delicate man should be attracted to athletes, given that rougher and more virile men are too. And if someone should object that wanting to go to bed together is something else – true enough, but only because the homosexual desire is alienated, as a general rule, in sporting fans, who reject it and sublimate it in a fanatical fashion.

Oscar Wilde once scandalised a headmaster by quipping that 'Football is all very well as a game for rough girls, but it is hardly suitable for delicate boys'.[6] But Wilde's irony here conceals the trauma often experienced by

2. See Chapter 5, section 4.
3. Konrad Lorenz, *On Aggression* (London: Methuen and Co, 1967), p. 242.
4. [Translator's note: Gianni Rivera was a star Italian footballer who played much of his life for A. C. Milan and was adored by the Italian public; Carlos Monzón was an Argentine boxer as famous for being one of the greatest middleweights ever as for his glamorous life, the image of which was sullied later by his domestic abuse and eventual murder of his wife.]
5. Marcel Proust, *Remembrance of Things Past*, vol. 2, (London: Penguin Books, 1989), p. 645.
6. Philippe Jullian, *Oscar Wilde*, p. 29.

homosexual adolescents, who, unable to sublimate the erotic desire that they feel for their school friends, find it terribly frustrating to battle with them in competitive sports, and suffer terribly at times on this account. In ancient pederastic Greek society, love and gymnastics were not posed against each other. The officers of health and hygiene of our communities, on the other hand, do not easily release those who are said to be homosexual from obligatory physical education: a rare case, but it's often in such small breaches that homosexuality is not considered pathological.

The homosexual idea of sport is very different from the traditional one. The gay schoolboy who detests physical education dreams of a world in which physical exercise, sexual satisfaction and affection are no longer separate and opposing spheres. He knows very well, in fact, that his schoolmates, while kicking each other, actually desire one another. Instead of punching and beating, play should rather consist in people offering themselves physically to one another,[7] with the erotic character of sadomasochism being openly recognised and combined with affection. The struggle of bodies can very well end up in a kiss and forms of sex that are both tender and violent, and team meetings could well be transformed into a collective encounter in the scrum (a development already foreshadowed in rugby).

Today, the connection between Eros and sport is veiled with hypocrisy, even if hugging and kissing is already commonplace after a goal is scored. (What is the real goal?) And we know how in the locker room after the game, tousled and sweaty youths heatedly discuss their exploits in language full of sexual expressions, particularly the word 'fuck'.

In the municipal Turkish baths of London's East End, where young and not so young working-class heterosexuals regularly get together to massage each other's naked bodies on the steam room benches, and the scent of mint and saffron fills the air, it is enough to close one's eyes for a moment and simply listen, to be struck by the incessant repetition of 'fucking' this and that. The desire to fuck is so strong, and at the same time so tightly repressed, that it is continuously expressed in language and never concretely (or almost never, but my lips are sealed).

For its side, cunning capital is moving in to exploit the homosexuality that lies within and behind sport. The latest American sporting

7. [Translator's note: In the Italian, Mieli returns once more to his earlier pun around the word *battere* [to strike], which carries a dual connotation of hitting and cruising for sex. See Footnote 4 in Chapter 1.]

magazines, for example, publish gay ads in their back pages. And, in the more 'advanced' capitalist countries, fashion imposes on gays the attractive and provocative garb of the athlete. On a Sunday afternoon in New York's Central Park, you get the impression that a cycle race is taking place: racing bikes, shorts and muscular thighs are de rigueur, the scene is perfectly set. Still, what goes on in the bushes, would undoubtedly surprise the heterosexual who happens by.

At times, too, the bodybuilding cult has provided a medium linking sport with manifest homosexuality. A British magazine of the 1950s, for example, advertised itself as: 'The finest, most thrilling International Physique Photo magazine. Packed with superb pictures of the World's most flawless physiques. Hi-Fi reproduction on glossy art paper. Plus inspiring articles by today's Champion body-builders'.[8] Inside, photographs of nude males in the pose of Greek statues: 'Stars from all over the world'. Another issue of the same magazine was titled 'Men and Sex', even though there was not a single article inside on male sexuality. Apparently there was no need to justify the title.

Alcohol, patriotism, and other drugs. Male Bonding and Friendship

In the same way as sport, patriotic enthusiasm allows a converted expression of latent homosexual desire:

> Bleuler refused to accept that alcohol destroys sublimations. To support this view, he cited the tendency to a 'patriotic' sublimation that is frequently encountered after the consumption of alcohol. But when a drunken man induces those around him to join in expressions of 'patriotic' enthusiasm, we would rather see this as an ill-disguised homoeroticism than as sublimation.[9]

The Italian Alpine division must have felt that something hit the mark when they demanded (and obtained) the confiscation of Pasolini's *Salò, or 120 Days of Sodom* on the grounds that the film showed their troops in a scene deemed 'morbid and perverted'.

Looking more closely at drink, Ferenczi also maintained that 'the alcohol played here only the part of an agent destroying sublimation,

8. *Man's World,* (April 1957).
9. Ferenczi, 'Alcohol and the Neuroses' (1911), no English translation.

through the effect of which the [patient's] true sexual constitution, namely the preference for a member of the same sex, became evident'.[10] It is plenty well known how drunkenness releases homoerotic impulses in many who are heterosexual par excellence. Once a man gets drunk, he will fall prey without difficulty to gay seduction.

Marijuana, hash, LSD, etc., and in fact all 'mind-expanding' drugs frequently bring straight people face to face with their homoerotic desire and/or the problem of its repression, especially if they find themselves in the company of homosexuals. They can then either abandon themselves to the formerly repressed impulse, to experience, or else resist this and end up in 'paranoia'.[11]

Moreover, just as Ferenczi recognised the ill-disguised presence of homosexual desire in expressions of patriotism, so we can similarly see the same thing behind all male bonding, the military and police variety above all, as well as other forms of friendship between people of the same sex. According to Freud:

> After the stage of heterosexual object-choice has been reached, the homosexual tendencies are not, as might be expected, done away with or brought to a stop; they are merely deflected from their sexual aim and applied to fresh uses. They now combine with portions of the ego-instincts and, as attached components, help to constitute the social instincts, thus contributing an erotic factor to friendship and comradeship, to *esprit de corps* and to the love of mankind in general.[12]

The 'bosom buddy' of childhood and adolescence is in fact the 'object' of the child's desire, in the broad sense and hence also sexual. Mutual and collective masturbation among school friends expresses the erotic charge that ties them together, even if it is generally only the very young gay boy who can openly and without hypocrisy indulge in sexual relations with his peers. The others are already aware of the suppression of homoeroticism, and accept erotic play with their friends only as a palliative masturbatory outlet ('girls won't let us'), refusing to admit the deep homosexual desire that unites them.

10. Ferenczi, 'On the Part Played by Homosexuality in the Pathogenesis of Paranoia', p. 162.
11. See Chapter 5, section 2.
12. Freud, 'Psycho-Analytic Notes on an Autobiographical Account of a Case of Paranoia', p. 61.

Among adults, heterosexual male friends, colleagues, mates or comrades all fail to conceal from the gay eye the homosexual substratum of their relationships. Business partnerships, political rackets, gangs, bars and men's clubs are the unhealthy sites of latent homosexuality, for which they provide only a wretched gratification. Here, men exhibit the symbolic phallus, confirming their own fixation on the cock while speaking of 'women' or 'cunts', vigorously slapping one another on the back and issuing tacit requests to get fucked in the ass: 'Dickhead! Nutsack!' Clearly, men speak amongst themselves of male sexuality, and if they are heterosexual, then their homosexual desire can get worked out only in language.

Male bonding is the grotesque staging of a paralysed and embittered homosexuality, which can be grasped, in the negative, in the denial of women, whom they speak of phallocratically, without any genuine consideration, reducing them to a hole and therefore to *that which is not.* The suppression of homoeroticism is here always bound up with the oppression of women by men. Negated homosexual desire makes its resurgence via the negation of woman. In male language, woman is totally transformed, she becomes woman-for-man, a fetish-medium between men, the alienated go-between for men whose sole and constant preoccupation is the incessant assertion of a fetishistic, overweening, individualistic, male-bonding, and negative virility. Virility is simply the neurotic and cumbersome introjection by men of a homosexual desire for one another which is both very strong and tightly censored: it coarsens and hardens the male human being, transforming him into a crude caricature of maleness. There is nothing more ridiculous and wholly fragile than this would-be virile heterosexual who boasts of his violent and 'absolute' potency and in this way only negates himself, forcibly repressing the human being – particularly the 'woman' and the queer – within himself, and making himself a cop for the phallic power system. There is nothing more feeble than this 'virile' male who beneath it all fears impotence and castration, since in reality he already is, as an absolute male, a mutilated human being.

To quote Ferenczi once again:

> With male neurotics who feel themselves unkindly treated by the physician *homosexual obsessions* may appear, which often refer to the person of the latter. This is a proof, which might almost be called

> experimental, that friendship is essentially sublimated homosexuality, which in case of denial is apt to regress on to its primitive level.[13]

In all relations of friendship between male heterosexuals, the homosexuality that is latent and inhibited finds expression in the form of obsessive heterosexuality. The heterosexual is obsessed with the need to prove to his friend his exclusive attraction towards women, and to exorcise the homosexuality on which his friendship with the other man is based. Friendship, therefore, cannot be genuine: it is founded on a misconception and a mutual (anti-)homosexual complicity (or rather, on mute homosexual complicity, on alienated homosexuality). The liberation of homoeroticism, therefore, is not just the negation of homosexuality as it presently is, but also the supersession of the present forms of friendship between people of the same sex. If homosexuality comes out, then a certain type of 'friendship' cannot but give way to new erotic relations and open emotions.

Hetero-queens. The Cult of the Gay Superstar

Hetero-queenery, too, must be seen as a phenomenon closely connected with the sublimation of homoerotism. The hetero-queen is a heterosexual who, while unaware of the gay component of his own desire, and thus not having homosexual relations, has all the ways (if not the savoir faire) of a queen.

We can see this, for example, in the radical chic[14] of the left, the Stalinist-Maoist dress of *L'Uomo Vogue* as pioneered by Luca Cafiero[15] and others; the 'plum-coloured jacket with wide reveres' and the handbag – 'which, now that everybody carries one, is no longer necessarily a gay symbol'[16] – of the working-class militant of Lotta Continua; the jeans and leather of the Autonomists, a fetish taken over from the leather-queens, which objectifies and sublimates their homosexual desire; the

13. Ferenczi, 'Transitory Symptom-Constructions during the Analysis', *First Contributions*, p. 209. (Ferenczi's emphasis.)
14. [Translator's note: One of Mieli's complicated puns, riffing both on *checche* (queens/fags) and *radical chic*.]
15. [Translator's note: Cafiero was an important leader of Movimento Studentesco, an extra-parliamentary far left student organisation.]
16. See my article 'Il radical chic e il chic radicale', in *Fuori!* 7, (January 1973).

Arbasinian[17] preciousness undergirding Sergio Finzi or 'Little Hans'; the pinstripes and cigar of Verdiglione who, so tanned, would cut quite the figure, cognac in hand, at the Napoleon (the refined club for well-heeled homosexuals in central London).

For their part, even the very critics of the left often exhibit the radical chic variant of hetero-queenery. Take, for instance, the glossy paper, 'elegance' and 'unscrupulous' intellectual show-off evident in the publications of certain Situationist theorists (like Simonetti or the disguises of Sanguinetti or the bunch of frescoes and the novella of the thirties titled *Madness* that Pinni Galante brought me one time I was recovering in hospital). All these expressions of hetero-queenery reveal, to the eyes of conscious homosexuals, the queen within so many men whom no one would suspect of being gay. The Situationist critique of the society of the spectacle, in the language of certain Situationists, becomes itself spectacular, to the point that they come to act out through this mask their real desire for, and to be, queer.

Besides sport and sporting mania, patriotic enthusiasm, male bonding and friendship, hetero-queenery and radical chic, a certain quantity of unconscious homosexual desire is also channelled into the myths of singers and movie stars. This phenomenon is ever more common, to the point that in the USA and Britain, in particular, the latest idols of popular music rouse their massed teenage fans to delirium by a repertoire of sinuous movements, 'transsexual' vocal modulations, ostentatiously effeminate clothing and sophisticated make-up – by the patent ambiguity, in short, which they display, from the Rolling Stones to Roxy Music, Lou Reed and David Bowie. This phenomenon has reached paradoxical heights. The New York Dolls, for instance, a group of young men who come (or came) on stage in full drag, are completely heterosexual, and yet at least in its intent, their show is not in fact a parody of homosexuality and transvestism, but rather an exaltation. The great majority of their audience are heterosexual too, and yet the success of these singers is rightly attributed to their undisguised exhibition of a 'complex-free' homosexuality. Nor do their audience worship them as something ridiculous, but precisely because they appear provocatively gay.

This is a case of a repressive desublimation that is immediately resublimated. Capital liberalises desire while channelling it into a consumerist

17. [Translator's note: The reference is to Alberto Arbasino, the Italian novelist, whose 1959 epistolary novella *Il ragazzo perduto* [The Lost Boy] details the narrator's romance with a bourgeois Milanese man.]

outlet. Far from being genuinely liberated, homosexuality thus plays a key role in the totalitarian capitalist spectacle. Nowadays, there is no commercial 'artistic' expression which does not take into account, to a greater or lesser extent, the homoerotic content of desire. But in the 'age of its technical reproducibility,' the 'work of art' makes a high contribution to the commodification of homoeroticism.

As a general and conformist rule, a homosexual is seen as justified if they are an artist, since according to popular conception, artists are always outrageous, non-conformist, and mad, so they might as well be 'inverted' as well. In the eyes of 'normal' people, art, in the last analysis, redeems the anomaly of sexual depravation: 'even Michelangelo, Leonardo, Shakespeare, Rimbaud, Verlaine, Proust, Cocteau, etc. were like that'. Similarly, homosexuality is tolerated, as an exception, when accompanied by an 'artistic' expression, because it can then be relegated to the sphere of imagination, fantasy, and sublimation, and it does not directly interfere with relations that are currently considered 'normal'. Homoeroticism is all very well in the cinema, in books, and in painting, but not in bed, and above all: 'Not in *my* bed, for the love of God and the Blessed Virgin Mary!'

Capital makes us wallow in this form of tolerance. But if homosexuality really 'circulated' freely (as the ideology of permissiveness claims) as 'common currency', the consequences would be such as to seriously (or rather, *gaily*) endanger the heterosexual institutions and the unstable equilibrium on which the capitalist state is founded. And this is why the 'liberal' state is liberal only up to a certain point.

For the present system, to liberalise means above all to prevent and block any genuine liberation. And the liberalisation of homosexuality, as I have already shown, is in the first place its commodification, driven by capital – often via the medium of 'artistic' expression – in such the industries of the gay ghetto in cinema, publishing, clothing: in short, in the industries of fashion.

But if homosexuality, like feminism, is currently in fashion, its commodification does not alter social custom[18] substantially. Or rather, if there has been a change in custom, this has only taken place at a snail's pace, whereas ephemeral fashions assert and outmode themselves at a

18. [Translator's note: Mieli makes a pun around the multiple senses of the word *costume*, which can refer simultaneously to a social custom, a costume, and a men's suit.]

gallop. The streets of London are thronged with young heterosexual couples who are dressed, made-up and coiffured in the manner of their gay rock-star idols. But they are still heterosexual couples and – apart from a few rare exceptions who only prove the rule – so they remain.

Homosexuality has thus been elevated to a myth, on the condition, paradoxically, that the homosexual essence is kept hidden. The heterosexual rock fan idolises his star, and pays for his success, because in his eyes only a star can swish his hips with his head held high and mascara-smudged eyes. Like a mirror framed by glitter, the rock idol reflects the fascinated light of the homoerotic libido that his audience projects onto him. The cult of the gay superstar is the reverse side of the two-faced mask that heterosexuals wear in front of homosexuality. The face they usually show is immediate disdain and disparagement for the fag who stands at the corner of the street, who dares to smile at them in the underground.

Jealousy, Masochism and Sadism; The Homosexuality Within Heterosexuality

I already indicated in the first chapter the recognition by psychoanalysis of a veiled homoerotic desire in some mechanisms specific to so-called 'normal' jealousy ('competitive' jealousy, as Freud also described it): 'That is to say, a man will not only feel pain about the woman he loves and hatred of the man who is his rival, but also grief about the man, whom he loves unconsciously, and hatred of the woman as his rival; and the latter set of feelings will add to the intensity of his jealousy.'[19]

It is particularly jealousy of the 'delusional' kind, which also contains elements of the two other types, 'competitive' and 'projected', that reveals most blatantly the homoerotic substrate that is common to all three:

> It too has its origin in repressed impulses towards unfaithfulness; but the object in these cases is of the same sex as the subject. Delusional jealousy is what is left of a homosexuality that has run its course, and it rightly takes its position among the classical forms of paranoia. As an attempt at defence against an unduly strong homosexual impulse

19. Freud, 'Some Neurotic Mechanisms in Jealousy, Paranoia and Homosexuality', *Standard Edition,* Vol. 18 (London: Vintage, 2001), p. 223.

> it may, in a man, be described in the formula: '*I* do not love him, *she* loves him!'[20]

And according to Ferenczi, 'jealousy of men signifie[s] only the projection of [one's] own erotic pleasure in the male sex'.[21]

Jealousy, therefore, is envy: envy of the woman able to get off with the other man. In spoken language, you often hear the idea of jealousy confused with the idea of envy: to say 'I'm jealous of you because you've got a beautiful car' is the vice versa of what you cannot say, that is: 'I am envious of you, my dear, because you do it with the butcher's boy'.

The achievement of homosexual awareness and the liberation of gay desire shatters the closed world of the traditional heterosexual couple, and above all, dispels the murky fog of possible betrayals, infidelities and jealousies that weigh upon it, poisoning our days and nights. Jealousy too, therefore, is based on a serious misunderstanding of homosexual desire. It gnaws at the liver of the heterosexual male if his woman gets off with another man, because he is unaware that if he, too, were to make love with this other man, with other men in general, then he would have taken the most important step towards overcoming his tribulations and transforming jealousy into enjoyment. It may well be true that jealousy today often involves an indirect expression of masochistic tendencies, and thus in a certain respect is a pleasure in itself. But it is also true that masochism can be enjoyed in a more satisfactory, conscious, direct and communicative way.

Giuliano De Fusco has pointed out to me that a person aware of his masochism exerts himself to bring out the 'contradiction' in his partner, by which he means the inhibited sadism, or, in the wider sense, the sadistic and masochistic impulses of those who do not recognise their own sadomasochistic propensity. The true masochist is adept at inducing his partner to liberate his aggression and become aware of it. This involves an increase in emotion and enjoyment for both parties, and the masochist ultimately manages to see the person as he 'really' is, uninhibitedly. In a love relation, the genuine masochist sees himself the object of an amorous aggression, permitting him to directly and openly enjoy the pleasure of jealousy; 'betrayal' becomes an act of love, since it reveals aggression and hence enhances pleasure and passion.

20. Ibid., p. 225.
21. Ferenczi, 'On the Part Played by Homosexuality . . .', p. 161.

But conscious sadomasochism is certainly not the same thing as the sadomasochism implicit in the 'normal' couple. As Giuliano De Fusco observes, this relationship reflects the alienated and alienating sadomasochism with which capitalist society is permeated, which is authoritarian and repressive, and which, by negating the human being, sadistically negates also his sadism, imposing on him a subhuman and humiliating condition, and debasing his masochism.

Just as a loving desire for people of the other sex is today reduced by the system to a stunted and phallocratic heterosexuality, while desire for people of the same sex is severely repressed by a society that transforms this into an instrument of capitalist power, by forcing it to remain latent or desublimating it in an alienating manner, so too are the sadistic and masochistic tendencies divided, repressed, and exploited by capital, which distorts them so as to make them serve its own rule. The revolution will also be the (pro)positive liberation of sadism and masochism, and a free community in which masochistic and sadistic desires will find open expression and take on a new and transformed form, quite different from the 'sado-masochism' of today. With masochism and sadism, too, the revolutionary critique also attacks the prejudice that sees sadism and masochism as simply 'perversions', mere distortions of Eros, denying their intrinsic importance, their ability to bridge the gulf between Eros and Thanatos, between good and evil, and to overcome – in practical and emotional life – the dichotomy of opposites founded on repression.

In the words of Georg Groddeck:

> It is therefore not true that pain is an obstacle to pleasure. The truth is that on the contrary it is a condition of pleasure [. . .] To brand as perversions these two inescapable human desires which are implanted in every human being without exception, and which belong to his nature just as much as his skin and hair, was the colossal stupidity of a learned man. That it was repeated is intelligible. For thousands of years man has been educated in hypocrisy, and it has become second nature to him. Everyone is a sadist, everyone a masochist; everyone by reason of his nature must wish to give and to suffer pain; to that he is compelled by Eros.[22]

Today – it's never too late! – liberation requires an awareness of sadistic and masochistic desires. The masochist cannot restrict himself to living

22. Groddeck, *The Book of the It*, p. 73.

out these tendencies hypocritically or with an inadequate consciousness, as the police apparatuses of the established left would like. The great history of love is filled with sadistic and masochistic fantasies, which should also find clear expression in our everyday life, in interpersonal relations and in our relations with animals, so that our reality does not remain essentially superficial, cut off from what lies beneath, but instead gets to the bottom of things, and even beyond.

Among us homosexuals, the propensity to form exclusive couples is far less strong than among straight people. And the values of gay promiscuity are many, most of all because it opens the individual up to a multiplicity and variety of relations, and hence positively gratifies the tendency that everyone has to polymorphism and 'perversion'. It thereby facilitates the satisfactory course of any relationship between two people, because neither of them clings too desperately to the other, demanding that he should give up totalising relations with other people too. The revolutionary homosexual struggle demands the erotic and emotional recognition of every human being in the community and the world. Each of us is a prism, a sphere, is mobile, and beneath and beyond the contradictions that presently oppose and negate us, each of us fits potentially together with anyone else, in a 'geometry', both real and imaginary, of free intersubjectivity – like a wonderful kaleidoscope to which new and precious stones are steadily added: children and new arrivals of every kind, corpses, animals, plants, things, flowers, turds ...

Finally, if heterosexual jealousy displays a sharp if disguised form of homosexuality, a psychological defence against the genuine surfacing of a homoerotic desire, we can also frequently establish how the libidinal choice of an 'object' of 'opposite' sex reveals the presence of elements that unconsciously satisfy in a palliative fashion the latent homosexual tendency of the 'subject'.

According to Freud, 'everyone, even the most normal person, is capable of making a homosexual object-choice, and has done so at some time in his life, and either still adheres to it in his unconscious or else protects himself against it by vigorous counterattitudes'.[23] It often happens that the homosexual choice is induced to opt for an 'object' of the other sex. In this case, the heterosexual 'object' partially satisfies the censored homoerotic component of desire. The converse is also true for us homosexuals

23. Freud, 'Leonardo da Vinci and a Memory of his Childhood'. *Standard Edition*, Vol. 11 (London: Vintage, 2001), p. 99, note.

Homosexuality, therefore, very often hides within heterosexuality. It is no accident that French feminists have maintained the homosexual character of all heterosexual relations that presently exist, so that Luce Irigaray can speak of 'so-called heterosexuality'.

Violence against homosexuals as negative extroversion of censured homoerotic desire. The hypocrisy of the heterosexual male.

When someone provokes us he does not know
that this is his desire starting to show . . .[24]

We have seen how, in the present society, sadism almost always presents itself in an alienated form. This happens, for example, when sadistic tendencies are accompanied by the repression of another component of desire and the complementary overvaluation of one particular expression of Eros. In the same way, we can recognise a form of alienated sadism, combined with an inverted homosexual impulse and an ostentatious display of heterosexuality, in the acts of aggression that straight people commit against us gays.

The witch-hunt against queers (and here the 'casual' association between the words recalls the particular connection that exists between the persecution of witches and the extermination of faggots) is nothing more than an expression of alienated sadism, alienated through its connection with a negative extraversion of repressed homosexual desire and the need to shore up heterosexuality with force, both internally and against overt homosexuals. Freud, however, wrote that 'poets are right in liking to portray people who are in love without knowing it . . . or who think that they hate when in reality they love'.[25]

We homosexuals have to cope every day with more or less violent persecutors. We cannot be too careful, since those who might beat us up or murder us lurk on all sides, in the heart of the city and its periphery, in small provincial towns, in parks and even in the country. Are these aggressors just 'common criminals'? We certainly have no intention of

24. From the song 'We Are Queers and Queens' ['Noi siamo froci e checche'] from the theatrical production *The Misled Norm, or Rather, Go Fuck Yourself . . . All Right!* [La Traviata Norma, ovvero: vaffanculo . . . ebbene sì!], presented in Milan, Florence, and Rome in the spring of 1976 by the company Our Lady of the Flowers [Nostra Signora dei Fiori] of the Homosexual Collective of Milan.

25. Freud, 'The Psychogenesis of a Case of Homosexuality in a Woman', p. 167.

taking over this bigoted, summary, bourgeois and reactionary definition. And in that case, all heterosexual males would be common criminals, as their customary anti-homosexual attitude makes them permanent accomplices in the violence perpetrated against us.

The attackers and killers are pushed onto the scene (the 'gay' scene) and seduced and led to crime by prevailing morality, by the male supremacist and heterosexual ideology which the system upholds (and which upholds the system). It is capitalist morality that leads them to violence and aggression. If a government minister makes a speech attacking homosexuality as a social pest, while priests condemn 'sinful and unnatural' sexual practices from the pulpit, if it is customary to drag homosexuals from their insecure meeting places and haul them up before harsh and blatantly unjust courts, if self-appointed moral vigilantes see homosexuality as a form of 'moral pollution', if leftists see fags as a sign of bourgeois decadence,[26] then is it any surprise that so many marginalized young proletarians kids, defined as 'sub-proletarians' by the Marxist dunces of the left, should take gays as their scapegoat? You've got to take it out on someone,[27] and capital, cleverly, always manages to divert popular rage away from itself. The homosexual survives alone and practically defenceless against all and through all – when he does survive . . .

But if homoeroticism is a 'vice' as far as society is concerned, a 'perversion' and/or a 'criminal deviation', then the very oppression of homosexuality, the verbal and physical queer-bashing, and the rampant persecution that has always been launched at us offers to heterosexuals further indirect ways of expressing their own latent homoerotic impulses. This censored homosexuality is often externalised in the form of witless sadism, aggression that is either gratuitous, or 'justified' by stubborn and reactionary anti-gay prejudices.

Often – as Genet explains – to attack a homosexual is to put one's heart at peace, considering that,

> if a queer was like this, a creature so light, so fragile, so airy, so transparent, so delicate, so broken, so clear, so garrulous, so musical, so tender – one could kill it. Since it was made to be killed; like Venetian

26. More recently, the attitude of the majority of 'leftists' has changed, and many have jumped from one extreme to the other, some even seeing 'feminists and homosexuals as the movement's super-ego'.

27. [Translator's note: Mieli uses a colloquial Italian expression: *Con qualcuno bisogna pur prendersela.*]

> glass it waited only the big tough fist which could smash it without even being cut (save possibly for an insidious sliver, sharp, hypocritical, slitting and remaining under the skin). If this was a queer, it wasn't a man. For the queer had no weight. He was a little cat, a bullfinch, a fawn, a blind-word, a dragonfly, whose very fragility is provocative and, in the end, it is precisely this exaggeration which inevitably invites its death.[28]

The very existence of the homosexual, his 'anomaly', his 'depraved' desire, and his weakness that comes from marginalisation and exclusion demand punishment in the eyes of the heterosexual, that shining knight of the Norm. In actual fact, however, 'the punishment [is] a favour like the crime'.[29] For if overt expressions of homoeroticism are 'normally' considered a crime, and if heterosexuals feel legitimate enjoyment in condemning them to punishment, this pleasure is at bottom a negative satisfaction of the repressed wish to make love with a queer. 'I cannot get off with him because I'm normal; so I beat him and rob him. His presence suggests to me a physical relationship that I can't accept, so I respond to it with physical violence'. Paradoxically, however, we homosexuals can recognise the secret lover in those who mistreat and chastise us.

This anti-gay violence, which derives from the repression and blaming of homoeroticism, is also to be found among men who have occasionally had sexual relations with other men, and might even still do so (as we have already seen in the previous section). Stilitano, for example, the hardest of the hard, Genet's 'lover', insults queens;[30] and in prison the tough guys, the lords of the jail, the manly bullies who the queens secretly 'contaminate' through long cohabitation, put down homosexuality at the same time as they practise it, and are ever ready to meet an unwelcome advance with a punch in the mouth.[31] The absurdity of their conception of sex and sex roles shows the deeply absurd essence of patriarchal 'normality'. In the hypermasculine atmosphere of prison, only passive homosexuality is considered shameful, whereas 'a male that fucks

28. Jean Genet, *Querelle de Brest*, translated by Kate Millett in *Sexual Politics* (New York: Columbia University Press, 2016), p. 344.
29. Sartre, *Baudelaire*, p. 81.
30. Jean-Paul Sartre, *Saint Genet, Actor and Martyr* (New York: Grove Press, 1963), p. 318.
31. See Bianca Maria Elia, *Emarginazione e omosessualità negli istituti de rieducazione* (Milan: Mazzotta, 1974), though on the whole this is a thoroughly bad book.

a male is a double male'.[32] The 'double male' requires an inverted and abject appendage, a 'surrogate cunt', and he bases his glory and prestige on the subjection of others.

Kate Millett shows the strong similarity between the relation of butches and queens in prison, and the opposition between the sexes involved in 'normal' heterosexuality.[33] In prison, where homosexual relations offer the only gratification for erotic desire apart from solitary masturbation, homosexuality itself generally takes the form of a mere reflection of the asymmetrical relationship of the heterosexual couple (which thus reveals its true face). Even in prison, the 'heterosexual' male remains privileged, behaving as a straight man, and basing his 'power' on the submission of the 'weakest', the queen.

But it is not always so. In his amazing film *A Song of Love,* for example, Genet has himself given us a most poetic and delicate (as well as quite sexy) picture of love between men in prison. And I myself, in an English prison, got on well – sometimes very well – with other prisoners.

Yet Genet always has the heterosexual equation in mind. In the 'eternal couple of the criminal and the saint',[34] we are given the tragic-erotic representation of the eternal heterosexual couple of the totalitarian phallic male, who is always a criminal in his relations with women, and the woman who, given that she loves him, desires him and is subject to him, cannot but be a saint in her love life. But woman as the slave of man is in a certain respect similar to the effeminate queen, Genet himself, whom the macho 'heterosexual' at once fucks and demeans.

For Genet, the 'eternal couple of thy criminal and the saint' is above all the duo of the beautiful brute ('*un assassin si beau qui fait pâlir le jour*') and the homosexual who desires him and at the same time is negated by him, who is martyred in his passionate love because the criminal whom he loves is first and foremost his egoistic and violent oppressor, 'indifferent and bright as a slaughterhouse knife'.[35]

Genet's, play *The Maids* was conceived and written to be performed by men dressed as women.[36] The negated femininity of the heterosexual man in his relation to women is represented very well by a fictitious femininity, reduced to a mere appearance. Today, this negated femininity

32. Jean Genet, *Our Lady of the Flowers* (London: Panther Books, 1966), p. 226.
33. See Kate Millett, *Sexual Politics*, pp. 336–61
34. Jean Genet, *The Maids* (New York, 1961, p. 63.
35. Genet, *Our Lady of the Flowers*, p. 63.
36. Jean-Paul Sartre, *Saint Genet,* p. 61.

is above all the being of women, who can really exist as women only beyond the negation criminally inflicted on her by men. Secondly, this femininity is also the repressed 'feminine' component of the man himself, and 'Genet will make a relentless effort to discover a secret femininity in all the toughs who subdue him'.[37] Finally, an oppressed femininity is present in Genet, in his desire to really become a woman, and in the concrete impossibility of this.

In the heterosexual phallocentric universe, femininity, for the man, is reduced to a mere aura of sanctity around the brute power of the phallus. As a general rule, for the heterosexual man (as Fornari typically writes in his narrow-minded apology for heterosexuality), 'if the male genital did not exist, then the female genital would appear a meaningless organ'.[38] It is only too clear that the phallus in the brain prevents the heterosexual man from seeing beyond his own dick: for him, society today is made up of cunts. If I did believe in the idea of a vanguard, I would say that the vanguard of the revolution would be made up of lesbians. In any case, the revolution will be lesbian.

The 'common criminals', then, only echo the anti-woman and anti-homosexual criminality that is common to all straight men. If someone murders a homosexual, he has simply acted, in the words of Paolo Volponi, 'out of the collective sense of right, in the very name of our society and its norms, whether he has done so out of horror of homosexuality, or to punish it, with a pronounced feeling of social justice'. As Volponi goes on to say: 'The murder is collective, representing and acting on behalf of a social feeling and passion and knows not only' how to interpret the anti-gay tendency of all 'normal people, but 'also that he is supported and protected' by them.[39] All heterosexuals are responsible for the violence directed against us gays.

The heterosexual male, moreover, is distinguished by his hypocrisy. Mignon, the butch who 'mounts' Divine, refuses even to define himself as homosexual, even though Divine, with whom he makes love, is a man.[40] But if femininity is reduced to an appearance here, with the queen serving the 'double male' as a mere surrogate for a woman, then so too is heterosexuality. The 'double male' feels himself heterosexual twice over,

---

37. Ibid., p. 132.

38. Franco Fornari, *Genitalità e cultura* (Milan: Feltrinelli, 1975), p. 59.

39. Paolo Volponi, 'Il dramma popolare della morte di Pasolini', *Corriere della Sera* (21 March 1976).

40. [Translator's note: Mignon (which might be translated as 'Darling') and Divine are characters in Genet's *Our Lady of the Flowers*.]

even more than 'normal': of this we can be sure because of his need to reassure himself and the way he's always ready to break anyone's teeth if they dare to call him a queer. His conviction of remaining heterosexual, even in a sexual relationship with a man, does not even clash with the male supremacist ideology he embraces, which is in itself hypocritical and absurd. If the butch who fucks the queen sees himself as heterosexually 'normal', his bad faith is not substantially different from that of those doctors who, as we saw in the first chapter, would define him without hesitation as only 'pseudo-homosexual'.

In the same way, the 'heterosexual' man, married with children and who makes love with a transvestite or drag queen, believes himself 100 per cent 'normal', in the logic of heterosexuality: he is comforted by appearances, and in his eyes the transvestite is like a woman. In actual fact, when dressed for battle, female prostitutes and male transvestites are largely similar, at least in terms of this external appearance. It is not difficult, then, for a man to reproduce through himself the fetish of 'woman' that men like.

What really excites the transvestite's client, however, is the man underneath that fetishistic representation of 'woman'. Firstly, in his male supremacist view, femininity is simply a fetish, and so it excites him only fetishistically, which is to say as an object, as a hole. And secondly, what he is directly interested in is not an interpersonal relationship, but simply his narcissistic relationship with himself, even if in an alienated mode, through phallic fantasies and gratifications that overspill the narcissistic pleasure itself and require the partner-object as a pretext. So what in essence excites the transvestite's client is simply his own self, but it is himself as he really desires to be, and discovered beneath the make-up and gown of the transvestite, to his eyes fetishistically attractive in a 'feminine' way. The homoerotic components of desire of those 'heterosexuals' who have sex with transvestites is too severely censored for them to openly desire a gay relationship (I know this myself, as a part-time transvestite). They can only escape their homosexuality through the parody of a heterosexual relation. But in this parody, they act out the tragedy of the repression of Eros.

The Torturer is the Victim's Accomplice. Victimisation and Masochism

If, as I have shown, the heterosexual who attacks a gay man both discloses and exorcises his own homosexuality, then the aggressor, the torturer, stands in secret complicity with his victim. The concept of complicity here must be understood by bearing in mind the negative conversion of homoerotic desire into aggression on the part of the heterosexual. Moreover, for him to become unconsciously complicit with the homosexual, his own victim, it is necessary for him to view homosexuality as a crime and the victim as guilty. It is clear that this imposition of guilt does not involve any real guilt on the victim's part, he being a victim precisely because he is innocent, but it legitimates aggression on the part of the heterosexual. To recapitulate: the (hetero) torturer is the accomplice of the (gay) victim; and the idea of complicity thus refers to the unconscious attraction that the heterosexual has towards the homosexual, despite his conscious imposition to him of guilt. It refers to a homosexual act which does not take place, but which is unconsciously desired by the heterosexual, and which he subsequently translates into violence.

This view, then, is the reverse of the thesis maintained by Liliana Cavani in *The Night Porter*, a thesis that, while superficially similar, is in reality opposite ('the victim is the accomplice of the torturer'). Still, might not the two theses be complementary?

Not necessarily. In the Nazi concentration camps, for example, the extermination of the pink triangles expressed a collective sadistic conversion of the SS's homoerotic impulses (an alienated sadism insofar as it is bound up with the alienation of homosexuality), rather than a masochistic support by the homosexuals for their sadism.

All the same, it cannot be said that the homoerotic desires of the Nazi persecutors were always latent. If the SA were notoriously homosexual, many SS men, too, did not flinch from sexual relations with other men. In a social context in which gay desire was severely oppressed, we can understand how male homosexuality could find expression only on condition that it assumed hypermasculine and paradoxically anti-homosexual forms. As Francesco Saba Sardi has written:

> Under Nazi rule, in fact, it was a specific type of homosexual, weak and 'decadent', who was the object of persecution, certainly not the rough barrack-room bugger. The mincing queen of the boulevards and gay ghettoes was taken away; he was not sufficiently war-like. The rough SA or blond SS man, however, so loved by their sergeant or *Sturmbannführer*, were deemed more virile and militaristic, more worthy of trust and membership in their 'service', if they did not abandon themselves to frivolous affairs with women.[41]

41. Francesco Saba Sardi, 'La società omosessuale', *Venus* 7 (November 1972), p. 40.

Those who were slain were the homosexuals who did not fit the hyper-masculine uniformity of Nazism and who, by the very nature of things, by their physical appearance and mentality, were excluded from the phallic, fanatical and war-like display of the regime, which demanded men, in the absolute sense, or, more precisely, 'double males'. Indeed, the extermination of homosexuals under the Third Reich offers the clearest picture, the very quintessence, of the infernal quotidian persecution inflicted on gays by capitalist society. If today it is a collective homo-erotic desire, unconscious insofar as it is repressed, that is externalised in the forms of verbal and physical aggression against the openly gay, then under Nazisim it was frequently men who were themselves manifest homosexuals, but chained to the system and infested by its violent and martial ideology, who served as the instruments of deadly repression of homoeroticism. The system set homosexuality against homosexuality: and it still does so today, albeit in a more subtle and hypocritical fashion.

And yet the image of the more or less impassive tough guy, the 'torturer', is still a widespread erotic fantasy among us gays. Genet is no exception: it is impossible to deny that manifest homosexuality is frequently bound up with forms of masochism. But how could it be otherwise, in the context of a violently anti-homosexual Norm? How could you go after a heterosexual man, with his 'normal' sadism, without putting your own masochism to the fore? For it is clear that we queens do not just desire other queens, but feel erotic attraction for 'all' people of our own sex, whether homosexual or not.

Many of us, indeed, prefer straight men as sexual 'objects'. What attracts us in them is their maleness, and in general we find heterosexual men more male because heterosexuality, based as it is on the marked differentiation between the sexes, tends to make the man male in an absolute sense, the opposite of the female. Supported and gratified by the Norm, the heterosexual often appears to us like Nietzsche's 'sensually healthy and beautiful beast of prey'. French queens call these heterosexual males whom they so adore *'bêtes'*, and they are certainly beastly in both senses of the word.

Thus we frequently desire someone whom we cannot love, the very prototype of the 'normal' straight man who persecutes us. There is undoubtedly an inherent contradiction in the very strong sexual attraction we experience for men who particularly detest us, the personifications of phallocentric power. As Daniele Morini of the Milan Homosexual Collectives wrote: 'Paradoxically, I really discover my body only in contact with my imagination of the male. It is easy to see that the content of this imagination is alienated and that my partners are reactionary fantasies.'[42]

The erotic fantasies that spring to our consciousness very often reflect those stereotyped figures embodying the heterosexual Norm that has modelled society and the species. Our prevalent desire for the *bête* is in a certain sense the internalisation of the figure and role of the oppressor. To exclusively or especially desire the straight man means supporting those who oppress us, and contributes to perpetuating the reactionary characteristics that historically distinguish him.

But the struggle for homosexual liberation leads to disinvesting and transforming precisely the most immediate 'objects' of homosexual desire; above all, it liberates desire and multiplies its streams, helping us to overcome any such exclusive erotic fixation. On top of this, it provides the homosexual with a sense of dignity which gradually leads him to abandon alienating relations with straight men, and/or to assist these men to change in a new and positive direction, retrieving the humanity and, above all, the femininity that is suffocated by their bitter and phallocratic attitude. The homosexual, by liberating himself, sets the heterosexual an example of gay strength and dignity, of a new way of being human, which is no longer based on interpersonal negation, but on mutual understanding, desire and satisfaction. The homosexual can lead the straight man into a relationship that is genuinely gay, and not some clumsy imitation of heterosexual fucking. The struggle of revolutionary homosexuals against straight men seeks to transform these 'objects' of desire into free and open human beings, no longer intransigently and exclusively heterosexual, no longer alien, but rather like ourselves; so that we can truly make love with them, with one another, and can find in gay, uninhibited and free intersubjective relations the collective strength required to subvert the system as a whole. This positive goal inspires the gay struggle against heterosexual men, who are themselves inevitably chained to the status quo.

The homosexual who, in his anger, neither goes nor sees beyond the objective of a drastic negation of the male, remains caught in a contradictory trap, even if his 'dictatorial' attitude has a certain historical justification. The contradiction stems from the fact that it is neither

42. 'La Bella e la Bestia', in the Milan Homosexual Collectives' *Il Vespasiano degli omosessuali* (Milan, 1976).

possible to negate the straight man definitively, while at the same time continuing to desire him, nor to abolish this sexual attraction voluntaristically. Doing so, we risk suffocating ourselves and our imagination, because this straight man is already inside of us, from the moment that we desire him sexually. We cannot kill him, because in so doing we would kill ourselves. We cannot fall into the illusions of William Wilson who struck his double, or of Dorian Gray, who died by stabbing his own portrait. We need rather to reanimate the human being who lies frozen beneath the virile sclerosis of the heterosexual male, freeing him (and ourselves) from the phallic 'spell'. In this sense, the desire of the homosexual for the heterosexual is revolutionary: in spreading homosexuality, it unchains Eros.

Revolutionary homosexuals have decided to no longer play the role of victim and have begun to reject, once and for all, being simply an exception that proves the rule. The task facing us is to abolish forever a Norm which debases and oppresses us. The role of victim is no longer gratifying enough, nor indeed has it ever been. (Even if it would still be worth our while to write a detailed martyrology of gay persecution.) We intend to enjoy freely, without interference, our own homosexuality and that of others, just as our own (and others') masochistic tendencies. But this does not mean continuing to play the victim's role. For if the victim's counterpart is the sadistic libertine, the counterpart of the masochist is not a sadist – a Mars in leather, haughty and resplendent as a god. The sadism of De Sade was not the masochism of Sacher Masoch, even if there can be no sadism without collateral masochistic expressions, nor a masochism devoid of sadistic impulses. It is not by accident that we speak of sadomasochism as a unity. And yet the traditional sadistic libertine does not select a masochistic victim (what point would there be in hurting someone who enjoyed it?), nor the masochist a sadistic dominator. 'It is too readily assumed', writes Deleuze, 'that the symptoms have only to be transposed and the instincts reversed for Masoch to be turned into Sade, according to the principle of the unity of opposites'.[43]

On the terrain of liberation, however, a sexual encounter between prevalently sadistic and prevalently masochistic people really is possible. The liberation of sadomasochism and the liberation of homosexuality will overcome the traditional counterposed roles of sadism and masochism.

43. Gilles Deleuze, 'Coldness and Cruelty', in Deleuze and Leopold von Sacher-Masoch, *Masochism* (New York: Zone Books, 1991), p. 13.

Deleuze's investigation of these tendencies appears somewhat restricted, for in a certain sense he hypostatises forms of masochism and sadism that have only a contingent and historical existence. This is what Larry Rosàn of the American Eulenspiegel Society wrote in an editorial titled 'Gaudeamus Igitur':

> We know there are natural sadistic and masochistic elements in a very large proportion of people. And the majority of us are aware that the attraction of a naturally sadistic or masochistic personality is far greater, from the point of view of pleasure, than the mere exploitation of those patterns of domination and submission that are inveterate and sustained by our society, such as 'police against prisoners', 'rich against poor', and so on. There is a profound psychological difference between the 'true personality of a slave' and a 'potentially rebel prisoner' who is only the unwilling victim of circumstance. This is why Eulenspiegel stresses voluntary relations. As we see it, 'limitation to voluntary partners' is not an exception to our freedom, but rather a part of it. We want to be free from submitting to social authority, or to those persons who use us as unwilling victims! (And in fact we sado-masochists, in particular those of us who are sadistic dominators, are actually more vulnerable than others to sudden repression on the part of the state and the police, that corrupt and obscure abyss of primitive and conflictual sado-masochist desires, jealous and resentful of us for freely celebrating and enjoying the mystique of sado-masochism.)[44]

Those homosexuals who are effectively and predominantly masochistic are therefore forced to combat the negative role of victim that the system inflicts on them. It is no accident that masochists are to be found among the most radical protagonists of the gay movement, the most decisive opponents of homosexual victimisation and anti-gay social violence. Indeed, it is those homosexuals who adapt to the role of victim out of inertia and a sense of guilt that we recognise as the real victims, rather than the masochists who under it all are enjoying themselves. (Even if it should not be ruled out that long adaptation to suffering might bring out in many people masochistic impulses that were formerly repressed.)

The question of homosexual masochism is indeed an intricate one. It frequently presents itself in an alienated form, as a result of false guilt

44. Larry Rosàn, *'Gaudeamus I gitur', Pro. me. thee. us* (New York, Spring 1975). [Retranslated from the Italian.]

and the internalised condemnation, and is still confused with the evident mechanism of sadistic extraversion of latent homoerotic impulses on the part of heterosexuals. Clearly the homosexual question is less explored and less understood by the heterosexual Norm. We gays know a lot about the straight couple (we still often have a parent on our back, and also, whether we like it or not, in our head), while 'normal' people base their ideas on the repression of homosexuality. The act of legitimising the persecution of those who are 'deviant', or nowadays the act of tolerating them, dispenses 'normal' people from investigating the reasons that spur them either to persecution, or else to the new convenient solution of 'tolerance'. 'The social consensus around their own form of sexuality does not spur them to question it, and through it the whole of their private life' (Corrado Levi).

For us who are 'deviant', understanding the reasons for our oppression is indispensable if we are to find the correct direction in which to lead our struggle for liberation. Just as only the feminist standpoint can show the patriarchal essence of our present civilisation, and only revolutionary criticism can shed light on the real 'nature' of the rule of capital, so can only the gay standpoint discern the real content of the Norm to which we are opposed, and recognise in the concrete human subjects who uphold this Norm the contradiction implicit in the Norm itself. Heterosexuals are what they are, and exclusively so, because they deny the homosexuality that is latent within them, sublimating it and/or converting it into aggression.

Sublimated homoeroticism as the guarantee of social cohesion. Homosexuality in Dante

Freud emphasised only the peaceful sublimation of homoerotic desire. 'After the stage of heterosexual object-choice has been reached, the homosexual tendencies are not [...] done away with [...] they are merely deflected from their sexual aim and applied to fresh uses'.[45] He indicated an underlying homosexual content in those types of sublimation that are translated into dedication to the community and to public interests: 'In the light of psychoanalysis we are accustomed to regard social feeling as a sublimation of homosexual attitudes towards objects.'[46]

45. Freud, 'Psycho-Analytic Notes on an Autobiographical Account of a Case of Paranoia', p. 61.

46. Freud, 'Some Neurotic Mechanisms in Jealousy, Paranoia and Homosexuality', p. 232.

Freud accordingly deemed the sublimation of homosexuality to be publicly useful. His conception derived, by generalisation, from establishing the existence of a good number of homosexuals who were distinguished by a special development of the social instincts and their devotion to public welfare. According to Freud, this dedication was explained by the fact that 'the behaviour towards men in general of a man who sees in other men potential love-objects must be different from that of a man who looks upon other men in the first instance as rivals in regard to women'.[47] Homosexual desire is transformed into a force of social cohesion. By accepting the sublimation of homoeroticism in social sentiments, the law of the jungle is restrained and transformed, given that heterosexual society is a system of rivalry, jealousy and competition.

But the sublimation of homoeroticism is based historically on its suppression: it is the bulwark of social cohesion for a system which directly or indirectly condemns overt expressions of homosexuality. If homosexuality is liberated, it will cease to sustain this system, come into conflict with it and contribute to its collapse. At the same time, a liberated homosexuality is an important condition for the creation of communism, which is the (re)conquest of human community. And the realisation of this true community is inconceivable without the liberation of homoeroticism, which is universal, and which alone can guarantee genuinely totalising relations between persons of the same sex. (Communism is the rediscovery of bodies and their fundamental communicative function, their polymorphous potential for love.)

The 'particular' development, highlighted by Freud, of the social instincts among open homosexuals calls to mind Dante's *Divine Comedy* where, amongst the 'sodomites' condemned to Hell, we find numerous prestigious and influential public figures:

All these, in brief, were clerks and men of worth
In letters and in scholarship – none more so;
And all defiled by one same taint on earth.[48]

Dante generally speaks of them in elegiac tones: ('Stamped on my mind, and now stabbing my heart, / The dear, benign, paternal image of you'),[49]

47. Ibid.

48. The Divine Comedy 1: Hell, trans. D. L. Sayers (London: Penguin, 1949), p. 164. (Canto XV, lines 106–8.)

49. Ibid., lines 82–3.

despite their being judged guilty of a sin so grave and mortal that it goes unnamed (*'pecatum illud horribile inter Christianos non nominandum'*). The two Cantos of the *Inferno* devoted to the 'sodomites' (XV and XVI) feature not even a single word that explicitly defines the nature of the crime 'against nature' that cost them their damnation (indeed, 'Sodom' is mentioned only in Canto XI, where Virgil explains the order of the lower circles). They are exemplary men (such as Brunetto Latini, described as one who in his lifetime taught Dante himself 'the art by which men grow immortal'[50]), but who committed a terrible fault which was itself enough to see them cast forever into the bowels of Hell.

A band of 'sodomites', however, appear also in *Purgatory* ('Paradise waits for you ...'); hence Dante does not view the sin 'against nature' as necessarily irredeemable. This is genuinely surprising, if we take account of the exceptionally harsh legal and religious penalties that homosexuals faced in Tuscany and the whole of medieval Europe;[51] nor does Dante explain why these people are expiating in Purgatory the crime for which 'Caesar, in a triumph once heard them call "*Regina*" against him',[52] whilst others, including Brunetto's 'dear, benign, paternal image', belonged to the 'troop' of those who would suffer forever the infernal torments.

Besides, if in *Inferno* the 'sodomites' occupy the pit and are thus separated from the 'lustful' (i.e. heterosexuals, contained in the second circle), in Purgatory both 'sodomites' and heterosexuals meet up and gaily embrace:

> I see there every shade on either side make haste and kiss another, not stopping, content with brief greeting; so within their dark troop one ant touches muzzle with the other, perhaps to enquire of their way and fortune.[53]

Plenty gay, too, is the image with which Dante describes, in *Inferno*, the first band of 'sodomites' who meet him and his guide:

> Hurrying close to the bank, a troop of shades
> Met us, who eyed us much as passers-by
> Eye one another when the daylight fades

50. Ibid., lines 84–5.
51. See Chapter 2, section 3.
52. Purgatory, translated by J. D. Sinclair (London: Bodley Head, 1948), p. 341.
53. Ibid., Canto XXVI, p. 339. Lines 31–6.

To dusk and a new moon is in the sky,
And knitting up their brows they squinnied at us
Like an old tailor at the needle's eye.[54]

How often, still today, at night, and in our gay cruising places, do we still squinny in the same way? And, above all, check out the new arrivals? 'So was there cruising in the Middle Ages, then?' Without doubt, *chérie*.

Dante transposed into the highest of poetry the homosexual desire latent in him (that said, because of the poverty of historical references in our possession, we're not authorised to consider his a rare case of completely sublimated homosexuality). On the subject of the 'sodomites' he goes on to write:

Could I have kept the fire off, there below,
I'd have leapt down to them, and I declare
I think my tutor would have let me go;

But I'd have burnt and baked me so, that fear
Quite vanquished the good-will which made me yearn
To clasp them to my bosom then and there.[55]

A gay interpretation might read what lies behind the metaphor of these verses:

> Could I have kept off the persecution for homosexuality (*the fire*: in Dante's time homosexuals were condemned to be burned), I would have been buggered along with them (or by them, with them), and I think that Virgil would have tolerated it, allowed it (*would have suffered it*: it's well-known that Virgil was a queer;[56] *sofferto*, from *sofferère* or *sofferire* derived from the Latin *suffere*, composed from *sub*, under and *ferre*, to bear: Virgil would have borne Dante below, where he would have inducted him into homosexuality); but because I would have suffered the pain of persecution (*I'd have burnt and baked me so*),

54. The Divine Comedy: Hell, Canto XV, p. 162. Lines 16–21.
55. Ibid., Canto XVI, p. 169. Lines 46–51.
56. See p. 88 above.

> fear conquered the desire (*good-will*) that made me eager (*made me yearn*)[57] to embrace him.

On the other hand, as Serge Hutin writes, 'everything in the *Divine Comedy* is constructed in such a way as to conceal from the profane the true convictions of the author: Christian esotericism and the doctrine of the Fedeli d'Amore, whose initiation rites and esoteric practices are made known in the poem ...'

> The *Divine Comedy*, a work that is Catholic in appearance, [...] thus constitutes a summa – for those in a position to read it – of Christian Hermetism. Dante and his friends belonged to a secret society, that of the Fedeli d'Amore, linked undoubtedly with the Rosicrucians, and the immortal masterpiece of the great Italian poet is an exposition, veiled but sufficiently explicit, of the secret doctrine of this templar confraternity whose members directed their amorous poetry to a 'Lady', in reality the symbol of the order and its secret doctrines, the symbol of esoteric Christianity par excellence.[58]

'Could I have kept the fire off': the fire, therefore, perhaps represents not only the persecution of homosexuality, but also the proof through which the occult is revealed, where one goes beyond 'normal' perception (that of everyday hell). Access to magic is symbolized in this passage by fire, which is also the essential initiation phase of hermaphrodism. Thus the 'journey into madness' is experienced in part as a passage through the flames, as a direct confrontation with the terrifying Dharmapala, a farewell to the repetition compulsion and an escape from the unhappy routine of everyday life, assuming risk and rising to a higher dimension of existence (the foundation of the burning feeling being a dream of love for the Buddha). Like Freud and Ferenczi, we come to see homosexuality as the principal cause and 'agency' of so-called 'paranoid delirium'.[59] The choice of fire is also a pact with the Devil, who is ready to meet you as soon as you are ready; you cannot avoid enjoying a real homosexual

57. [Translator's note: In Italian, the sense is even stronger: the word is *ghiotto*, which carries the sense of a gluttonous greed or craving for something delicious: to translate it more precisely, then, we might say that Dante's narrator is *craving* to embrace those below – or, more colloquially, *hungry for their touch*.]
58. Serge Hutin, Histoire des Rose-Croix (Paris: Le Courrier du livre, 1971), p. 22.
59. See Chapter 5, section 2.

friendship with him, if for no other reason than because the Devil is androgynous or gynandrous, or better, assumes every form, and can make his appearance as a fascinating queen or an Australian woman. To 'sell one's soul to the Devil' means, among other things, to discover and acknowledge one's own *anima* or *animus* in the Jungian sense.

Behind the repression of homosexuality lurks a sense of homosexuality as a *bridge* to the *unknown* (or perhaps, to that which we know already without knowing). Still today, too many people are afraid of actually crossing to the other side. The revolutionary gay movement proposes this great adventure to everyone. Reformist homosexuals, on the other hand, think that it is possible to camp en masse on the bridge itself, obstructing passage to those who wish to go further.

In any case, it will only be possible to go beyond when homosexual desire is completely liberated. And beyond this gay totality, there is everything else: *'Paradise' waits for you ...*

Notes on Platonic Eros and on Homosexuality within Religion

> 'I would maintain that there can be no greater benefit for a boy
> than to have a worthy lover from his earliest youth,
> nor for a lover than to have a worthy object for his attention.'
>
> – Plato[60]

That importance, which Freud brought to light, of sublimated homosexuality as the guarantor of social cohesion (albeit always threatened), also recalls the utopian legislation envisaged in Plato's *Republic*. The supreme power there is ascribed to the philosophers; but the *Symposium* teaches that the true philosopher is also the 'perfect lover';[61] the Platonic theory of love is predominantly pederastic, and the perfect experience of pederasty is described as ultimately free from the 'vulgar' gratification inherent in the sexual realm. This notwithstanding, a passage in the *Phaedrus* ultimately concedes that the said philosopher, as 'ideal lover', may indeed lie with his beloved.[62] And even leaving the *Phaedrus* aside, it is not

---

60. Plato, The Symposium 178c, translated by W. Hamilton (Harmondsworth: Penguin, 1966), p. 42.

61. Ibid., 204b; p. 83. See also the entire speech of Diotima, from which this is taken, as well as the eulogy Socrates delivers on the drunken Alcibiades, 212e–212b; pp. 97–8.

62. Plato, Phaedrus, translated by W. Hamilton (Harmondsworth: Penguin, 1978), 255e–256a; p. 64. He is speaking here of the ideal relationship between perfect lover

possible to reduce the entire notion of Eros contained in the *Symposium* to the words of Socrates alone: a dialogue cannot be mutilated, sending the dialectic on its merry way. In reality, Plato presents the amorous and sensual passion of the young and intoxicated Alcibiades as ultimately fine, just as he does the sublime erotic elevation of Diotima-Socrates and the words of Phaedrus and Pausanius; and the primordial myth of the three sexes espoused by Aristophanes – androgynous, masculine and feminine – is again a Platonic one.

The *Republic*, the *Symposium* and the *Phaedrus* are all dialogues recognised by modern criticism as being roughly contemporary with each other. In them the doctrine of love and its affinity with philosophy is developed and refined: in reading them, we can thus conclude that for Plato, the ideal society must adhere to philosophical pederasty, and the ideal eroticism corresponds to a form of pederasty that is essentially sublimated. It is only in his later work, the *Laws*, that Plato explicitly condemns homosexual practice: 'homosexual intercourse and lesbianism seem to be unnatural crimes of the first rank', and 'suppressing sodomy entirely'.[63]

In actual fact, the Platonic conception of sublimated homosexuality is in a certain sense already a symptom of the decadence of the Greek pederastic tradition. In the second half of the fifth century BCE, according to Carlo Diano,

> [homosexuality] became a subject of debate, not so much ethical as philosophical and political. Because the 'gilded youth' who had found in the 'wisdom' of the Sophists a new form of *aretè*, and who in both politics and life were pro-Spartan, had made this their distinctive

---

and beloved, who alone have not given way to the passionate and violent assault of the rebel steed of the soul. Nevertheless, the beloved also 'feels a desire to see, to touch, to kiss [his lover] and to share his bed. And naturally it is not long before these desires are fulfilled in action. When they are in bed together, the lover's unruly horse has a word to say to his driver, and claims to be allowed a little enjoyment in return for all that he has suffered. But his counterpart in the beloved has nothing to say; but swelling with a desire of whose nature he is ignorant he embraces and kisses his lover as a demonstration of affection to so kind a friend, and when they are in each other's arms he is in a mood to refuse no favour that the lover may ask …' See Léon Robin, La teoria platonica dell'amore (Milan: Celuc, 1973), and Thomas Gould, Platonic Love (London: Routledge & Kegan Paul, 1963).

63. Plato, Laws, Book 1 636c and Book 8, 841d, in Complete Works (Cambridge: Hackett, 1997), p. 1330 and p. 1502.

> badge, the common people, who had their voice in comedy, condemned it and ridiculed it mercilessly. One significant fact was the varied ways in which the assassination of Hipparchus and the expulsion of the Pisistratides was presented. In the democratic tradition, Harmodius and Aristogiton were only champions of freedom, and the love that bound them was passed over in silence; in the aristocratic tradition they were champions of freedom, but as such heroes both of *eros* and *arete*.[64]

This 'populist' and heterosexual ideology, which Diano accepted, prevented him from pursuing his research any deeper. It was enough for him to judge aristocracy and oligarchy as evil, and homosexuality still worse, for him to deduce quite naturally that democracy could not but be contrary to homosexuality. This is just one of those 'clear' conclusions to which deep-rooted anti-gay prejudice leads our dear professors.

On the other hand, the assertion of democracy and the anti-homosexual taboo in Athens was accompanied by the negation of the Dionysian spirit, which up till then had been characteristic of Greek antiquity, and the gradual crystallisation, in philosophy, of the opposition of subject and object, of spirit and matter, that subsequently marked Western thought through the centuries up to our own time. Yet this philosophical contradiction reflects social fracture and sexual alienation. Masculine thought entered the neurotic and dichotomous phase that distinguishes it still today. It is only from a bourgeois point of view, according to which the present world market of democratic states appears as the best of all possible worlds, that the establishment of (slave-owning) democracy in Athens presents itself as a positive achievement (and from which the rejection of homosexuality can be derived). In his adulation of the democratic and anti-homosexual 'people', Diano reveals his own spirit as a slave of capital.

Historical research by revolutionary homosexuals has not yet managed – as far as I know – to show the real motivations that provoked the decline of the Greek homosexual tradition in the second half of the fifth century. At all events, the Platonic doctrine of Eros is not as Diano claims 'the negation or at least the superseding of a barbaric custom and a perversion of nature'. Plato was rather a theorist whose thought reflected the gradual imposition of the anti-homosexual taboo in antiquity, and the incipient collapse of the ancient Greek political system.

64. Carlo Diano, 'L'Eros greco', Ulisse 18, (1953), p. 705.

On the other hand, the inherent question of the importance of sublimation in the Platonic doctrine of love is fairly controversial and complex: this is one of the reasons why it seems useful to me to distinguish, following certain French scholars, *amour platonicien* and from that *amour platonique* so distorted by the meaning attributed to it in that vague common conception.[65] It is true moreover that the concept of sublimation, as posed in the psychoanalytic context, is a poor fit with interpretations of a philosophical theory that so long predates our own day. Abstaining from sexual relations does not, for the perfect Platonic lover, mean rejecting the beloved as an 'object' of his erotic desire, denying the presence and the forces of the 'rebellious horse of the soul'; whereas when we talk in everyday terms about sublimation in a relationship between persons of the same sex, we almost always mean a process strictly bound to the repression of homosexual desire, which does not directly surface in consciousness.

The pre-existential eschatology of the *Phaedrus*[66] illustrates the reasons by which, in the Platonic utopia, only the philosophers are predestined to rule: they alone dispose of the true Eros and the spiritual impulse to attain, by means of *anamnesis*, the Ideas. Their souls are the only ones that, prior to the fall and incarnation, are able to pass beyond the vault of the heavens to follow in the wake of the gods. They alone are able to contemplate the Good, the Beautiful, Justice, Temperance and Science. They alone, in this earthly life, can recall in love the pure perception of the Beautiful and can in public life renew the ideal virtues.

According to Hans Jürgen Krahl, there is an important connection between idealism and the primacy of male homoeroticism in Platonic thought. In fact – and in the light of the deep separation (*chorismos*) between form and matter that characterised Plato's doctrine – 'form, the purest unity, is the determining masculine moment; this determining force is the autonomous good. Matter is the undetermined moment that must in this way be determined; it is non-being which, like a position of feminine dependence, derives from the bad.' And again:

> To love women is shameful. The sexual act is restricted to procreation. True love is that of equal for equal, and pederastic homosexual love

65. See Léon Robin's introduction to Plato's Phèdre (Paris: Editions les Belles Lettres, 1961).
66. See Phaedrus, 246a–248e, pp. 50–53.

> inspired by Eros originates in the sphere of pure identity. The bottomless *chorismos* – which in Nietzschean terms is ascribed a moral valuation – has torn the pleasure principle away from the act of procreation. This latter has become a mere restriction on reality and thus does not have a true essence.[67]

Krahl's interpretation seems to me in certain respects speculative, in others idealistic, from the moment where in his attempt to reveal the homoerotic substratum of Platonic idealism, he has recourse to a reduction of homosexuality to the Idea, and of the Idea to homosexuality, which is not a Platonic conception. For Plato, homoeroticism is more of a mediation between matter and the Idea, given that – for him – the pure contemplation of the Beautiful proceeds from the immediate attraction towards beautiful (male) bodily forms. The Beautiful cannot be reduced to the intuition of the Beautiful present in homoerotic desire: it is one thing to fall in love with a single beautiful person, quite another to love Beauty for itself. 'Between the two situations there is a whole hierarchy of possible states, through which the soul has to pass in its ascent, by way of steps that are always more universal, from love for the particular caducity of the earthly to that for the eternity of the ideal' (Guido Calogero). And the *chorismos* between immediate homoerotic desire and the pure perception of the Beautiful is in reality founded on a whole series of dialectical, practical and concrete mediations – as shown by Diotima's speech – and on a profusion of that supra-rational 'mystic spirit' which makes Plato's work beautiful as well as supremely intelligent.

In any case, if Krahl had taken it in the rear, if he had tried real desire for men, he would probably have interpreted 'the determining masculine moment' in a less formal fashion, and noticed that the 'pure identity' between men is sunk in the bowels of matter, and hovers as an irresistible, sensual lure between one and others. On this basis, he might have understood that Platonic idealism, beyond its partial rejection of heterosexuality, is also founded on an inhibition of carnal homosexual desire, which – as I noted – is finally condemned explicitly in the *Laws*. In separating matter and form, the work of Plato reflects a certain separation of Eros from the body, and from the male body just as from the female. It is

67. Hans Jürgen Krahl, 'Ontologia ed eros: una deduzione speculativa dell'omosessualità. Schizzo lemmatico', in Costituzione e lotta di classe (Milan: Jaca Book, 1973), p. 133.

not homosexuality, therefore, on which Plato's idealism rests, but rather the rejection of homosexuality. Even so, this rejection is not blind sublimation: it is in the face and the body of the beloved that the philosopher receives the imprint of the Beautiful, the trace ('phantasm') of the god pursued from the soul's first embodiment. For Plato, however, the trace of the Beautiful is lost in unrestrained sensual satisfaction, in which one exhausts a love. We will need to explain what historical motives induced Plato to establish an incompatibility between carnal love and the philosopher's access to ideal virtue, the Beautiful in itself.

In the patriarchal society of ancient Greece (in particular Crete, Sparta, Corinth, Thebes, Calcide in Eubea, and Attica), the anti-homosexual taboo was unknown, and the subordination of women determined the privileged, often sacral, assertion of homosexual love between equals. With Plato and his age, actual homosexuality entered a crisis. There remained however – and here Krahl is right – the judgement of superiority attributed to emotional and intellectual (but not sexual) relations between men. Athenian democracy proved to be less homosexual, but certainly not less masculinist.

According to Krahl, a better disposition towards heterosexuality is encountered in all those dialectical thinkers intent – as against Plato – on establishing a real mediation between form and matter. However,

> the decisive reception of the Platonic *chorismos* came with the Pauline reinterpretation of the homosexual Jesus. Flesh is sinful matter that has rejected God, the pure identity of the Trinity. The act of procreation is a rigid duty. Paul banished that sphere of identity, of same-sex love, into which Plato had transposed the pleasure principle. Homosexuality is love of God, of Jesus – of the Word become flesh – hence the monastic life, a pure and ascetic pleasure. Such a sensuality, directed towards the abstract beyond and radically modified in its function, transforms any erotic element in Europe into a neurotic one (paralysed homosexuality).[68]

Religion, as a universal obsessional neurosis of humanity, also results in large part from the sublimation of homosexual desire. In the words of Wilhelm Reich: 'Clinical experience shows incontestably that religious sentiments result from inhibited sexuality, that the source of mystical

68. Ibid.

excitation is to be sought in inhibited sexual excitation'.[69] Like the obsessional neurosis of children, wrote Freud, religion 'arose out of the Oedipus complex, out of the relation to the father'.[70] The dissolution of the complete Oedipus complex involves both an identification with the father and an identification with the mother. The first serves as a substitute for the libidinal cathexis towards the paternal object; the second as a substitute for the libidinal cathexis directed towards the mother:

> The broad general outcome of the sexual phase dominated by the Oedipus complex may, therefore, be taken to be the forming of a precipitate in the ego, consisting of these two identifications in some way united with each other. This modification of the ego retains its special position; it confronts the other contents of the ego as an ego ideal or super-ego.[71]

And Freud goes on to argue:

> It is easy to show that the ego ideal answers to everything that is expected of the higher nature of man. As a substitute for a longing for the father, it contains the germ from which all religions have evolved.[72]

Both love and fear of God are the neurotic result of a love for the parents that is censored by the incest taboo and the taboo against homosexuality, the result of a sensual love for those closest that is reduced to *agape, caritas.* The gap between Eros and *agape* is filled with the presence of God, whose laws condemn the love of the flesh. In reality, however, it is the condemnation of carnal love for the parents that helps lay the foundations for belief in God, by establishing within us, through identification with the parental sexual 'objects' which have had to be renounced, a severe censor, a Lord, an ego ideal, whose 'voice' repeats the commands and duties of the parents. 'The self-judgement which declares that the ego falls short of its ideal produces the religious sense of humility to which the believer appeals in his longing'.[73]

---

69. Wilhelm Reich, *The Mass Psychology of Fascism* (London: Penguin, 1975), p. 210.
70. Freud, 'The Future of an Illusion', *Standard Edition,* Vol. 21 (London: Vintage, 2001), p. 43.
71. Freud, 'The Ego and the Id', *Standard Edition,* Vol. 19, p. 34.
72. Ibid., p. 37.
73. Ibid.

But the forced renunciation of the parental 'objects' also means a severe repression of homosexuality. The boy's desire for the father, and the girl's for the mother, are neurotically transformed into the worship of God. Desire is so strongly present, and at the same time burdened by so imperious a taboo, that it ends up covering its object with the absolute veil of an illusion: divinity. God is transcendent, among other reasons, because the father will not go to bed with his son. The repression of Oedipal desire is so radical that it fills the whole of life with a terror of the unknown, and this repressed content emerges only at the risk of being snarled back by the Cerberus of repression: *primus in orbe deus fecit timor*.[74]

It may well be unnecessary to emphasise that these ideas on religion cannot claim to provide an exhaustive key to the vastness of the subject involved. It is enough to indicate the other angles from which the question has been approached in philosophy, by Kierkegaard, Feuerbach and Marx among others. Then we can refer to the interpretation of psychoanalytic anthropology that sees 'the primal scene' and its traumatic infantile introjection as the principal factor in establishing belief in gods and demons (Róheim), or again to the very different bearing of religious themes in so-called 'madness' (Schreber, to take only a particularly famous case), and so on.

And yet it is precisely the religious experience of 'schizophrenia', which has very little in common with institutionalised neurotic religion and with customary or 'adopted' faith, that displays the sublime and fundamental nexus existing between (homo)eroticism and that which lies behind the veil of Maya, across the bridge. While the patriarchal religion of transcendence is based among other things upon the sublimation of homosexual desire, the magical experience of the hidden and normally unconscious universe, the journey to that other place which is here, the 'know thyself', passes necessarily by way of manifest homosexuality.

Anal Eroticism and Obscene Language. Money and Shit

To those who want to give the proletariat the religion of a name, a (false) consciousness, a suit-and tie and a halo, a credibility for the respectable, it is legitimate to counterpose a proletariat that is violent

74. [Translator's note: Which translates to: *fear made the first gods in the world*].

and wild, unconscious, autonomous, and the trinity: SHIT, DEVIL, REVOLUTION.[75]

It is necessary at this point to stress the relationship that exists between the rejection of homosexuality and the repression of the anal component of Eros. In his *Three Essays on Sexuality,* Freud showed the temporary concentration of infantile libido on the anal erogenous zone: the anal phase that lies between oral eroticism and a fixation on the genital zone that is generally definitive. The stabilisation of sexual impulses on the genitals almost always provokes a repression of anal desires, which may even be absolute – except, as a general rule, in 'cases' of overt male homosexuality, and a few others.

As Geza Róheim ironically put it, 'when . . . excretory functions have become "not nice" we have reached a high stage of culture'.[76] But even Queen Elizabeth goes to the toilet. The present repression of anal pleasure, coprophilia and urophilia, is the result of a historically specific suppression. The anal desire displayed by every child reveals a potential for pleasure that is latent in every adult, and reflects (in the development of the individual) an atavistic erotic expression of the species, which has been progressively more negated over the millennia, and particularly in the last few centuries of capitalism.

The demand for the restoration of anal pleasure is one of the basic elements in the critique made by the gay movement of the hypostatising of the heterosexual-genital status quo by the dominant ideology. As the French gay liberationists expressed it:

> We have to ask the bourgeoisie: What is your relationship with your asshole, apart from having to use it to shit with? Is it part of your body, your speech, your senses, in the same way as your mouth or ears? And if you've decided that the only purpose of the anus is to defecate, then why do you use your mouth for other things besides eating?[77]

In his essay on anal eroticism, Freud shed light on the causal relationship between the unconscious fixation of repressed anal eroticism and certain expressions of character, such an obsessional and sometimes manic

75. Luciano Parinetto, 'Analreligion e dintorni', *L'Erba Voglio* 26, (June–July 1976), p. 24.
76. Geza Róheim, *The Riddle of the Sphinx* (London: Peter Smith, 1934), p. 231.
77. FHAR, *Rapport contre la normalité*, p. 55.

attachment to orderliness, parsimony and obstinacy. In concluding his analysis, he added:

> If there is any basis in fact for the relation posited here between anal eroticism and this triad of character-traits, one may expect to find no very marked degree of 'anal character' in people who have retained the anal zone's erotogenic character in adult life, as happens, for instance, with certain homosexuals. Unless I am much mistaken, the evidence of experience tallies well on the whole with this inference.[78]

In my own experience, it is indeed rare to meet gay men who enjoy being fucked and are at the same time obsessively orderly, stingy and stubborn. But that is not the point.

The point is, that if you get fucked, if you know what tremendous enjoyment is to be had from anal sex, then you necessarily become different from the 'normal' run of people with a frigid ass. You know yourself more deeply. How right De Sade was in writing:

> Ah, did you but know how delicate is one's enjoyment when a heavy prick fills the behind, when, driven to the balls, it flutters there, palpitating, and, then, withdrawn to the foreskin, it hesitates, and returns, plunges in again, up to the hair! No, no, in the wide world there is no pleasure to rival this one: it is the delight of philosophers, that of heroes, it would be that of the gods were not the parts used in his [sic] divine conjugation the only gods we on earth should reverence![79]

Of all the aspects of homosexuality, I would say that the one feared above all by heterosexual men is anal intercourse. This is undoubtedly due not just to the repression of their anal desire, but also to their fear of castration – in essence, the fear of falling off the masculine pedestal into the 'female' role. The fear of castration, in every male, is the counterpart of his phallic conception of sexuality as erection. Any male heterosexual goes wild at the idea of 'not being able to get it up'. If he can't, his virility goes up in smoke, and so he is deeply worried about this eventuality, as

78. Sigmund Freud, 'Character and Anal Eroticism', *Standard Edition*, Vol. 9 (London: Vintage, 2001), p. 175.

79. Donatien Alphonse François de Sade, *The Complete* Justine, Philosophy in the Bedroom, *and Other Writings* (New York: Grove Press, 1966), pp. 277–8.

repression has made him identify with the virile model, making him into a wretched guardian of the heterosexual order. The man fears losing his virility because, more than anything else, he fears losing his identity: and he knows very well that behind the boastful facade, this virile identity is fragile indeed, just as the equilibrium in which he balances between rigid phallicism and fear of castration is decidedly unstable.

The absolute male, insofar as he is a mutilated being, is exclusively 'active'. And any heterosexual man, who prides himself on identifying absolutely with the male, considers the 'passive role' as shameful, abject and 'effeminate'. For people of this kind, to be fucked means to 'be ruined'. But if we remove the negative connotation of being 'taken from behind', so typically and neurotically masculine, then being fucked can be seen as the great pleasure that it is, a meeting and fusion of bodies, a gay entertainment, delicious both in the ass itself and in the mind. As a general rule, the more fear a man has of being fucked, the more he himself fucks badly, with scant consideration for the other person, who is reduced to a mere hole, a receptacle for his blind phallic egoism. Someone who likes being fucked, on the other hand, will himself know how to fuck 'artfully'. He knows how to give pleasure, as he knows how to receive it, and he unblocks the restricted fixation of stereotyped roles. To fuck then truly does become a relation of reciprocity, an intersubjective act.

The psychoanalytic conception of the sexual 'object' derives from the male heterosexual's sadly crippled view of sexual intercourse. And if Rank indicated the origin of neurosis in the condition of the foetus in the maternal womb, we would go even further, and see in heterosexual coitus itself, from which life proceeds and specifically in the male supremacist and neurotic manner in which this is generally conducted, one of the primary causes of the universal neurosis that afflicts our species.

Heterosexual males also fear the excremental aura of anal intercourse. 'But Love has pitched its mansion in / The place of excrement' (Yeats).[80] We gays know this very well, and our condition is most close to the joyous redemption of shit – if we have not already attained this. Even as far as shit is concerned, too, the repressive disgust conceals a rich enjoyment.

---

80. W. B. Yeats, 'Crazy Jane Talks With the Bishop', *Selected Poetry* (London: Macmillan, 1978), p. 161.

Many of the pejorative expressions used by straight people to put down homosexuals refer to the anal erogenous zone. In his essay on the use of obscene language by militants of the (former) extra-parliamentary left, Mauro Bertocchi emphasises how, in the use of such vocabulary:

> The terms selected generally display a strong inhibition or obstacle, and certain recurrent identifications can be observed. The sexual organs, both male and female, are synonymous with stupidity, intellectual and political inadequacy [e.g. 'cunt' or 'prick' in the English equivalent], with bad actions, politically 'incorrect' practices, anger and bad temper (e.g. 'cock-up', 'balls-up' or to 'fuck something up'). Impotence and the passive sexual condition, e.g. passive homosexuality, on the other hand, are synonymous with bad luck, disability or being cheated, swindled or damaged by one's own incapacity (e.g. 'to be buggered', or expressions such as 'get stuffed', 'asshole', 'up yours', etc). Active homosexuality, on the other hand, is the symbol of shrewd ability, in the same way as heterosexual activity (e.g. to 'bugger' someone, 'fuck someone up', etc).'[81]

Active homosexuality, then, is seen in the perspective of the 'double male'. All the expressions that Bertocchi discusses derive from attitudes of aggression and disdain towards women and queens. But we know very well that verbal – and not only verbal – violence and disrespect represent the extraversion under a negative sign of a repressed and unconscious desire. (But unconscious up to what point?) Freud stressed that: 'An invitation to a caress of the anal zone is still used today, as it was in ancient times, to express defiance or defiant scorn, and thus in reality signifies an act of tenderness that has been overtaken by repression'.[82]

The presence of anal and scatological desires, in other words, is discovered by analysis of the terms involved in their negation: shit!

Bertocchi sees it as important to establish the significance assumed by the use of such expressions in the very complex discourse constructed by so-called revolutionary groups:

> What does a sentence like the following really mean: 'Comrades, it's no fucking good going ahead with these four shitty queers, we'll

81. Mauro Bertocchi, 'Compagni spogliatevi!', *Fuori!* 5 (November 1972).
82. Freud, 'Character and Anal Eroticism', p. 173.

> only end up getting buggered'? The meaning is clearly contradictory and shows two different levels, one dominant and the other subordinate, one strictly political and ideological, the other sexually abusive, referring to male and female erogenous zones and degrading them into mere organs and orifices, and referring to basic functions (ejaculation, excretion) to give them connotations of disgust, satisfaction and aggression.[83]

But what I see as still more interesting is that these expressions ultimately communicate, beneath the male supremacist and violent attitude, a latent desire that is homosexual, anal and scatological. Anyone who is subject to the suppression of homoeroticism, femininity, anality and coprophilia that is perpetrated by the dominant subculture, finds himself forced to express and thus communicate his own unconscious and forbidden desires, which are inherent to the sphere of Eros, by way of 'signifiers' which, in the appearance and meaning given them by consciousness, express their rejection, negation and condemnation. In this case, as in so many others, psychoanalysis furnishes revolutionary criticism with the instruments needed to fill the gap between phenomenal appearance and reality: and we know that, from a Marxist position, 'science' is distinguished precisely by this capacity to descend from the appearance of phenomena to their intrinsic reality.

In our case, the question is to individuate the homosexual, transsexual, anal and scatological desire that lies behind the bombastic surface of these anti-woman, anti-gay and anti-coprophile pornographic expressions. Once again, Bertocchi notes:

> *Busone* [bugger], *frocio* [queer], *culattone* [bum-boy] are among the most common and widely used insults. On the other hand, the erotic fixation on the genitals, and above all on the phallus, gives rise to such frequent expressions as *che sborrata!* [lit. *what a cumshot!*], signifying political success, enthusiasm, self-assertion, in the conception that equates male genital orgasm with total success.[84]

Mauro Bertocchi also underlines the close affinity between the abusive sexual vocabulary used by the left, and the traditional anti-woman and anti-gay language of fascism.

83. Ibid.
84. Ibid.

We must finally turn to investigate the relations between the capitalist sublimation of anality in money ('*pecunia olet*', Ferenczi recalls)[85] and the repression of homosexuality.

Norman O. Brown detects in Luther the emblematic connection between anality and capitalist rationality, insofar as his historical figure, in addition to his thought (so rich in explicit anal references) and indeed the whole complex process of the Reformation, reflect the rise of the mercantile bourgeoisie in fifteenth century Europe.[86]

San Francisco's Museum of Erotic Art holds a caricature of Martin Luther dating from the time of the Counter-Reformation, which depicts him with a tiny homosexual companion, bent on anal sex, right in the middle of his head: unknowingly, by way of the petty vulgarity of this 'slander', Catholic propaganda against Luther clearly underlines the central place occupied by anality (and homosexuality?) in the thought of the reformist monk.

For Luther, this Earth is dominated by the Devil: Satan's anus is enthroned at the centre of the world, filling it with excrement and farts (all those sinners, popes, usury, hypocrites dedicated to 'good works', etc.). Luther clearly bases his own negative and disdainful notion of the Devil (whom he may have had the occasion to meet personally) on the repressed problematic of scatological (as well as homosexual) desire. And yet, as he himself admits, the fundamental assumption of the Protestant religion (the doctrine of justification by way of faith) came to his mind 'on the privy in the tower'.[87] Norman O. Brown carefully emphasizes the non-causality of this excremental site: 'Psychoanalysis, alas! cannot agree that it is of no significance that the religious experience which inaugurated Protestant theology took place in the privy.'[88] Martin Luther probably did not acknowledge that the innovatory religious discovery destined to immortalise him came to him from the Devil: it was Satan who suggested it to him while he was sitting on his own throne.

When he encountered the Devil, Luther's response was to treat him aggressively (and to fart in his face), and to order him, blinded with hate, to "'lick (or kiss) my posteriors" or to "defecate in his pants and hang them round his neck", and threats to "defecate in his face" or to "throw

85. Ferenczi, 'Pecunia Olet', *Further Contributions to Psycho-Analysis* (London, 1926).

86. Brown, Life Against Death, pp. 202–33.

87. Ibid., p. 202.

88. Ibid., p. 203.

him into my anus, where he belongs'".[89] These insults to the Devil, like those of heterosexual males who insult us gays, display in the very insult their repressed desire. It is not hard to understand how in reality their injunctions, threats and injuries, the coprolalia to which they give vent, express a homosexual-coprophilic wish distorted by repression and yet communicated under the blind and negative sign of aggression.

It is clear that the Devil (or whoever) could not refrain from torturing Luther night and day; Satan indeed goads and torments those who, in treating him ill, attack only themselves, ranting against their own deep desire. As Freud put it, 'the devil is certainly nothing else than the personification of the repressed unconscious instinctual life'.[90] According to Baudelaire, however, 'the finest trick of the Devil is to persuade people that he does not exist'. Freud's opinion would thus itself be Satanic to the core.

In any case, it is precisely the repression of the instincts, the rejection of (homo)sexuality and anality, that made Luther the enemy of Satan. And this is in spite of the fact that he knew full well how he was carnally governed by the Devil as lord of this earthly life, this perverse world in which the reformer demanded chastisements greater than those that had destroyed Sodom and Gomorrah. The contradiction of Lutheranism ('the devil possesses me, but I oppose his rule with all my strength') finds an escape route in the religious hope of a second coming of the redeeming Christ. So it is that God and the Devil come to be opposed, casting a light on those who – like us – do not know 'if God is the devil or the devil God'.[91]

Above all else, Luther had to oppose God to the devil so as not to fall into the shit and the Satanic embrace, he had to be able to find a means of pure, spiritual fideistic escape that would bear him suspended through the air. His religion had necessarily to take a form that, well aware of being strictly chained to money, to 'things', and to the Earth (while unaware that money in fact just tied it to shit), elaborated a 'spiritual' ideological compromise – a historic compromise – that elevated him, in appearance, above the shit fetish into which the Earth was transforming. The capitalist world is not shit, and it is not the paradise of the coprophiles whom it indeed represses; it is rather the monstrous shit fetish.

89. Ibid., p. 206.
90. Freud, 'Character and Anal Eroticism', p. 174.
91. Brown, Life against Death, p. 217.

And when someone says, 'these goods are shit, this pâté is shitty', he fails to realize that shit isn't as disgusting as a lot of canned goods, and that there is also a part of faeces, its delicious and exquisite core, that is comparable only to the most costly pâté de foie gras. In 1872, Rimbaud wrote to Verlaine:

> Work is further from me than my fingernail is from my eye. Shit for me! Shit for me! Shit for me! Shit for me? Shit for me! Shit for me! Shit for me! Shit for me! [...] Only when you see me positively eating shit will you no longer find that I'm too expensive to feed![92]

The distorted scatological notion of the Devil thus led Luther to found the specific religion of capitalism (the real domination of capital subsequently leads to an entente cordiale between Catholics and Protestants), of the universe of usurers and money traders that he saw as the real emanation of the Devil. For our monk, in fact, the world of the mercantile bourgeoisie was the realm of Satan; and yet, this was truly the world that had adhered to the Reformation and made it its own. 'To see the Devil as lord of this world is to see the world as a manure heap, to see universal filth: "*Scatet totus orbis*," says Luther. The avarice of Leipzig is the Devil's work and by the same "filthy".'[93]

Erich Fromm, Brown adds,

> in one of his real contributions to psychoanalytical theory, showed the connection between Freud's anal character – with its orderliness, parsimony, and obstinacy – and the sociological type of the capitalist as delineated by Sombart and Max Weber. And Weber, of course, followed by Troeltsch, Tawney, and others, postulated a far-reaching connection between the capitalist spirit and the ethic of Protestantism.[94]

Psychoanalysis has repeatedly recognised the connection between money and shit. In Freud's words, 'the connections between the complexes of interest in money and of defaecation, which seem so dissimilar, appear to

92. Arthur Rimbaud, letter to Paul Verlaine, Charleville, April 1872, in Œuvres complètes (Paris: Gallimard, 1960), p. 283. (Translated by Evan Calder Williams.)
93. Brown, Life Against Death, p. 226.
94. Ibid., p. 203.

be the most extensive of all'.[95] The *Lumf* (turd) complex[96] scatologically determines people's attachment to money: 'What the psychoanalytical paradox is asserting is that "things" which are possessed and accumulated, property and the universal precipitate of property, money, are in their essential nature excremental'.[97] Many cults and myths of antiquity, and several superstitions today, explicitly place money in a very close relation with the products of excretion. The phylogenic origin of the symbol, in fact, is frequently intuited, and at times it can be discerned by ontogenic study. Ferenczi attributed to psychoanalysis 'the task of separately investigating the phylogenesis and ontogenesis of symbolism, and then establishing their mutual relation'.[98] Psychoanalysis recognises that,

> children originally devote their interest without any inhibition to the process of defaecation, and that it affords them pleasure to hold back their stools. The excreta thus held back are really the first 'savings' of the growing being, and as such remain in a constant, unconscious inter-relationship with every bodily activity or mental striving that has anything to do with collecting, hoarding, and saving.[99]

But compulsory sexual morality represses this infantile scatological pleasure and traps children into the socially pre-established model whose economic structure is the anxious and coerced sublimation of Eros in general and coprophilia in particular. Educastration gives rise in us to a disgust for what had originally aroused great pleasure and interest: the taste of turds is transformed into the turd complex, and the coprophilic tendency is directed towards substitute objects in the sphere of play and sublimation. In the society of forced labour, major economic gratification ('power') is given by money, but 'money is organic dead matter which has been made alive by inheriting the magic power which infantile narcissism attributes to the excremental product'.[100] The magic ('schizophrenic') trip reveals to the initiate how dogs, decidedly copro- and urophilic, are the richest animals (or how they are generally

95. Freud, 'Character and Anal Eroticism', p. 173.
96. Freud, 'Analysis of a Phobia in a Five-Year-Old Boy'.
97. Brown, *Life Against Death*, p. 292.
98. Ferenczi, 'The Ontogenesis of the Interest in Money', *First Contributions*, p. 319.
99. Ibid., p. 321.
100. Brown, *Life Against Death*, p. 279.

far richer than humans), and leads the initiate to try coprophagy. The ingestion of shit reveals the symbolic significance of many things, enabling us, for example, to clearly grasp the very deep influence exerted on us by advertising. Subliminal communications play on the various tendencies of Eros that are 'normally' sublimated, in order to persuade us to buy. The purchase of goods is then the illusion of re-obtaining erotic faculties which have been repressed, and which have become substrata of social oppression. With the just conscience of a child, one of my nieces, who was sent to the asylum, stole a check from my brother (her father) who had stolen her pleasure. Are we dealing with theft as a game or rather the thieving nature of exchange?

The psychoanalytic equation of money and shit permits us to assert that in the present society, the capitalist or bureaucratic functionary has the same anal character as the general equivalent for commodities. Ferenczi maintains that,

> the capitalistic interest, increasing in correlation with development, stands not only at the disposal of practical, egoistic aims of the reality-principle, therefore – but also that the delight in gold and in the possession of money represents the symbolic replacement of, and the reaction formation to, repressed anal-erotism, i.e., that it also satisfies the pleasure-principle. The capitalistic instinct thus contains, according to our conception, an egoistic and an anal-erotic component.[101]

Capitalist ideology rejects and condemns manifest anal eroticism, or else it effectively ghettoises it, since the rule of capital is based, among other things, on the repression of anality and its sublimation (but this sublimation, and its sophisticated fruits, are 'enjoyed' in fact only by a very few – Onassis himself had to have a special plane fly daily to Paris to supply him with fresh bread, to have the real deal.) It is the function of ideology to obscure the authentic 'nature' of capital, to negate the human, corporeal foundations that sustain it: the whole shoddy mess is held up by our alienated labour, our repressed libido, our estranged energy. Taking full account of this leads to the acquisition of a revolutionary consciousness and a revolutionary libido. As Luciano Parinetto

101. Ferenczi, 'The Ontogenesis of the Interest in Money', p. 331.

writes: 'the proletarian revolution too must pass through the asshole'.[102] The (re)conquest of anality contributes to subverting the system in its foundations.

If what in homosexuality especially horrifies *homo normalis,* that cop of the hetero-capitalist system, is getting fucked in the ass, then this can only mean that one of the most delicious bodily pleasures, anal sex, bears in itself a remarkable revolutionary force. The thing for which we queens are so greatly condemned contains a large part of our subversive gay potentiality. I hoard my treasure in my ass, but my ass is open to everyone ...

---

102. Luciano Parinetto, 'L'utopia del diavolo: egualitarismo e transessualità', *Utopia* (December 1973).

4
Crime and Punishment

Homosexuality Passed Off as Heterosexuality

Georg Groddeck opens Letter 27 in *The Book of the It* by maintaining: 'Yes, I hold the view that all people are homosexual, hold it so firmly that it is difficult for me to realise how anyone can think differently.'[1] Public opinion, however, holds dearly to the myth that sees homosexuality as a problem concerning only a limited number of people, i.e. gay men and lesbians. Yet this is not the case. To cite some statistics, the Kinsey report of 1948, despite being rather dated, revealed that some 46 per cent of the US male population had either had both homosexual and heterosexual relations, or had at least consciously responded to the erotic attraction of both sexes, while only 4 per cent had exclusively gay relations and 50 per cent exclusively heterosexual. On the basis of Kinsey's investigations, 'persons with homosexual histories are to be found in every age group, in every social level, in every conceivable occupation, in cities and in farms, and in the most remote areas of the country'.[2]

Some 50 per cent of men, therefore, have at one time or another had, at the very least, conscious homosexual desires. And yet how many openly admit this? Very few. The suppression of homoeroticism is such that many people who have occasionally had gay contacts, or even continually do so, maintain that they are not homosexual, and may even, absurdly enough, deny outright the homosexual character of these relations. It's no surprise: anyone who is surprised in reality sails, more or less consciously, in the same boat of those who behave and speak so hypocritically.

Groddeck goes on to say:

> We all spend at least fifteen or sixteen years, most of us spend our whole lives, with the conscious or at any rate half-conscious reali-

1. Groddeck, *The Book of the It*, p. 230.
2. Kinsey, Pomeroy and Martin, 'Homosexual Outlet', p. 9.

sation of being homosexual, of having behaved as such more or less often, and of still behaving so. It happens with all people that at some time or other in their lives they make a superhuman effort to throttle this homosexuality, which in words is so despised. And the repression is not even successful, so, in order to carry through this lasting, daily self-deception, they support the public denunciation of homosexuality and thus relieve their inner conflict.

Denial of the blatant evidence of one's own homosexual relations and impulses forms part of this 'quasi-repression' of homosexuality. To quote Kinsey again:

> The homosexuality of certain relationships between individuals of the same sex may be denied by some persons, because the situation does not fulfill other criteria that they think should be attached to the definition. Mutual masturbation between two males may be dismissed, even by certain clinicians, as not homosexual, because oral or anal relations or particular levels of psychic response are required, according to their conception of homosexuality. There are persons who insist that the active male in anal relations is essentially heterosexual in his behaviour, and that the passive male in the same relation is the only one who is homosexual. These, however, are misapplications of terms ...[3]

Ideas of this kind, according to which the 'active' party in anal intercourse is still essentially heterosexual, show at the very least a 'confused' identification between the other sex (other than the male, given that the definition of heterosexuality necessarily involves a distinction between the sexes)[4] and a simple hole; in other words, the other sex is that which is used as a hole. By applying absurd heterosexual categories to homosexuality, therefore, this conception gives away its obtusely male supremacist character, showing how heterosexuality itself is based on the negation of woman, and how male heterosexuality is made to coincide with the role of the person who fucks.

---

3. Ibid., p. 6.
4. F. Fornari, *Genitalità e cultura*, p. 11: 'The establishment of a heterosexual identity actually presupposes that each sexual partner has a sex that the other does not ...'

The other sex (woman) is a hole. It matters little whether this hole belongs to a female or a male body, since as a hole it is simply a nothing, merely a possible complement to the phallus, which in this patriarchal conception is everything. But this is solely the male refusal to recognise woman. Woman exists, and is woman, only beyond the role of a zero that the phallocratic system imposes on her.

Even in its 'interpretation' (or rather misinterpretation and mystification) of the sexual relation between men, the phallocentric worldview is absurd and the bearer of absurdities, precisely because it negates woman, and hence the human being, who is far from reducible to the mutilated monosexual role imposed by our repressive society and civilisation.

Yet the idea that only those men who take the 'passive' role in anal intercourse are really homosexual is extremely widespread, and brings to light the immediate association, in the phallocentric mind, between gay men and women. 'The "active" partner in anal intercourse is essentially heterosexual; so the "passive" partner belongs to the other sex. But the other sex is the female, and so only the "passive" partner in anal sex between two men is homosexual, and the homosexual man is a woman.'

In its patent absurdity, however, this male supremacist view reveals, when considered from the gay and critical standpoint, how homosexual men who get fucked are closer to transsexuality, and tend to overcome the polarity between the two sexes. If the rediscovery of transsexuality necessarily involves the liberation of anal eroticism, as well as homoeroticism, it is also true that only the present and long-standing repression of Eros leads us to think of the concepts of transsexuality, anality, homosexuality, bisexuality, etc, as separate. In actual fact, liberation means overcoming these presently divided categories, which only reflect conceptually the alienation of the human species from itself by the work of the capital-phallus. Liberation leads to the conquest of a new manner of being and becoming, both one and many, whether from the individual standpoint (the aspects of sexuality no longer being repressively separated, or in a state of mutual exclusion), or from the universal standpoint, since liberation leads to recognising individuals in their community (one and many) and in the world, and thus to resolving the contradiction between self and others, self and non-self. The revolutionary liberation of Eros and life cannot take place without a collective explosion of the unconscious, which is in very large measure itself a collective one. And the explosion of the id expands and 'dissolves' the boundaries of the ego. In other words, the ego no longer arrogates to itself the monopoly of subjectivity. Life is seen as reciprocal and communal. In the darkness of our underlying being, there lies dormant a species that is transsexual, and the desire for transsexuality and community. Communist intersubjectivity will be transsexual – but I shall come back to this point later on.

For the time being, we must return to the male supremacist fixation that makes homosexuality out to be heterosexuality. Kinsey, once again, wrote:

> Some males who are being regularly fellated by other males without, however, performing fellatio themselves, may insist that they are exclusively heterosexual and that they have never been involved in a homosexual relation. Their consciences are cleared and they may avoid trouble with society and with the police by perpetrating the additional fiction that they are incapable of responding to a relation with a male unless they fantasy themselves in contact with a female. Even clinicians have allowed themselves to be diverted by such pretensions. The actual histories, however, show few if any cases of sexual relations between males which could be considered anything but homosexual.[5]

Among all those 'heterosexuals' who refuse to see their erotic contacts with other men as homosexual, the 'double males' stand first in line. And the ideology of the double male is very dear, as a general rule, to those young 'hustlers'[6] who act as prostitutes to gay men.

The Murder of Pasolini

The death of Pasolini has kicked up a storm of interventions on homosexuality: but so far, what has been said and written has been disgraceful and unheard of (or more precisely: heard all too well), with the exception of what has been established by comrades of the homosexual liberation movement. Roberto Polce, of the Milan Homosexual Collective,

---

5. A. Kinsey, W. Pomeroy and C. Martin, 'Homosexual Outlet', p. 6.

6. [Translator's note: In this section and the following, Mieli uses the term '*ragazzi di vita*' (always in quotes): the term is explicitly linked to Pasolini, as it was the title of his 1955 novel. In English, it has been variously rendered as *street kids* or *hustlers*, the latter of which we use throughout, as it comes closer to the way in which Mieli references and theorises it. I have kept it in quotes, as Mieli does, so as to mark his suspicion about the applicability of the term, even as he engages it, given that he is at pains to detail the complicated position designated as hustling.]

recorded the following exchange near the State University of Milan on Monday, 3 November 1975:[7]

> 'Poor guy! They had good reason to do it, though, because it kills when they try to stick it in your ass, huh?'
>
> (Laughter)
>
> 'But do you know that now they think that carrying four caramels in your pocket is like carrying a concealed weapon?'
>
> 'Four caramels? What does that have to do with anything?'
>
> 'Everything! Four caramels are all you need to lure in a few young boys …'
>
> (Laughter)
>
> 'That said, even if he was an ass, when it came to writing and making movies, he was no idiot!'
>
> 'It's true. He sure could do that, you've got to admit. When you go to see one of his films, you leave the theater feeling all worked over.'[8]

The same day, on the walls of the University of Rome was written, in huge letters: 'You did well to murder that fag.' Drawn beside it was a stick figure stylisation of Pasolini.

Once more in the street: 'How do you say Pasolini in English? Ass?'

At this point, it seems relevant to return to the communique from *Fuori!* (the Turinese collective) that appeared in *Corriere della Sera* on 13 November 1975:

> THEY KILLED PASOLINI. HOMOSEXUALS ACCUSE THIS. Pasolini was just one of the thousands of homosexuals who get blackmailed, assaulted, 'suicided', and massacre. He was not murdered because he was a man of culture, politics, or poetry, but because he was homosexual. The homosexual is seen to be weak, blackmailable;

---

7. [Translator's note: The day immediately after Pasolini was murdered.]

8. Roberto Polce, 'Pasolini', in *Re Nudo* V (December 1975), pp. 60–61. [Translator's note: The Italian expression that Polce records is *tutto unto*, literally 'all greased' – as if one leaves his films oiled through and through. There's no exact idiomatic English equivalent, but it's worth noting how this latently echoes the bleak joke about his death being the consequence of a painful assfucking – an echo that surely didn't escape Mieli, in terms of its heterosexual anxiety and desire to both mock Pasolini yet be thoroughly 'lubricated' by his films.]

crimes against homosexuals find too much justification and unspoken consensus.

HOMOSEXUALS ACCUSE THIS.
We accuse the radio, the television, and the newspapers, guilty once again of passing off as criminal news or a by-product of generalized rampant violence what in fact testifies to the violence exercised daily against those who, because they are homosexual, are marginalized, humiliated, and oppressed.

WE ACCUSE those intellectuals and politicians who in their statements of mourning have objectively falsified the real meaning of the murder of Pasolini; that this was above all the murder of a homosexual, a crime equal to thousands of others in which unknown homosexuals lose their lives and to which no one pays any mind or makes a big deal. We accuse all those citizens who are complicit in furthering this climate of ignorance and terror that circulates around the figure of the homosexual. They are as guilty of the death of Pasolini as the murderer himself.

REMEMBER AND MOURN Pier Paolo Pasolini, in the name of the millions of anonymous homosexuals who are constrained every day to live a life filled with fear and violence.[9]

We still don't know – and we won't know any time soon … – what really happened that night in Ostia. Nor is it certain if the killer acted alone or with others. There are those who see in Pasolini's a political crime: Pasolini was 'inconvenient' because he was a man of the left, not just because he was homosexual. And I don't think it's worth much to add my own dark hypotheses – however 'original' they may be – to all the others. Because in any case, I think Pasolini was killed by one or more of those 'street boys', or by one or more 'prostitutes'. There could be plenty of different motives for the crime, it could have been carrying out an order; what is certain is that Pasolini was killed in this situation because he was homosexual, because only homosexuals find themselves in situations like that. And – as the *Fuori!* text spells out – in situations like that, homosexuals are killed every day.

---

9. *Il Corriere della Sera*, 13 November 1975. For the reactions of readers, editors, and owners of *Corriere* to the publication of this text from *Fuori!*, see 'Sbatti il Fuori in terza pagina', in *L'Espresso*, n. 47, XXI, (13 November 1975).

Many heterosexuals are asking: 'Who is the culprit? Pasolini for having a sexual liaison with a minor? Or the minor for having killed him?' And, to resolve the question, they have decided: 'Both are guilty. One is a corruptor. The other a killer. It couldn't have ended differently.'

The more 'open' journalists on the left, who have refused this image of the corruptor, are posing in their own way another 'problem of consciousness': 'Who is the authentic victim? The murdered bourgeois? Or perhaps the subproletariat induced to commit crime?' But they reach no clarifying conclusion: the repression of gay desire prevents them from confronting the fundamental problem, that of a conflict linked to the suppression of homoeroticism (rather than that of class differences between Pasolini and he who killed him).

Consider what Roberto Polce wrote, in an article on Pasolini's death:

> It seems to me that two things are essentially unclear: 1) there exist two equally fundamental contradictions, that of class and that of gender; 2) it is necessary to keep the two distinct in order to be able to give a correct interpretation to any event.
>
> So: many have said that Pelosi was subproletariat while Pasolini represented the boss, for which he was killed – poor guy. We must have compassion, but we must have even greater compassion and solidarity than must be shown towards the boy. We must say that yes, it is true that the boy is part of a subaltern class and was/is a victim of the ruling class, but it is also true that, taking full account of the ideology of the social classes that exploit and repress him, as a supposed heterosexual he hurled his violence against a homosexual who, like women, is within the structure of sexual contradiction always the victim, the loser, the one who gets killed. And a heterosexual who does violence to a homosexual always represents in this case, regardless of his class, the one who holds the power and who abuses it . . .
>
> *And we say that heterosexual 'power' is one face of capitalist power.* [Having received news of Pasolini's death] when we still knew nothing of what the investigation would reveal, we said to ourselves: it's clear enough what happened – the sixteen year old supposedly heterosexual (but in reality homosexual even if repressed) boy from the slums [one of those 'heteros' of which Kinsey writes, who denies their own homosexuality while all the while having homosexual relations][10] went with

10. [Translator's note: Both of these brackets mark interjecting annotations that Mieli makes into the passage from Polce.]

Pasolini in his car under some pretense, agreed upon or not, and was all too ready to explode at him, responding in an attempt to offset his sense of guilt derived from the collapse, even if minimal, of the model of normalcy imposed on him with violence since childhood. In beating and punishing Pasolini, the boy was unconsciously convinced that he was indirectly punishing and torturing his own homosexuality. In murdering him, he unconsciously believed he was murdering his homosexual side, eliminating it once and for all.

When the inquiries went ahead, this discourse was itself clarified. The hypothesis outlined above came to seem consistent with the facts because Pelosi was revealed to quite likely have a hustler, i.e. a homosexual who fucks for money, even if only at the beginning: a queer who doesn't have the strength to freely live out his homosexuality, shaking himself free of the rules of patriarchal society he was forced to swallow since childhood (in a proletarian neighborhood where virility and adhesion to bourgeois norms are everything). And being young and good-looking, he was able [to] satisfy his sexual urges while getting paid, thereby giving economic justification to his queerness, striving in this way to suffocate his sense of guilt for the acts that he had been taught were abnormal and outside of the Norm [...] We know well enough because all this has happened. Because Pasolini was killed. [...] A homosexual was murdered, not by a violent and delinquent boy from the slums but by the phallocratic patriarchal system, by the bourgeoisie and their terroristic ideology. This time it is on the front pages of the paper, but only because he was famous and a great artist. One can go beyond his homosexuality and pardon it like some extravagant weakness or sickness, provided that the one who bears its stigma is a big name Somebody. But if the one who gets killed was one of us, just a fag, a fag and nothing more, then it is nothing but silence and squalor sketched in a couple lines, wedged between news of a purse-snatching and the story of a family who died from mushroom poisoning. And if Pasolini was inconvenient (as they like to say) THEN WE ARE ALL THE MORE SO. We're sick of this shit. We are plotting the revolution, and we're bringing all our weapons, all our fury and violence. So listen up: there weren't two monsters, nor was there one monster and one victim (played interchangeably by Pier Paolo and Pino la Rana). There was just two victims. Two victims of the same violence

> that plays out everywhere and assumes every form, dons every mask, whether subtle and hidden or unmistakable and clear as day.[11]

We're dealing with the violence of the system: and the only monster is the 'automated monster', capital itself. (Just as monstrous are all those who, more or less directly, apologise for a crime perpetrated by capital against a homosexual, for those innumerable crimes that capital has always carried out or encouraged against us.)

So in memory of Pasolini, homosexual director: enough with the permissible but guilt-tripped homosexuality between street kids and the fires of Canterbury; between an Oedipus, a pig, a theorem, and Salò;[12] between *Death in Venice* and the death of Visconti's Ludwig at the bottom of a lake. Instead, we shout: 'LONG LIVE THE REVOLUTIONARY ASS IN CINERAMA!'[13]

Hustlers

As we have seen, besides all those who consider themselves and are generally considered to be homosexuals, and on whom the repressive consciousness of straight people inflicts a particular stereotype, there are many other homosexuals who are far more repressed as far as their sexuality goes, and particularly their homosexuality. These include the 'double males', and all those male heterosexuals who have often had, or still have, homosexual relations, even while constantly maintaining their heterosexuality. Many of them live on the margins of the homosexual 'world' proper, on which they become parasites and – often – executioners. These are the prostitutes, the 'hustlers', or rather all those working-class youths who prostitute themselves to gay men, and whom the journalists of capital (and its left wing in particular) today designate as 'sub-proletarian' so as to avoid recognising in their actions and 'lifestyle' a specific expression of the proletariat subjected to the system.

---

11. Polce, 'Pasolini', pp. 60–61.
12. [Translator's note: Mieli is here riffing off of, and running through, the titles and central figures of many of Pasolini's films, from his first fiction film (the hustling street kids of *Accattone*) to his last (*Salò, or the 120 Days of Sodom*).]
13. Piero Fassoni, 'Anonimo londinese ma non troppo', in *Fuori!*, n. 5 (November 1972). [Translator's note: Cinerama is a widescreen colour film format that uses three separate 35mm projectors to produce an enormous image: to call for the revolutionary ass in Cinerama is hence to call for the most lavish, spectacular depiction possible.]

'Hustlers' are homosexual but do not consider themselves such, in so far as they generally also feel a form of attraction towards the female sex, or at least towards their objectification of it. Their homosexuality is sufficiently repressed that they tend generally to restrict themselves to the 'active' role (which is in reality passive par excellence), and to mystify even this, they make out that their main interest is not pleasure, but rather the money they can extort from their 'effeminate' partner. These young men's rejection of their own homoeroticism runs very deep: capital and the ideology of heterosexual primacy have instilled in them a disparagement for homosexuality in general, and for queens in particular.

The system cheats them in two ways. Besides castrating them economically and socially right from birth, it gives them palliative gratifications that are bound up with phallic privilege, gratifications that lead them to behave in a way that is functional to the rule of capital. Enslaved in this way, their anger and hate are directed not against the system but rather against those who appear even lower than themselves: women and queers.

Masculinism shows itself to be the most serious obstacle to the communist revolution: it divides the proletariat, and almost always makes working-class heterosexual men into guardians of the repressive sexual Norm which capital needs in order to perpetuate its domination over the species. These working-class heterosexuals have been corrupted: they accept payment in the system's wretched phallocratic coin in return for holding in check the transsexual revolutionary potential of women, children and homosexuals, in exchange for the gratification that they receive. The 'hustlers' are no more corrupted than the worker enrolled in the Communist Party, who insults 'queers', mistreats his wife and beats his children.

But, to take up the discourse of Roberto Polce, the rejection by those so-called 'hustlers' of their homoeroticism derives not only from their internalisation of the dominant ideology and from the violently and openly male supremacist 'culture' of the streets, but also from their need to forcibly deny the evidence of their continuous homosexual relations. The misery and violence seen daily on the streets, the sum of the frustrations they undergo, their economic struggle for survival, and the anxious need to deny their own homosexuality, all this spurs them to vent themselves in one way or another. And today, there is no scapegoat more immediate, more susceptible to a bullying attack, than the homosexual himself, i.e. the *other* homosexual, the overt queen.

By attacking homosexuals, 'hustlers' demonstrate that they are not only parasites on the gay world, but also its executioners, carrying out the sentences that the system has already pronounced by its marginalisation and condemnation of homosexuality, which is confined in more or less clandestine and insecure ghettoes, or generally kept apart and separate from the rest of society.

Even in this case, of course, there are exceptions that prove the rule: not all 'hustlers' are hateful, violent and phallocratic. (Remember, for instance, Harold's 'rule'?)[14] There are even some who are sympathetic. And yet, as a homosexual, all I can say is that these are essentially just somewhat less bad.

In any case, if things are to get better, we must hope that ever more 'hustlers' will transform themselves into unrestrained drag queens, after being seduced by us gays in the liberation movement. Anyone who believes that homosexual relations cannot result in births will be confounded: in fact a growing number of gays come to see the light.

So, once the 'hustlers' have been transformed into comrades, we will also be able to all go whore ourselves, however temporarily, to 'infect' the last self-assured heteros left in the world, joining utility to the delightful and the revolutionary. Because as long as anality remains sublimated to money, as long as capital has not yet been brought to ruin, then the gay movement needs some cash, in order to buy Chanel n. 5 and some curlers when we want to make ourselves beautiful and there's no looting on the horizon, just a young proletarian party in Parco Lambro or a soirée at Covent Garden.

For the time being, however, we are still a long way from reaching a revolutionary understanding with the 'hustlers', and it is still through them that the system punishes homosexuality, even with death – no less ferociously than the Nazis, but far more subtly and with greater effect. Today, the system no longer needs to exterminate gays *en masse,* it is enough to strike at some, for the most part in an extremely indirect manner, keeping its own hands 'clean', but still managing to impose on all others a reign of terror.

The most 'developed' countries, as we have seen, decidedly refrain from any direct bloody repression of homosexuality, providing instead a

14. [Editor's note from original volume; Mieli refers here to the comedy *The Boys in the Band* by Mart Crowley, which William Friedkin adapted into a film in 1970 [*The Birthday Party*] and which was released in Italy under the title *The Birthday Party for Dear Friend Harold.*]

'comfortable' if expensive ghetto. If you want a safe hustler, you can get one for $100 from the Model Escort Agency in Los Angeles. If homosexuals do not want to risk being beaten up or murdered, then they only need to pay: the King's Sauna and Incognito Bar will open their doors. In this sense democracy is progressive when compared to Nazism: it makes greater profits from the commercialisation of homosexuality.

Capital, in fact, kills two birds with the same stone. On the one hand, it vents anti-gay social violence through the attacks of 'criminals' (who, as a general rule, are those 'bisexuals' whose homosexuality is most repressed). In this way the system offers many marginalised young kids the opportunity to let off steam by having a go at people whom the capitalist and phallocratic ideology relegates to a place even below their own, the 'inverts' (not to speak of women, slaves of the slaves). Capital thus makes a timely manoeuvre to divert from itself the anger and violence of the street, caused by the misery it has itself produced.

On the other hand, by inciting the hustlers, capital manages to terrorise the gay world proper. The system generally inhibits gays from defending themselves and making themselves respected (by fostering guilt and an inferiority complex), while it incites against them enemies who are genuinely formidable, i.e. criminalised proletarian youths for whom violence is part of everyday life. It is not hard to understand how, finding themselves defenceless in this way, gay people often seek protection from others, instead of from themselves: and where can they find it, if not in the system? This explains how in the USA, for example, one wing of the GLF wanted to increase the number of policemen patrolling cruising grounds, where homosexuals were regularly murdered. (Have you ever spent the night in Central Park? Or in the Circolo Massimo?)

The stereotype of the cowardly and reactionary homosexual, who looks for individual security within the system, in personal success and in *L'Uomo Vogue* – a stereotype which very many gays still identify with today – has its roots in the sum of humiliations and acts of violence that are suffered, and in the constant anxious tension provoked by the risk of enduring this. We gays know all too well how, on the street and in cruising grounds, in cinemas, parks, toilets, etc., we constantly face not only the risk of arrest, but also of being beaten up, robbed, ridiculed, humiliated and even killed; while in the intellectual and artistic milieu, or even among people with a bourgeois education, this risk is generally absent, or at least attenuated. It is one thing to be oppressed and exploited by one's analyst, something else to be oppressed with a knife.

It is understandable, then, how many gay people fear revolution, seeing in it the revolt of their tormentors, and thus their own demise. Nor can we refute those who prefer things to remain as they are, rather than seeing in power those same proletarians who daily insult, attack and hypocritically reject gays. No matter whether these proletarians call themselves fascist, 'communist' or extra-parliamentary; in substance, their violent anti-homosexual attitude is all the same.

The system, however, is able to meet the 'deviant' half-way.

> Behave yourself properly and live out your perversion in the little ghettoes we can control and regulate, and then we'll protect you. If you go cruising in parks and public toilets, you're just looking for trouble. Better stay at home! Better still, come to the Super Cock International Privacy Club, where you'll find a restaurant, a strip-tease show, porno films, psychedelic toilets, and perhaps even a fire-escape.

The 'Protectors' of the Left

The leftists – above all the PCI, but equally all the organisations who proclaim themselves to be revolutionaries – were slow to adopt a similar attitude of 'protection' in their encounters with us gays (and only just now are things 'changing'...): they have always denied homosexuality without mediation, they have refused it while exalting the tough and virile figure of the productive – and evidently reproductive – worker. They have mocked homosexuals, defining them in terms of the corruption and decadence of bourgeois society, while they themselves, the left, do their part to fix gays into a position of the *qualunquismo*[15] counterrevolutionary. At the same time, they sustain an image of the revolution that is grotesquely bigoted and repressive, founded on sacrifice and the hellish proletarian family, and caricaturally virile, founded on productive-reproductive labour and on brute militarised violence, all the while hailing the model of countries that define themselves as socialist yet which liquidate homosexuals in concentration camps or in 'institutes for re-education', as in Cuba or

15. [Translator's note: *Qualunquismo* refers, initially, to a short-lived Italian political movement, 'L'Uomo Qualunque' (which we might translate as 'the everyman'), which tried to remove the influence of party politics, but the expression more generally came to designate an indifference to politics (often used pejoratively by the left to describe those only concerned with their own livelihoods or family).]

China, for example. It is scarcely surprising, then, that gay people saw only the system itself as their 'salvation'.

When the homosexual liberation movement started in Italy, the left did their best to hush and discourage it. I remember one time when Luca Cafiero, at the head of a handful of *katanghesi*[16] from Movimento Studentesco, came to stop us from handing out *Fuori!* fliers at the entrance of the State University of Milan. Every one of us can itemise the interminable series of insults, provocations, and at times physical attacks that we've endured from leftist militants. Those of us who have temporarily been part of such groups know all too well the amount of humiliation and frustration that makes up the militancy of a queer in the heterosexual left. The leftists did everything they could to extinguish our movement: they were obstinate in labelling us 'petit-bourgeois *qualunquisti*' precisely from the moment in which, to the contrary, we started to come out in a revolutionary way. Already in 1971, Joe Fallisi could write that the left served, above all, 'to *modernize* reformist politics and to impose (under the skies of Spectacle) the new ideological images of the "protester", the "tough", the "extra-parliamentary", the "new partisan"'.[17] And if the reformist politics of the left are phallocentric and heterosexual, their ideal protestor is the 'tough guy with a big cock and muscles of steel', who sets even the fascist bullies to flight.

> [These extra-parliamentary groups] are formed from the wreckage of an old shipwreck, one which they themselves have patched up. They

---

16. [Translator's note: The *katanghesi* were the organized forces of Movimento Studentesco (MS), and their name is derived from the Congolese secessionist State of Katanga, which declared independence in 1960. Given that this was hardly a revolutionary secession but rather one led by white European mercenaries, the name seems an exceedingly odd choice. However, according to some accounts (including one from Paolo Torretta, who claims personal knowledge of the situation), it involved a series of odd borrowings, drift, and forgetting, starting from a *Le Monde* report on the occupied Sorbonne where someone present claims to have himself been a mercenary in Katanga, before the word became an accusatory term leveled against the militants of Movimento Studentesco and one that they seem to have adopted in response. The name is indicative of the sort of inspiration and borrowing from struggles of decolonisation and Global South independence movements that was common in the Italian extra-parliamentary left in the late 1960s and early 1970s – as well as the frequent blindspots of such borrowing. For the Italian account of why members of MS came to use this name, see: http://www.linterferenza.info/contributi/i-katanga-spiegati-alla-mia-nipotina/]

17. Joe Fallisi, 'Lettera a Irene', in *Comune Futura*, n. 2 (November 1976).

> have risen back to the surface only because it is the real movement, the revolutionary movement, which slowly but inexorably *returned*. But if they reappear in the wake of this New Proletariat that today has *just started* to make itself evident – and which therefore does not yet have clear class consciousness – it is because they are the reflux of a reflux, and they do so only in order to recuperate it.[18]

It's no accident that yesterday's extra-parliamentary groups are today seated in Parliament.

Today, the real revolutionary movement includes, above all, the movement of women and homosexuals who struggle against the system and against the heterosexual phallocentrism that sustains it and chains to it the (male) proletariat himself. Conversely, the organisations of the left, fundamentally male and macho, heterosexual and anti-homosexual, make apologies for the public and private capitalist Norm, and hence for the system itself.

Fallisi reminds us that,

> the first phase of the worker's movement was the sectarian phase. And these associations and sects of the 19th century (Owenist, Fourierist, Icarian, Saint-Simonian, etc) were effectively the 'yeast' of the working class movement at its origin. Then, as soon as they had been left behind, they were obstacles that soon become reactionary. In sum, they were the childhood of the worker's movement [. . .] But because they made possible the foundation of the First International, it was necessary for the proletariat to move beyond that phase. Now, as in the last century, we need to overcome the stage of sects, the proletariat must overcome – truly – the stage of *groupuscles*.[19] Albeit with the difference, compared with the situation a hundred years ago, that, today the official little groups (Stalinist, 'anarchist', Trotskyist, etc) are the acritical products of an anterior defeat, one that unfolded during the '20s, so that they don't even have the function of a revolutionary 'yeast' that the sects once had, and they cannot be the polarizers of radical situations, just those who come after, trailing in the wake, with all the stultifying weight of ideological mystifications. And because as they

18. Ibid.

19. [Translator's note: Mieli uses the French word, which here refers to small far left political organisations, the majority of which stand willfully outside of any pretense toward mass political engagement.]

> cannot comprehend the New Proletariat [. . .], they can only hope to *recuperate* it, proffering their sham gold of Politics, and ultimately they will only be discarded. When the real movement matures, when it is conscious-in-itself and reunified, it will pass swift judgment on all its so-called 'representatives.'[20]

In short, from '71 to today, times have changed. If the extra-parliamentarians ended up in parliament, it is, however, also true that the movement of revolutionary women has shaken society as a whole and has put in crisis even those groups who declare themselves to be revolutionaries yet are still to this day strongholds of masculinist bigotry. The same movement of homosexuals who are conscious, revolutionary, or at least open to a vision of a world different from the traditional one, can no longer be ignored by the politicians of the left. For the parties, big and small alike, it is now necessary to recuperate homosexuals too. I think that not even Stalin, by this point, would turn in his grave.

The heterosexual left tries a similar recuperation in their interactions with the homosexual question, albeit on a more minor scale than that of their confrontations with feminism. Until very recently, for the extra-parliamentary leftists the thieving and 'fascist' minister was obviously also 'queer'. ('Enough, enough, with pederastic clergy!', they chanted in the streets during the demonstrations of '68 and '69.) Today, however, it might happen that a homosexual shows himself to be a 'good comrade', an 'invaluable activist in the service of the proletariat', while it is opportune that all the 'good comrades' keep in mind the inherent contradictions of the sexual sphere. The contrast is unmistakable. On one side the term 'inverted' is used as an insult. On the other, the wolf dresses in sheep's clothing, preaching acceptance and comprehension for the homosexual comrades, those 'wild dogs' who often don't feel like they belong in those so-called revolutionary groups who label Rumor and Colombo as queer, just as they call Andreotti a hunchback and Fanfani[21] a dwarf, while Fanfani, that arch-swaggart,[22] keeps up the

---

20. Ibid.

21. [Translator's note: The names here are all of Italian prime ministers: Mariano Rumor, Emilio Colombo, Giulio Andreotti, and Amintore Fanfani.]

22. [Translator's note: Mieli here makes a particular pun on Fanfani's name, calling him *arcifànfano*, or 'arch-swaggart'. The rest of the phrasing continues this sort of linguistic play, such as the fact that the same word (*morale*) can be used for 'morale' and 'morality'.]

morale of national morality, deprecating divorce as the bearer of vice: adultery, prostitution, abortion, juvenile delinquency, female homosexuality, druggy kids and pederasts . . .

In essence: if antifascism gathers in a single bunch the Christian Democrats, the Communist Party, the socialists, etc, and the ex-extra-parliamentarians of the left, the united front against homosexuality (the Hetero Holy Alliance) truly reconciles 'opposite extremes' and rivals across the 'democratic arc'. And if the Christian Democrats, in a climate of conspiring with fascism, makes a huge show of its own antifascism, so the ultra-left groups often behave themselves like real fascist rackets in their interactions with homosexuals, even as they also give a little nod of solidarity and tolerance.

For nearly all the militants in the groups, the homosexual question is of secondary importance and 'superstructural', only concerning a minority: 'we must tolerate the homosexuals, so that they don't bust our balls, making us discuss our heterosexuality and acting like we also take it in the ass'.

We could cite, for instance, an article that appeared in *Il Manifesto* and commented on the 'proletarian festival' days in Licola during September 1975:

> One moment when everyone perked up their ears to the speakers playing on the radio all through the forest was when a comrade of the *Fuori!* collective from Milan was speaking. There had already been a lot of commotion around the stand of this collective early in the afternoon [. . .] The Milanese of *Fuori!* choose a life of provocation. Tricked out in a violent and exaggerated manner, with sequins and gold gleaming, they sell their paper, accosting people in an accusatory manner, saying to them: 'You deny your own homosexuality' The reactions were, to a small degree, panic and intolerance only to a small degree (in general, though this is another way of ignoring the problem), but mostly the comrades reacted by saying, 'Look, I don't give a shit what you do or what you want for me, all fine, provided that you stop bothering me.'[23]

This last type of reaction enables us to grasp, behind the appearance of a new and more open attitude, the actually closed mentality of the

23. *Il Manifesto*, (20 September 1975).

heterosexual 'comrades'. And, as a general rule, I would reply: Dear comrade, have you ever wondered why you clam up when someone puts into question the repression of your homosexual desire? Your withered homosexuality? And don't tell me: 'You can do what you like among yourselves, but don't interfere with me', *when you are not free to desire me*, to make love with me, to enjoy sensual communication between your body and mine; when you rule out the possibility of having a sexual relation with me. If you are not free, then how can I be free? Revolutionary freedom is not something individual, but a relation of reciprocity: my homosexuality is your homosexuality. And as for the sequins, they are neither over the top nor violent, at least not any more than my desire to enjoy your homosexuality, *our* homosexuality, dear comrade …

'Incredible, ineffable, and rather entertaining', was, however, the 'theoretical contribution' of Lotta Continua's paper (again still referring to the days in Licola):

> A party always shows the contradictions within the people. We can give a few examples: the immense camp was lively all day, as seated under the tents and below the pines, people were playing music and cards, passing a joint or drinking house wine, with workers going up the booth of the feminists to ask for information, with huge throngs at that of the comrades from *Fuori!* At the debate over the proletarian struggles in Naples, a PCI worker starting criticizing the festival because there were too many signs and writings on music and homosexuality; and he was interrupted by one of the organized unemployed: 'You cannot say this, because on our committee there's a fag who fights the hardest of all.'[24]

To the contrary: I believe that homosexuals are revolutionary today in as much as we have overcome politics. The revolution for which we are fighting is, among other things, the negation of all male supremacist political rackets (based among other things on sublimated homosexuality), since it is the negation and overcoming of capital and *its* politics, which find their way into all groups of the left, which characterize them, sustain them, and make them counterrevolutionary.

On the other hand, my asshole doesn't want to be *political*, because it is not for sale to any racket of the left in exchange for a bit of putrid oppor-

---

24. In *Lotta Continua*, (23 September 1975).

tunist and political 'protection'. Meanwhile, the asshole of the 'comrades' in the groups will be revolutionary only when they have managed to enjoy them with others, and when they have stopped covering them up with the ideology of tolerance for the queers. As long as they hide behind the shield of politics, the heterosexual 'comrades' will not know what is hidden behind their thighs. '*Politique d'abord*', wrote Cavour to the countess of Castiglione ...[25]

As always, it is only rather belatedly, in comparison to the 'enlightened' bourgeoisie, that the leftist groups have begun to play the game of capitalist tolerance. From declared hangmen, a thousand times more repugnant than the hustlers and fascists, given all their (ideological) declarations of revolution, the militants of these groups have transformed themselves into 'open' interlocutors of homosexuals. In their minds, they act out fantasies about becoming well-meaning and tolerant protectors of the 'deviant', and in this way gratify their own virile image, already well on the decline, at a time when even the parishes of the ultra-left have suddenly to improvise 'feminist' speakers for 'their' women. Moreover, the fantasy of being *protectors* helps them to exorcise the problem of the repression of *their* homoerotic desire. Under it all, the activists of the left aspire, as always, to become good cops. But they don't know that real cops often get in there more than they do, and that when this happens, they make love with us gays. When will there be a free homosexual outlet for the militants of the far left?

As good cops for the system, the little groups are doing their utmost to construct an 'alternative' ghetto for us 'deviants', and since they do not want to pollute their serious and militaristic organisations with anything gay, they prefer to concede us free access to the rubbish-heap of the counterculture. For the time being, however, the left is more stupid and clumsy than the system's traditional Mafia, and in no position to create for us homosexuals attractive ghettoes comparable with those constructed by the capitalist 'perversion' industry.

Again, though, even for this counter-culture of ours it's a bit *too much* to accept the presence of fags, and at the festivals for the 'young proletariat', there are provocations and attacks against women and us. The

25. [Translator's note: Mieli uses the French, which translates to 'politics first' (or 'politics above all'). The reference here is to Virginia Oldoini, who was sent to Paris in 1856 in hopes of gaining Napoleon III's support for Italian unification. Her cousin, Count Cavour, urged her to get that support by any means necessary: which in this case meant becoming the emperor's mistress for a time.]

masculinist, aggressive, fatally broken, and heteromaniacal atmosphere of these festivals is for us seriously heavy: and anyone who says that we are 'paranoid' simply means that we are quick to grasp the intolerability of an environment created by people who can scarcely even tolerate us, by the hidden aggression of phallocentric 'comrades', and by the negation of homosexuality that – in the typical form of male bonding – both unites and divides them at the same time, and certainly divides them from us.

But times are finally changing. The groups are now giving us a certain space of our own: a weekly broadcast on the 'free' radio, and two or three regular pages in the underground press. This is a space well guarded by the cops of the left, whose function to reinforce the lack of confidence that gay people have in themselves and convince them of the need to put themselves in line with (and at the whim of) this or that powerful protector, especially since 'if it wasn't for the left, we would have fascism' – a new scarecrow to replace that of revolution, so that everyone, homosexuals included, will remain well lined up, separate and tidy on the democratic and antifascist parliamentary benches.

Those homosexuals who appeal to the left are only preparing a new prison for themselves, providing new energy to keep alive these organisations and the male supremacist, anti-woman and inhuman ideology that they propound.

To the enthusiastic militants of the ultra-left, one can only ask them to abandon their fixations and illusions: to abandon, that is, the stereotypical, oppressive, and closed manifestation of their erotic desires, and to abandon at the same time all the existing political organisations which can only continue to survive by channelling the revolutionary necessities of their components into a 'new' familiar delirium. Liberated in itself, and not just abstractly from society, real gay desire means liberating real revolutionary passion from the repressive chains of the political. No longer politicians, the real revolutionaries will be lovers.

We conscious homosexuals can only find the strength to defend ourselves and to live in this homicidal and homocidal society only in ourselves. No kind of delegation is possible any more. Paternalism and appeal to the democratic pretensions of the groups can only construct a new ghetto. Only an intransigence that leads us to tell things the way they are, and to act together in a coherent way without renouncing any aspect of the communist world that we bear within us – only this can put in crisis, in *gay crisis*, the men of the political organisations, forcing them to abandon their role and thus to abandon these organisations.

Only the strength, determination, and charm of the oppressed can lead his oppressor to recognise himself in him and to recognise in him his own desire, can direct the violence of gay people (up till now almost always turned against ourselves), and the violence of youths who are anti-homosexual but homosexual underneath (up till now turned against open gays), against the system that oppresses both the victim and the murderer, the system that is the real murderer, always unpunished and ever ready to defend itself against its victims. Only we homosexuals can discover and express this gay strength.

5
A Healthy Mind in a Perverse Body

'Non-Desire' and Negation

'Can we maintain, then, that the day when desire has extended to incorporate non-desire (or so-called non-desire), the revolution will have been accomplished?' That is the question posed by the anonymous author of 'Les Culs Energumènes' ('The Demonic Assholes'), the concluding essay in the *Grande Encyclopédie des Homoséxualités.*[1]

The existence of non-desire is largely a question of the existence of negated desire. On the one hand, this involves defining the obstacles that are erected against a complete understanding of desire and – a far more complex undertaking – individuating the historical motivations for this. On the other hand, however, these obstacles should not be hypostatised; we are not trying to justify the present situation. This is what is done in the reformist perspective of homosexual integration, which sets up the obstacle of 'absolute' heterosexuality as a hypostatised opposition to the liberation of the gay desire. It sees society as forever marked by the parental couple, and seeks only to induce this to tolerate its 'perverse' offspring.

One of the main objectives of the revolutionary homosexual movement, however, is to reject this naturalistic hypostatisation of the status quo. Desire is 'normal' in as much as it corresponds to a prevailing Norm. And if the ideology of the present system spreads belief in the absolute character of its laws, basing itself on equating the Norm with normality in an absolute sense, our task on the contrary is that of delineating the historical limits of the Norm and showing the relative character of this concept of 'normality'.

Almost everyone who rejects the existence in themselves of a gay desire takes this rejection as fixed and final. 'We don't want to do that', they say, 'it's useless to insist, because we just don't want to'. And yet

1. 'Les Culs Energumènes', in *Grande Encyclopédie des Homoséxualités* (Paris: Recherches, 1973), p. 226.

almost always, as the author of 'Les Culs Energumènes' observes, when someone expresses their 'non desire' in this fashion, we should really hear a different sentiment behind their professed words: 'Don't insist! The patriarchal capitalist society has inscribed this rejection in my body and in my mind'.

In the light of psychoanalysis, it is truer to say that negation represents 'a way of taking cognisance of what is repressed'. 'The content of a repressed image or idea can make its way into consciousness, on condition that it is *negated*' (Freud).[2] To negate an 'object' of desire, in other words, is a particular way of affirming it. It is 'a kind of intellectual acceptance of the repressed, while at the same time what is essential to the repression persists'.[3] Negation is the primal act of repression; but it at the same time liberates the mind to think about the repressed under the general condition that it is denied and thus remains essentially repressed.[4]

From our recognition of the universal character of the homosexual component of desire, we deduce the existence of a veiled affirmation of homoeroticism even when this is explicitly negated. 'The unconscious knows only desire', as Freud put it, while on the other hand, 'the essence of repression lies simply in turning something away, and keeping it at a distance, from the conscious'.[5] As Norman O. Brown comments: 'Stated in more general terms, the essence of repression lies in the refusal of the human being to recognise the realities of his human nature'.[6]

If any human being, even a homosexual, overtly rejects his own homosexuality, all he does is repress this and adjust to the repression. For heterosexuals, it is obvious and 'natural' to be exclusively what they are; they correspond to the model that the system has obliged them to identify with. Nor are they consciously aware of the weight of this repression of homosexuality. Their blatant, 'normal' erotic behaviour conceals (but at the same time discloses) repression far more effectively than that of those who do not disguise their anomalous and 'abnormal' sexual desire, which the dominant subculture rejects, considers pathological and/or perverse, or at best merely tolerates. On the other hand, if

2. Freud, 'Negation', *Standard Edition,* Vol. 19 (London: Vintage, 2001), p. 235. (Freud's emphasis.)
3. Ibid.
4. Brown, *Life Against Death*, p. 321.
5. Freud, 'Repression', p. 147.
6. Brown, *Life Against Death*, p. 4.

for someone who is considered 'normal' being heterosexual is a 'natural' thing, we might note with Husserl how, 'all the things he takes for granted are prejudices, that all prejudices are obscurities arising out of a sedimentation of tradition'.[7] Departing from a heterosexual standpoint, it is necessary to suspend judgement completely on all sexuality, to avoid falling constantly back into the current prejudices. Before expressing value judgements, a far-reaching investigation is required (although for a heterosexual, to know homosexuality would be to become homosexual). We must overturn the entire common conception of desire, if we are to see its hidden dimensions. At bottom, 'non desire' is the 'other face of love'; alienation also involves the rejection of that side of ourselves which culture (in the Freudian sense) and prehistory (in the Marxist) have suppressed. Alienation is separation from ourselves: for how can we know ourselves in depth, and rediscover a full community of intersubjectivity beyond the anguish of an individuality hemmed in by reification, without revealing the repressed – or at least latent – content of our desire?

If we can say, as Franceso Santini observed, that 'patriarchal capitalist society has inserted this rejection in my mind and body', then we can also say that, 'capitalist society has inscribed *this* desire in me'.

It is very difficult to understand what human desire really is. On the one hand, because it is repressed; on the other, because this repression also manifests itself in the form of the conditioning of desire in a certain mode. There are a monstrous quantity of desires and needs that are ceaselessly imposed by capital. '*All* the physical and intellectual senses have been replaced by the simple estrangement of *all* these senses' (Marx).[8]

Today, the liberation of desire means, above all, liberation from a certain type of imposed desires. Exclusive heterosexual desire, for example, is a coerced desire, the result of 'educastration'. Just as, in the majority of cases, sexuality liberalised within the present system negates and represses the free expression of Eros, showing itself polarised by objects of desire in the literal sense, which restrict it, mutilate it, and channel it into the death-dealing orbit of the directives of capital, estranging it from the human being to turn it back towards the fetish, the stereotyped fantasy,

7. Edmund Husserl, *The Crisis of European Sciences and Transcendental Phenomenology* (Evanston: Northwestern University Press, 1989), p. 72.
8. Marx, 'Economic and Philosophical Manuscripts (1844)', *Early Writings*, (London: Penguin,, 1992), p. 352. (Marx's emphases.)

the commodity. The coerced sexuality of capital transforms women and men into commodities and fetishes, and yet underneath their masked appearance as zombie and robot, as things, living beings are hidden, and a censored desire is struggling.

Everyday relationships and conscious desires generally play themselves out between masks, appearances, characters and personifications of a determinate type of value: good in bed, intellectual, tough, 'feminist', construction worker, housewife, 'revolutionary', businessman, cook, prostitute, etc., each worth so and so much, more or less. But just as commodities are in reality human labour, so the fetishes that pass each other on the street are women and men, i.e. gods. The cities of capital are the stage of an absurd spectacle, and it is enough to realise this, to see that there is neither a sense nor a human utility in this performance. All the more so in that the performance is a most poisonous tragicomedy, and its falseness is continuously denounced to the eyes of the actors-spectators by the real and physical death of the characters, which a conspiracy of silence forbears us to speak of. But if there is death, then so too there must be life. And this pushes it far beyond the performance.

The struggle to liberate desire, the 'underneath', is a struggle for the (re)conquest of life, a struggle to overcome the anxious, role-bound and ever threatened survival that we are forced into, to put an end to the neurotic and grotesque spectacle in which we are trapped, all more or less, by being negated, separated from one another and from ourselves. It is not a question of redeeming the noble savage (which is itself a bourgeois myth), but of releasing our aesthetic and communist potential, our desire for community and for pleasure that has grown latently over millennia. 'The *cultivation* of the five senses is the work of all previous history' (Marx).[9]

Even the charm of death can be rediscovered and enjoyed, once life has been re-found, and human beings live in harmony with their community, with the world, and with the other who is part of our own existence.

Today, our passions and senses come up against the wall of theatrical images introjected by force, by the force of inertia, like a dead weight: advertising, propaganda, pornography, false ideals, the myths that have transformed our desire all too frequently into anti-desire, into what is truly the negation of desire. The 'sex' of the system is the negation of sexuality, just as the art and music of capital are the negation of sight

9. Ibid., p. 353. (Marx's emphasis.)

and hearing, and the use of obscene perfumes and deodorants, and the miasmas of pollution, are the negation of the sense of smell. The food which we eat is the negation of taste, shit food, and synthetic shit at that, a fetish of shit. And the stinking metropolis is the negation of sight, of hearing, of smell, of taste, of touch, of everything: it is a tremendous mess that deafens, irritates and stupefies us. We no longer know how to dance, run, sing, look at one another or caress: 'We have become insensitive, as if covered with wax' (Silvia Colombo).

In the same way, as a rule, the institutionalised heterosexuality of the system presents itself as a mere fear of homosexuality, and a double fear at that, a negation also of love for the other sex. While the ideology of, and fashion for, 'homosexuality' that is spreading today among feminists, and among ever more heterosexual men in crisis, is too often reducible to the attempt to neutralise their homoerotic desire, to forestall it intellectually or downright voluntaristically, and to blame themselves for being heterosexual, true gay pleasure cannot flourish unless this false guilt is eliminated. And the feeling of guilt is largely bound up with the repression of homosexuality.[10]

Homosexuality and Paranoia

According to Norman O. Brown, man is a neurotic animal:

> Man the social animal is by the same token the neurotic animal. Or, as Freud puts it, man's superiority over the other animals is his capacity for neurosis, and his capacity for neurosis is merely the obverse of his capacity for cultural development ... For if society imposes repression, and repression causes the universal neurosis of mankind, it follows that there is an intrinsic connection between social organisation and neurosis.[11]

But Brown is simply applying to the entire course of prehistory the psychoanalytic category of neurosis (which he more or less hypostatises, shrouding the future overcoming of time and history in the mystical veil of the Nirvana principle). It is sufficient for us to consider the psychoneurosis that particularly characterises capitalist society and culture

10. See Chapter 6, section 4.
11. Brown, *Life Against Death*, pp. 9–10.

– even if, with respect to the 'superstructural' aspect of the history of philosophy, we cannot avoid noting, with Needham,[12] the neurotic character of the split between 'matter' and 'spirit' that exists throughout almost the whole of Western thought, from Socrates through to today: the Western neurosis of the separation between matter and spirit. In fact, even when we speak of neurosis and its universality, we must bear in mind that 'the most general abstractions arise only in the midst of the richest possible concrete development, where one thing appears as common to many, to all'.[13]

Today, of course, society as a whole is neurotic and schizoid. Capitalist ideology, phallocentric, heterosexual and Eurocentric, founds and constitutes the worldview of one-dimensional man, *homo normalis*, the fetishistic vision of the human being alienated from himself, from the world and from others by the work of capital. Just like the habitual neurotic condition of people considered 'normal', so the whole logic of capitalism is schizoid. Dissociated or rather riven between ego and non-ego, *res cogitans* and *res extensa*, desire and 'non-desire', sense and intellect, public and private, unconscious and conscious, mechanical materialism and teleological spiritualism, capitalist rationality governs the insane equilibrium of the 'sane' individual, more or less adapted to the schizoid social system. The individual who is healthy for Freud is schizoid for Laing.[14]

Psychiatry often uses the terms 'schizoid' and 'schizophrenic' as synonyms. But if so-called 'normal' life is in fact itself dissociated and schizoid, then the 'schizophrenic' alteration of the process of association is far from being the dissociation it is said to be. It is rather a superior and deeper ability to grasp significant relationships between things and/or events that we 'normally' define as connected only in a fortuitous way, or rather in a way that is obvious and banal. It is also a still more profound faculty to recognise the evident significance that is hidden in apparently casual relations. For this reason (despite the fact that there are undoubtedly certain borderline 'cases'), I use the terms 'schizoid'

12. [Editor's note from original volume: Joseph Needham (1900-1995). English historian, among the most renowned Western experts on the history of Chinese civilisation.]

13. Marx, *Grundrisse*, p. 104.

14. R. D. Laing, *The Divided Self* (London: Penguin, 2010). Norman O. Brown writes: 'The difference between "neurotic" and "healthy" is only that the "healthy" have a socially useful form of neurosis.' (*Life Against Death*, p. 6).

and 'schizophrenic' essentially in two opposite senses: the former as a synonym for 'normal', and to indicate the dissociated character of the commonly held vision of the world; the latter to denote the decidedly alternative and far less dissociated conception of the world which is customarily considered 'crazy'.

In the countries dominated by capital, a growing number of people end up sooner or later in mental hospitals or similar institutions. So-called 'schizophrenics continue to occupy a larger number of hospital beds than people suffering from almost any other ailment, and this number is constantly on the rise, day by day, and year by year'.[15] These 'schizophrenics' escape the one-dimensional rule of the divided self adapted to the customary arrangements of capitalist society; they experience a radically 'different' vision of the world, of life, and of *Lebenswelt*:[16] they are an irreducible challenge to psychoanalysis, and its interpretations almost always appear sorry and restricted in comparison with the grandiose multi-dimensionality of their *Weltsicht*.[17] And yet no other aspect of so-called 'mental pathology' has occupied and interested 'scholars' as much as 'schizophrenia'.

The term 'schizophrenia' is used by modern psychiatry to denote the 'mental disorder' that classical psychiatry defined as *dementia paranoides* or *dementia praecox* (Morel, Kraepelin).

But is there any relationship between 'paranoia' (or 'schizophrenia') and homosexuality?

According to Ferenczi (and also Freud and others), homosexuality results from certain factors constituting the 'pathogenesis' of *dementia paranoides* (paranoia) : 'In the pathogenesis of paranoia, homosexuality plays not a chance part, but the most important one, and . . . paranoia is perhaps nothing else at all than disguised homosexuality'.[18] Those

---

15. Silvana Arieti, *Interpretazione della schizofrenia* (Milan: Feltrinelli, 1978), p. 3.

16. [Translator's note: Mieli here uses the German term, which literally means 'life-world' and is associated with Edmund Husserl (who he has previously cited). For Husserl, the concept denotes not the world as such (in a metaphysical or ontological register) but rather the world as it is lived, known, and contextualised by individual subjects.]

17. [Translator's note: Echoing his previous use of *Lebenswelt*, Mieli here again uses the German term for 'worldview'. Unlike *Lebenswelt*, however, *Weltsicht* is not the common philosophical term for worldview (and associated with Hegel), which would be *Weltanschauung*.]

18. Ferenczi, 'On the Part Played by Homosexuality in the Psychogenesis of Paranoia', p. 157.

individuals who are considered 'healthy' and 'normal', and are far from any 'suspicion' of homosexuality, may, following the sudden surfacing of repressed gay impulses, transform their existence into a 'delusion' on the grandest scale. This is the famous case, for example, of Dr Daniel Paul Schreber, chief justice in Dresden, who suddenly 'went mad', the most thoroughly studied 'clinical case' in the whole of psychiatry.[19]

The 'paranoiac', according to Ferenczi, projects his homosexual interests onto persons of the same sex, but with a negative sign:

> His desires, which have been cast out from the ego, return to his consciousness as the perception of the persecutory tendency on the part of the objects that unconsciously please him. He can now indulge his own homosexuality in the form of hate, and at the same time hide (it) from himself.[20]

In the same way, Freud held that, with Schreber, 'what was characteristically paranoic about the illness was the fact that the patient, as a means of warding off a homosexual wishful phantasy, reacted precisely with delusions of persecution of this kind.'[21] Freud maintained, too, that the rejection of a homoerotic desire explains the 'persecution complex'. According to Arieti,

> The statement 'I (a man) love him' is something that the sick person cannot admit, which he seeks to negate with the contradictory statement 'I don't love him, I hate him'. 'I hate him' is then transformed, by projection, into 'he hates me.' In this way, a homosexual desire is transformed into a delusion.[22]

But if homosexuality, more or less latent, occupies a front rank position in 'paranoid schizophrenia', it plays an equally important role in the lives

19. See Roberto Calasso's essay 'Nota sui lettori di Schreber', published as an appendix to the Italian edition of Schreber's *Memoirs*. [Translator's note from first English edition: The English edition of this amazing book is published as *Memoirs of My Nervous Illness* (London Bloomsbury, 2001).]
20. Ferenczi, 'On the Part Played by Homosexuality in the Psychogenesis of Paranoia', p. 167.
21. Freud, 'Psycho-Analytic Notes on an Autobiographical Account of a Case of Paranoia', p. 59.
22. Arieti, *Interpretazione della schizofrenia*, p. 28.

of so-called 'normal' (and hence actually schizoid) people. Nor, on the other hand, can the scope of the 'schizophrenic' trip be reduced to a badly tolerated gay itch – however true it is that a homoerotic desire of a certain strength, and its inhibition, can lead the 'normal' individual into an 'anxiety state', a confusion that is propitious to the 'schizophrenic' explosion. Analogously, in the case of a self defined gay person, a satisfying erotic relationship with a person of the opposite sex can contribute – at a certain point in life – to the onset of 'madness.'

According to Silvano Arieti (whose opinion I share only in part),

> latent homosexuality is a frequent cause of paranoid states, but it is not a necessary factor; it leads to paranoid forms not because it is an indispensable cause of the paranoid process, but because homosexuality generates major anxiety in many individuals. The latent homosexual seeks to negate their own homosexuality because this form of sexuality is not accepted by society. In certain situations, however, such as when they meet a person to whom they show a special attention, they cannot by themselves negate their emotions. They feel themselves succumbing to their real impulses, and in hopes of evading them, they can resort to psychotic negation. The loved person becomes the persecutor, as Freud has shown in the Schreber case. The patient no longer accuses themselves of the homosexual desires, but rather other persons who accuse them of horrible things, such as being a spy, for example. Parents and their symbols come anew into their frame; and they accuse the patient of being a 'naughty child'. They are wicked, they are homosexual, they are a murderer, and a spy. All these accusations become equivocated under their emotive aspect.[23]

All the same, if the extraordinary 'voyage of madness' cannot be reduced entirely to a homosexual matter, it is however true – and worth reiterating – that for heterosexuals (i.e. latent homosexuals), homosexual experience or even the simple perception of a gay desire can represent the initial (or initiating . . .) push towards a 'schizophrenic' trip. The fear of homosexuality that distinguishes *homo normalis* is also the terror of 'madness' (terror of oneself, of the real depths therein). So, homosexual liberation really poses itself as a bridge towards a decisively other dimension: the French, who call queers *les folles* [the mad], aren't exaggerating.

---

23. Arieti, *Interpretazione della schizofrenia*, p. 131.

If the public execration of homoeroticism denounces the general repression of desire imposed with force in neurotic society, homosexual experience presents itself as that which allows access to the unknown, to the mysterious world that is constantly present in the unconscious. Counter to Arieti, I believe that for a 'normal' person the flowering of homosexuality is indispensable to the determination of 'schizophrenia', but not the sole condition, since our depths are more than homosexual – they are transsexual, polymorphous, and they reveal themselves therefore through various experiences, as the resistances that themselves oppose its liberation are varied.

For an open homosexual, for instance, from the perspective of the explosive erotic horizon (in the sense of 'schizophrenia'), there can be – beyond making love with women – a suite of urophilic-coprophilic experiences, and one finds also gerontophilia, pederasty, and zoophilia: what would be liberatory would be to ultimately disinhibit gay desire itself, and instead staring incest fantasies in the face, opting for tied-up masochistic slavery, for lucid sadistic pleasure and intense autoerotic concentration. What would be explosive would be exhibitionism and voyeurism with your head held high, and fetishism rediscovered beyond fetishistic alienation. What would be liberatory would be to confront the here and now, existence itself and death without trying to escape it, living in the fullness of time, with courage and also in terror, choosing risk and opposing once and for all the blinded, 'normal', and neurotic compulsion to repeat.

In any case, it seems pointless to me to try and establish the precise degree to which homosexuality enters into the 'pathogenesis' of 'paranoia' or 'schizophrenia', if one wants to call it that, when – as against the doctors – we do not consider 'schizophrenia' a mental sickness, but rather see it as a false premise to trace its etiology back to categories that are restricted and schizoid (because based on the dissociation between ego and id).

For the time being, we shall confine ourselves to noting how the analysis of 'clinical cases' of 'paranoia' reveals, by extension, the presence in every individual of homosexual tendencies, which can be more or less repressed in the course of life, depending on the situation. It was precisely in the context of his celebrated analysis of the Schreber 'case' that Freud maintained: 'Generally speaking, every human being oscillates all through his life between heterosexual and homosexual feelings, and any frustration or disappointment in the one direction is apt to drive him over into the other'.[24]

And yet Freud, revealing his own limitations in the face of Schreber's grandeur, still felt himself constrained to ask whether it was 'not an act of irresponsible levity, an indiscretion and a calumny, to charge a man of such high ethical standing as the former *Senatspräsident* Schreber with homosexuality?' No, because 'the patient has himself informed the world at large of his phantasy of being transformed into a woman and he has allowed all personal considerations to be outweighed by interests of a higher nature'.[25]

It follows that Freud, despite being forced to admit the presence of both homo and hetero tendencies in every individual, deemed it basically slanderous to reveal homosexuality in the case of an individual of 'high ethical standing' (which presumably Freud also considered himself), unless this person made explicit reference to his own gay desires and fantasies. Freud's thinking here shows a decisively contradictory turn. If, on the one hand, anyone can be viewed as (also) homosexual, on the other hand Freud could not escape the basic equation in which homoeroticism corresponds to a vice, an aberrant fault of which anyone can therefore be accused. This contradiction, an irrational element in the context of Freud's lucid (if hasty) analysis of Schreber's 'delusion', is historically understandable, if not justifiable, in its conformity with the morality of his time. (And it is not as if Freud's time was so distant from our own.)

It's funny to note how, in his correspondence with Groddeck – who always wrote him as 'Dear Professor' – Freud, who always responded 'Dear colleague', spontaneously changed 'colleague' for 'Doctor' (and wrote 'Dear Doctor . . .') in the reply to the letter in which Groddeck for the first time mentioned having been in love with him. Then again, Freud was no less of a repressed queer than the other famous ones.

Even though restricted by interpreting the extraordinary range of 'schizophrenic delusion' in terms of a 'distortion of homosexuality' (Ferenczi), which makes them somewhat reduced and simplistic, the analyses of paranoia by Freud and Ferenczi are almost perfectly fitted to understanding the anti-homosexual 'paranoia' of society and the anti-

24. Freud, 'Psycho-Analytic Notes on an Autobiographical Account of a Case of Paranoia', p. 46.

25. Ibid., p. 43

homoerotic actions of so-called 'normal' people. As Guy Hocquenghem has written, '"society" [. . .] suffers from an interpretative delusion which leads it to discover all around it the signs of a homosexual conspiracy that prevents it from functioning properly'.[26] The collective, censored, homoerotic desire is expressed under a negative sign towards us open homosexuals: the homosexual love that is socially latent is transformed into hate for us gays. It is clearly not we gay men and women who suffer from persecution mania, as it is we who are actually persecuted. It is society, rather, that maniacally believes itself threatened by our presence, which it defines as a 'social pest'. Trying to defend themselves from 'contamination', and to check this 'vice', they attack us.

This is no paradox: the 'paranoiacs', the 'schizophrenics', the so-called 'mad', are in reality far less paranoid than people considered 'normal'. And in a certain sense, the 'schizophrenic' conception of the world is superior, or at least less illusory, than the eknoic[27] – but actually paranoic – worldview of *homo normalis*.

As Norman O. Brown puts it: 'It is not schizophrenia but normality that is split-minded; in schizophrenia the false boundaries are disintegrating . . . Schizophrenics are suffering from the Truth.'[28]

On the other hand, to quote Wilhelm Reich:

> The schizophrenic world mingles into one experience what is kept painstakingly separate in *homo normalis*. The 'well adjusted' *homo normalis* is composed of exactly the same type of experiences as the schizophrenic. Depth psychiatry leaves no doubt about this. *Homo normalis* differs from the schizophrenic only in that these functions are differently arranged. He is a well-adjusted, 'socially minded' merchant or clerk during the day; he is orderly on the surface. He lives out his secondary, perverse drives when he leaves home and office to visit some faraway city, in occasional orgies of sadism or promiscuity. This is his 'middle layer' existence, clearly and sharply separated from the superficial veneer. He believes in the existence of a personal supernatural power and its opposite, the Devil and hell, in a third group of experiences which is again clearly and sharply delineated

26. Hocquenghem, *Homosexual Desire*, p. 55
27. [Translator's note: An eknoic state refers to a delusional state that is the consequence of affective excitability that reaches ecstatic levels.]
28. Norman O. Brown, *Love's Body*, p. 159.

> from the two others. These three basic groups do not mingle with one another. *Homo normalis* does not believe in God when he does some tricky business, a fact which is reprimanded as 'sinful' by the priests in Sunday sermons. *Homo normalis* does not believe in the Devil when he promotes some cause of science; he has no perversions when he is the supporter of his family; and he forgets his wife and children when he lets the Devil go free in a brothel.[29]

Any ' normal' person, therefore, is a latent 'schizophrenic' just as much as a latent homosexual. But the manifest 'schizophrenic' experience is in the highest degree something different from 'normal' everyday life: it reveals what we are 'in reality', the universal history concentrated in us, and the transsexual and communist potential with which we are pregnant.

The 'Schizophrenic' Trip and Transsexuality

> Come then, my pretty Dr Faust, the mantle is spread for the flight. Forth into the Unknown . . .[30]

We homosexuals know how little concern is shown for those who are 'deviant' in the society of absolute values (even if this lack of concern presents itself as exorcism, and hence in reality a very deep concern; otherwise repression could never be so harsh). Just as homosexuality is simply considered a 'vice' or 'perversion', and dealt with accordingly, so the 'schizophrenic', as a general rule, is nothing but an incorrigible 'psychopath', to be sentenced to the lunatic asylum, or else 'curable' by way of 'therapy', this being simply the violent negation of 'schizophrenic' freedom, the oppression of mind and body effected by the authoritarian imposition of electric shock, drugs and ultimately lobotomy, with a view to forcibly leading the 'patient' back into the confines of the established Norm. The 'schizophrenic' must submit to the arbitrary acts of neurotic, schizoid doctors, who understand little or nothing of what they call 'madness'. Psychiatric textbooks more or less explicitly admit as much.

The labelling of homosexuality as an 'aberration', or more fashionably, a 'variation', involves a false consciousness in dealing with its real content, recognising the vital passion that inspires it and the aspiration

29. Reich, *Character Analysis* (London: Prentice Hall International, 1955), p. 399.
30. Groddeck, *The Book of the It* (London, 1979), p. 11.

of human desire that it expresses. In the same way, the label of 'psychopath' reduces the existential universe of the 'schizophrenic' to a 'clinical case' to be condemned to imprisonment and derision (or to a pity that is cousin to this). If the homosexual is not understood, because there is neither wish nor need to understand him, and yet he is still persecuted, then the 'schizophrenic' is a person 'who does not understand', and hence acts out his forced submission to a psychiatric (or anti psychiatric)[31] reason which understands everything, to the extent that it can reduce it to the worn out, banal and repressive categories of an ideological illusion passed off as 'reality'.

As a rule, the 'mad' person is considered asocial. According to the psychiatrists, the 'irrationality' and 'paralogical thinking' of the schizophrenic 'jeopardises his relationship with the community and his adjustment to it'.[32] But this 'community' which psychiatrists speak of is the absolute negation of community. 'In the West, with the capitalist mode of production, a stage now marked by the autonomy of exchange-value, the last residues of community were destroyed' (Jacques Camatte). The human community is replaced by a material (*sachliches*) community of things governed by capital. As Camatte goes on to say:

> In reality, the movement of production presents itself as the expropriation of man and his atomisation – the production of the individual – and at the same time as the autonomising of social relations and the products of human activity, which become an oppressive power over against him: autonomisation and reification. Man is therefore separated from his community, or more precisely, this is destroyed.[33]

Thus it is not the community, but the totalitarian negation of community, to which the so-called 'schizophrenic' experience is maladapted. And if the 'schizophrenic', so defined, is asocial, then the homosexual too is

---

31. Psychiatrists involved in the 'anti-psychiatry' movement confront 'schizophrenia' with the same mental framework as that with which an eighteenth-century Enlightenment philosopher might have confronted the communist theme of human emancipation. A revolutionary critique of 'anti-psychiatry', and in particular the ideas of David Cooper, can be found in Giorgio Cesarano, *Manuale di sopravvivenza* (Bari: Dedalo, 1974)

32. Theodor Lidz and Stephen Fleck, 'Schizofrenia, integrazione personale e funzione della famiglia', *Eziologia della schizofrenia* (ed. D. Jackson), Milan, 1964, p. 414.

33. Jacques Camatte, *Il capitale totale*, p. 193.

asocial, a true social plague, since he refuses to form a family or even a straight couple according to the canons of prevailing socio-sexual law. In reality, it is the anti-homosexual taboo that leads to the negation of true community, by condemning totalising relationships between people of the same sex; it is the system that is asocial and inhuman, in as much as the real domination of capital constitutes the maximum negation of the human community in the entire course of prehistory that separates us from the dissolution of primitive communism.

It follows that the asocial result, as it is seen in the (pre)judice of dominant ideology, generally contains within it something that is profoundly human, frequently oriented towards the (re)conquest of true community. Perhaps the 'megalomaniac delusion' of a 'paranoic' grasps in solitary recognition the immense importance of the human subject and his life, and his 'persecution complex' shows a tragic awareness of the real persecution meted out to the human individual in capitalist society. Christ – if one may say it – rots today in the prisons and asylums.

But the time has come for general in(re)surrection, given the destruction that is heavy in the cancerous air of capital (the cloud of pollution at Seveso[34] was only the first of its kind), and the life that we are forced to repress can (re)surge free and communally in its full potential. It is time to put the brakes on the engine of the system and bring it to a halt. It is time to (re)conquer the planet and ourselves, if we do not want the machine that humans constructed, and which subsequently autonomised and turned against them, to end up bringing about a complete catastrophe. Adjustment to the system means accepting the extermination that is perpetrated against us; it means making ourselves accomplices.

Time is pressing: we can no longer meekly put up with the enforced status quo, continuing to identify ourselves with a sexual Norm that is functional and consonant with it, but which divides us from one another by insisting on the condemnation of homosexuality, which divides male from female by counterposing men and women, and which divides us from ourselves because it is based on the repression of our polymorphous desire, so rich and transsexual. We need men, who are today so obtusely phallocratic, to accept that they too are pregnant with a life that is not to be aborted, a 'femininity' that must not be crushed by the deadly destiny

34. [Editor's note from original volume: On 10 July 1976, a cloud of dioxin escaped from the Icmesa plant in Seveso, in the province of Milan, causing an ecological disaster.]

of this male-dominated society. They also must – but this is a gay 'must' – come to establish new relations both with women and with other men, and finally to understand and uncover in themselves the half that they have always repressed, coming to express and communicate to others a new mode of being and to become gay, conscious, open and anti-capitalist. There is no longer time to act as puppets of the system, wretched clowns who take themselves so seriously in order to repress the gay life within themselves, and to oppose the revolution and the affirmation of women that is the essence, flavour and content of the revolution itself.

The new world that we bear within us, and which some of us are beginning to realise, understand and express, finds its prophets, its forerunners and its poets in the 'mad' women and men of both present and past, who – far from being idiots – have in fact understood too much. As Reich put it:

> When we wish to obtain the truth about social facts, we study Ibsen or Nietzsche, both of whom went 'crazy', and not the writings of some well-adjusted diplomat or the resolutions of the communist party congresses.[35]

The social collective, the world, history and the universe, act and interact in the 'schizophrenic' trip. Existence takes on a different light, new and very old meanings are gathered in the air, in the streets, among people, in animals and plants. Consciousness expands: the 'mad' person begins to experience consciously a large part of what is 'normally' unconscious.

How exceptional are the *Memoirs* of the 'paranoic' Schreber, compared with the analysis that Freud made of them! Schreber's 'delusion' expands into the great orbit of religion, history, transsexuality; it is made up of peoples and wars; it sweeps aside the customary conceptions of time and space, and fuses life with death, as Schreber actually sought to live out his own death. In the words of Gilles Deleuze:

> Schreber's *Memoirs,* whether paranoic or schizophrenic (it matters little), present a kind of racial, racist or historical delusion. Schreber's delusion is one of continents, cultures and races. It is a surprising delusion, with a political, historical and cultural content.[36]

---

35. Reich, *Character Analysis*, p. 400.
36. Gilles Deleuze, 'Capitalismo e schizofrenia', *L'altra pazzia: mappa antologica della psichiatria alternativa* (Milan: Feltrinelli, 1975), p. 66.

In actual fact, for those who know what is really meant by 'schizophrenia', Schreber's *Memoirs* are not particularly surprising, for in any 'voyage into madness', the social collective, nations, and even the remote past and the cosmos are thrown into fundamental and transparent relief, which has little in common with the opaque ego-istic view of the world. Beyond the veil of Maya, many of the customary barriers between the self and others break down, both between the ego and that which is apparently 'outside', and between the ego and the 'internal' world of the unconscious. There is nothing surprising, therefore, about the Schreber 'case' as opposed to any other 'delusions'; the psychonazis themselves admit that, 'schizophrenic symptoms' are generally extremely similar. Schreber's experience is only surprising in comparison with the Norm, with the myopic survival of *homo normalis*, in the same way as are the adventures of so many other 'mad' people, whether present or past, who are not and never will be famous.

Deleuze is quite right, moreover, in maintaining that, in his analysis of the Schreber case, 'Freud does not deal with anything rigorously, and reduces the judge's delusion simply to his relationship with his father'.[37] The 'schizophrenic trip', on the contrary, reveals how our entire ontogenesis must be understood in the light of a phylogenesis 'projected' from the darkness of the unconscious towards the 'outside', and rediscovered in other people and the environment. For in all of us, in fact, history is present – even if this is still *prehistory*, lying latent, because repression has forced us not to see, not to feel, and not to understand, not to recognise ourselves in others. The ego and the illusion of 'normal reality' are the result of the individualistic atomisation of the species, an atomisation that followed and replaced the gradually destroyed community. So-called 'delusion' is therefore a 'state of grace', since in the individual affected the desire for community reawakens and seeks to assert itself in surroundings which are hostile to it and in fact its negation.

In a text published in 1924, 'Neurosis and Psychosis', Freud observed that while in neurosis the ego, because of its submission to 'reality', represses a part of the id, in 'psychotic' 'schizophrenia' the ego, in the service of the id, withdraws from a part of 'reality'. The ego accepts part of the id. In this case, 'the ice of repression is cracked' (Jung). But the id is also a 'collective unconscious'. What surfaces to consciousness, therefore, besides all personal reminiscences, is in part the contents of this collec-

37. Deleuze, *Semeiotica e Psicanalisi*, p. 9.

tive unconscious. And this, being 'detached from anything personal [. . .] is entirely universal, and [. . .] its contents can be found everywhere'.[38] It is the latent community that surfaces, and with it a certain 'primordial effervescence'. We can understand, therefore, how 'there exists an invisible world that is unappreciated – the true world, without doubt - of which our own is simply a marginal fringe' (Jean Cocteau).

The perception of transsexuality, one's own and that of others, is of particular importance in the 'schizophrenic' trip. Just as hermaphrodism is a gateway into magic, so the 'schizophrenic' adventure is magical because, in this sudden and progressive change in experience, a central element proves to be the (re)discovery of that side of ourselves which Jung defined as 'anima' or 'animus'. The transsexual aspiration generally remains relegated to the subconscious, and only rarely rises to the level of consciousness (Freud, for example, showed the 'bisexual' nature of fantasies).[39] Frequently, this happens only via the mechanism of negation. But the question of transsexuality is fundamental. In the words of Harry Benjamin:

> For the simple man in the street, there are only two sexes. A person is either male or female, Adam or Eve. The more sophisticated realise that every Adam contains elements of Eve and every Eve harbours traces of Adam, physically as well as psychologically.[40]

Although homosexuality itself 'rests' on the deep-rooted conception of and belief in the differences between the sexes, we gays are still in a position giving better access to a conscious validation of transsexual fantasies, of the transsexual 'nature' of desire. There is of course more than a short distance between here and Casablanca.[41] But in the 'schizophrenic' trip, all the same – in particular when undertaken by conscious homosexuals – the transsexual fantasy is transformed into the overwhelming effective experience of transsexuality. If we can take up the words of Jesus according to the Gnostic Saint Thomas, then one day 'the two shall be one, and the outside shall resemble the inside, and there

38. Jung, 'Psychology of the Unconscious', p. 65.
39. Freud, 'Hysterical Phantasies and their Relation to Bisexuality', *Standard Edition*, Vol. 9 (London: Vintage, 2001), pp. 155–66.
40. Harry Benjamin, *The Transsexual Phenomenon*, p. 14.
41. Casablanca is the site of a celebrated 'sex-change' clinic, the Du Parc clinic, directed by a French surgeon.

shall no longer be either male or female'. From being latent, transsexuality now becomes manifest.

Plato already taught that it was only by way of madness or mania that man could come to discern the truth of Love;[42] and in the *Symposium*, when Socrates speaks of Love, he quotes the wise woman Diotima of Mantinea.[43] Through this intervention, the language of philosophy was fused with the Eleusian mysteries; just as in the *Phaedrus*, the incantation Socrates speaks in praise of Love is completely full of mystical tones, the revelations of mythology and a poetry inspired by the divinity of the countryside and of nature.[44] In the same way, the 'schizophrenic' mystery rises to the highest peak of the truth of love.

I believe that if we are to try and overcome the limits of our rationalistic discourse on sexuality, we have to approach the erotic themes and contents of 'schizophrenia'; the erotic desire is a thousand times higher than the limitations of our intellectual conception of love, made up of 'romantic' themes (in the broad sense) and psychoanalytic categories, chained by the chastened and alienating functions of monosexuality and the repression of all other tendencies of desire. Such limitations risk leading us to foresee the stabilisation of an illusory peaceful coexistence between the sexes and between heterosexuality and homosexuality, falling back into the gloomy perspectives of latter-day bourgeois enlightenment. If the minority of open gays can unveil such hidden truth as to the 'nature' of the human being and our underlying desires, what profound truth on the human universe and the full significance of sexuality is disclosed by the experience of the 'mad'?

The classical conceptual categories, and the everyday language in which these are expressed, are ill suited to describe the sensations and experiences of 'madness'. For not only does the 'schizophrenic' often know and feel himself hermaphrodite or in the process of becoming so, at times he also discerns hermaphrodism in the people around him. If he is in contact with heterosexual couples, for example, he may find himself suddenly picking up their intimate and astonishing 'fusion'; on the telephone, a woman speaking to him about her husband can to his ears gradually but distinctly change her voice into that of the husband. She 'is' her husband, since he exists within her. The 'mad' person perceives

42. Plato, *Phaedrus* (Harmondsworth: Penguin, 1973), pp. 46–7 (244).
43. Plato, *Symposium* (Harmondsworth: Penguin, 1951), p. 79 (201d).
44. Plato, *Phaedrus*.

how other people (un)veil their own transsexuality. He understands the extent to which their conscience is a bad conscience, is unfaithful, since in his presence they pretend not to know what they show themselves to be. And since, as a general rule, they behave repressively towards him, the 'schizophrenic' can also conclude that they mistreat him because they repress themselves, because there is a mysterious law that threatens them, and in the service of which they act.

Perhaps I have tended to generalise from an experience of my own, which, after a varied trajectory, brought me into clinics for the 'mentally ill' some two years ago. True; it is wrong to generalise; and yet I feel that I have lived situations that are true, in as much as they contain within them something universal. And this is why I have exceeded what are considered the 'normal' bounds of extrapolation and generalisation.

The serious problem for me, rather, is to maintain in retrospect the reality I lived so strongly at that time. Other people invariably oppose this as a pit full of vain hallucinations, though in actual fact everything presented itself to me as fully evident, clear and irresistible. If life in the 'society of the spectacle' is a stage production, then I have refused to perform. For I had a vision of the extraordinary scope of existence, the richness which this absurd social constriction prevents us from naturally enjoying.

Today, far too often, we are all forced in part to perform, forced into that 'normal' hypocrisy that enables us to go around 'freely'. If this book is worth little, that is due above all to the falseness that is difficult to avoid in writing, being necessarily reproduced in daily life. All the same, as a friend said to me, it is more important to go forth than to drag along; in my case, this means proceeding coherently with my 'madness', with that which, once revealed, it is impossible to deny, and which forces us to live for the best. Didn't Freud say that the superego represents the unconscious and becomes the spokesman of its demands in consciousness?[45]

The transsexual sentiment was one of the reasons, and also one of the results, of a gradual alteration in my perceptions of my body and mind, of the 'external' world and other people. At times I felt myself really a woman, at times spiritually pregnant, at other times the reincarnation of a woman. Besides, to use a certain jargon, my hidden fantasies, and with these the 'archetypes' of the collective unconscious, became

45. Freud, 'The Ego and the Id', p. 36.

'projected' – or were rather encountered – 'outside'; the 'schizophrenic' experience enabled me to grasp many of the secrets hidden behind the recurring representations of the 'normal' past. Routine was shattered, and the repetition compulsion beaten. I could sense in any single act of the day the interaction between freedom of choice and 'conditioning', between myself, things and other people. The meaning of sexual attraction became brilliantly clear; it was the first sign and the most evident expression of intersubjectivity. Desire was sensual and candid, in turns humorous and serious, disgusting and consuming.

At the same time, the European metropolis seemed to me like a Mecca, its people entranced and terrified. Coincidences and surprises multiplied, and my hesitations when confronted with magical phenomena declined in the face of disconcerting evidence, sure encounters in which I realised fantasies that I had believed I had for ever to abandon to 'reality'. 'Reality' was replaced by truth.

'Madness' is materialist. To investigate the truths of what lies below, and, suspending prejudices without – yet – jettisoning them, to confront them with the succession of actual facts (Ferenczi saw materialism as the prototype of 'paranoiac' philosophy).[46] In the process, sensitivity grows more refined.

As Edgar Allen Poe put it: 'And now have I not told you that what you mistake for madness is but over acuteness of the senses?'[47] The transsexual perception is double: it discovers that the majority of people are at least half-buried. The city looks like the realm of the living dead. And yet other people's faces reflect the divine along with the ghosts and demons. In nature, in the sky, and in other people, the 'mad' person contemplates himself and the grandeur of life, without anyone else seeing within him. The unconscious sees itself…

Freud's references to the unconscious are far too close to Kant's utterances on the noumen, the thing-in-itself that is assumed but cannot be experienced. But the 'thing-in-itself, the truth, can be experienced. It is only 'narrow-minded and ignorant people [who] take the profound as if it were uncouth, and relegate the marvellous to the realm of fiction'.[48]

46. Ferenczi, 'Philosophy and Psycho-Analysis', *Final Contributions to the Problems and Methods of Psycho-Analysis* (London: Hogarth Press, 1955), p. 328.
47. Edgar Allen Poe, *The Tell-Tale Heart (and other stories)* (London: J. Lehmann, 1948), p. 25.
48. Ko Hung, *Pao Phu Tzu,* quoted by Joseph Needham, *Science and Civilisation in China* (Cambridge: Cambridge University Press, 1969), Vol. 2, p. 438.

If the non-ego can be taken to embrace both the id and the 'external' world, then 'mad' people demonstrate how awareness of the underneath bridges individuality and the barriers between ego and non-ego. Once the dual separation of both the 'external' world and the id from the ego is overcome, then it is clear that the ego is 'normally' nothing but an oppressive barrier (in as much as it is the product of oppression and based on repression) between our underneath and the cosmos. The id (the internal non-ego) and the 'external' world (the external non-ego) mutually illuminate one another, since they are always reciprocally determined. And if the 'schizophrenic delusion' is seen as solipsist (in the sense of the solipsistic or quasi-solipsistic doubt that is at times experienced), this is not a product of 'megalomania' or an accentuated individualism, but rather of the lack of a vital response on the part of others to the 'mad' person's need for communication and direct community. If other people insist on forcing him into their own dissociated and 'normal' individuality, then to the eyes of the 'schizophrenic' they may well all appear, from time to time, 'people made of shadows'.

But there are others and *others*. Some people come to assume a very great importance for the 'mad' person (who certainly does not travel alone): and if the 'schizophrenic' can be attributed a 'state of grace', then I believe – from my own experience – that this 'grace' can be communicated to others, once the initiating impetus is given. Faust would not be Faust without the devil.

Women and Queens

And indeed, devils do exist.

I have already indicated the possibility that, at a given moment in the life of a gay man, a satisfying erotic relationship with a woman can contribute to launching the 'schizophrenic' trip. And the 'schizophrenic' experience, as we have seen, is (among other things) a transsexual perception, the discovery of hermaphrodism. This enables us to understand how the liberation of Eros, the (re)conquest of transsexuality, also involves overcoming the resistances that inhibit relationships between male homosexuals and women, as well as between us and other men. A free man is gay and loves women

There is a widespread belief among many people that gay men are misogynist. Nothing could be more false: if we experience a heavy sexual attraction towards other men, this in no way implies that we hate women. On the contrary, we are in general far more disposed to develop relations of affection and friendship with women, feeling deeply akin to them in some respects, despite the fundamental difference that sees us as being, after all (or, according to many feminists, first of all), men just the same, and hence on the opposite side of the fence. The various levels of the revolutionary dialectic cut across one another, and the man-woman contradiction and the contradiction between heterosexuality and homosexuality are interwoven. If a gay male behaves in a way antithetical to the heterosexual Norm that is functional to the system, he is still willy-nilly, whether more or less consciously, tied to the phallocentrism that governs this system. On the other hand, a woman, who as such is potentially on the side of the revolution, can still fully submit to the heterosexual Norm, hence confirming herself in the role of slave and perpetuating male privilege and the repression of homoeroticism; she can more or less openly disparage erotic relations between people of the same sex, and repress her own homosexuality. The revolutionary struggle of women, however, tears a growing number of gay men away from the male union, and finds in them gay allies, always as 'men in crisis'; while the propagation of gay desire by homosexual women and men distances women more and more from the Norm, and leads to many encounters, on the terrain of homosexuality, between women and women, and between women and queens. The presence of revolutionary lesbians is by far the chief link between the gay and feminist movements: revolutionary lesbians form the homosexual movement of women, and we can foresee that the women's movement will become more and more homosexual.[49]

Eros also finds liberation via the creation of new erotic relationships between women and gay men. This is in no way a question of reforming the Norm. Heterosexuality is essentially reactionary, because, being based on the contradiction between the sexes, it perpetuates the phallocentric male, the prototype of the fascist male that the state, and hence the left within the system, always propagate. Revolutionary homosexuals reject heterosexuality as a Norm, as the base of the family, and the guarantee of male privilege and the oppression of women. They combat it, recognising it as the form of sexuality in the name of which the system has always attacked homosexuals and incited people to persecute them.

---

49. See Chapter 6, section 1.

But erotic relations between women and gay men need not be 'normal' and hence heterosexual in the more or less traditional sense. Our relations with women can instead be (and in part already are) gay, very little heterosexual, and not at all straight. The revolution is (also) prepared by new positive encounters between persons of opposite sex, and by the creation of gay friendships between women and men. Women and fags can make love in a new way which, despite the historical and biological differences between the sexes, and the inherent contradictions of power that are bound up with these, is in tendency and intention a new form of intersubjective pleasure and understanding; they can make love in a way that is outside the usual pattern of the heterosexual couple. I believe that very many women really prefer fags to straight men, and that, among other things, their sexuality finds greater satisfaction and response in making love with a gay than in the egoistic fucking proposed, and often imposed, by the heterosexual male. Above all else, we gays do not treat women as sexual 'objects'.

Among us homosexuals, however, many feel particularly inhibited in recognising and expressing our erotic desire for women. I think that this is very largely a product of our psychological subjection to a particular model of heterosexual masculinity that we were forced to internalise as a model, but which we could not identify with. We know that we do not fit this model, and at the same time we conceive heterosexuality as we see it on all sides, in every corner of the world, i.e. centred on male virility and the objectification of the woman. But this is heterosexuality as it was imposed on women. And the liberation of women cannot but negate this, since inherent to it is the sexual, and not only sexual, subjection of the woman to the male.

Consider, for example, the phallic 'problem': the male boasts of the 'power' of his cock, whereas we know that, most probably, we will not even get an immediate erection in making love with a woman. And yet this is a false problem: I am convinced that it does not matter to women. The erotic relationship is neither exclusively nor even primarily a genital one, and revolutionary women reject the authoritarian imposition of the phallus by the male, that boastful and alienating phallus that serves as a symbol and instrument of power in the heterosexual prison. (Between men, however, playing with cocks, even in a phallic way, can be very gay, it is gay, exciting and pleasurable for both involved, or for all three or four, etc.) Males should act out their phallic desire among themselves (nowadays even extended to fist-fucking), and stop imposing it on women. Even if women do occasionally desire the phallic relationship, I believe they will still find the 'ideal' partner or partners among gays, who really do love a penis, and not only their own (which moreover they love right to the end, without any disgust at their own sperm, for example, unlike the majority of heterosexuals), but also those of others.

Once the 'problem' of erection is dispensed with, which is therefore a pseudo problem, the fag will understand that it is fine to make love with a woman, and the woman will be happy to make love with someone who knows how to make love, i.e. with a gay man. One evening on TV I saw Ornella Vanoni, looking very fit, who was singing 'You Don't Know How to Make Love': she was seductive, but I felt involved and 'complicit'; a complicity that was intense, emotionally erotic, and involving a shared common knowledge (and desire) of the male. I think that even the genital relationship between women and gay men is more richly shaded, in terms of reciprocal sensual attention in contact, rather than the habitual 'wham, bam, thank you ma'am', over in a couple minutes, of the heterosexual male.

Making love with a person of the other sex always yields the renewed discovery of a body and form of pleasure that is different from one's own. But in order to fully and reciprocally enjoy this diversity, it is necessary to understand one's own sex, not only in the autoerotic mode, but also in the alloerotic. Homosexuality is superior to sexual individualism; it is the discovery of one's own sex, the recognition by desire of (all) people of the same sex. Homosexuality is the sine qua non for being truly able to love the opposite sex, and hence to love bodies that are different from our own.

It is clear, however, that the phallic fixation of the heterosexual male is a function of his concentration on himself, on his own cock, a function of his repressed and suppressed homosexual desire. It derives from the transformation into (alienated) autoeroticism of the desire for one's own sex that was in its original tendency (and still latently is) directed towards (all) persons of the same sex. The identification with the phallus on the part of the heterosexual male results from a kind of 'introjection' of the homosexual 'objects' which he has had to renounce. It is this blind rejection of the homosexuality that is hidden and secret in himself, which the heterosexual imposes on the woman as virility, rigid virility.[50]

50. On 4 November 1976, at the congress of Lotta Continua held in Rimini, a woman comrade made the following remark to the male militants: 'You refuse to ask

The desire for persons of the same sex, which is the first consequence of love of oneself, is forced to return – in the heterosexual male – to its earlier narcissistic dimension; males leap across to their heterosexual goal by repressing the middle term of homosexuality. A leap in the dark, hence their clumsiness. As Georg Groddeck has written:

> Man loves himself first and foremost, with every sort of passionate emotion, and seeks to procure for himself every conceivable pleasure, and, since he himself must be either male or female, is subject from the beginning to passion for his own sex. It cannot be otherwise, and unprejudiced examination of anyone who will consent to it, gives proof. The question, therefore, is not whether homosexuality is exceptional, perverse – that does not come under discussion – what we have to ask is, why it is so difficult to consider this phenomenon of passion between people of the same sex, to judge it and discuss it, without prejudice, and then we have also to ask how it comes about that, in spite of his homosexual nature, man is also able to feel affection for the opposite sex.[51]

It is impossible to speak dispassionately of homosexuality, since it is a repressed passion. In the same way, it is often true that what is more openly desired is not what is desired at a more fundamental level: perhaps it is heterosexual men, solely heterosexual on the surface, who really have the most powerful gay fantasies stirring in their unconscious. And to keep their homosexual desire latent, they continue to establish only superficial relationships with women, who, by involving them deeply, could only bring out the queen that is in them, the 'woman' within. I believe that the erotic desire for women is alive deep within me, being at bottom my own desire to be a woman; and now this is beginning to surface, beautifully, in my life.

We can put forward the hypothesis that heterosexuals, forced to repress their own very strong homosexuality, identify themselves with

---

yourselves where it is that your intolerance towards homosexuals comes from. It is the product of the fear that you have of traumatic penetration. You are terrified of the same thing that you do to us, and don't want it to happen to you. You don't know what it means to have your body expropriated, but you're still scared of it'. See Antonio Padellaro, 'La polemica delle femministe spacca in due Lotta Continua', *Corriere della Sera*, (9 November 1976).

51. Groddeck, *The Book of the It*, p. 230.

the 'objects' of this repressed desire; and that this is what leads them to be such masculine males or feminine females. We gay males, however, are effeminate, and in this we display our deep attraction for women. (The converse may be true for lesbians, but it is not a simple case of *mutatis mutandis*.) In other words, we can say that everyone invests himself with the connotations of his own repressed 'object' of desire. This strengthens the ego and accentuates individualism; the liberation of polymorphous, transsexual desire, of the unconscious, is the condition and essence (in a very material sense) of the community that is to be realised. It is the guarantee of genuine intersubjectivity, of a genuine 'us'.

However, our condition as homosexuals, our sexual ambiguity, the type of balance attained in us between subjectivised connotations and repressed connotations, is tendentiously hermaphroditic, it is the expression of transsexuality. With heterosexuals, conversely, the assumption on the part of the 'subject' of the connotations of the repressed homosexual 'object' leads to a double role playing, to the male being simply more masculine, that typical normal role playing which the feminist and homosexual struggle will end up exploding entirely, in the interest of freeing our repressed transsexuality. If the dialectic between the sexes and between the sexual tendencies is already a fact of social life, it simultaneously involves a large number of underlying levels that are not immediately apparent. The women's and gay movements are preparing the earthquake that will spur the collapse of the entire patriarchal structure.

The harsh persecution of homosexuality has led us gays to greatly constrict our identity as homosexuals. In order to defend and assert ourselves, we must before all else be able to resist, and be homosexuals. This is why the gay movement has particularly emphasised the theme of homosexual identity. Our first task has been to learn to recognise ourselves, to know and love ourselves for what we are, to extinguish the sense of guilt that has been forcibly imposed on us. Only then can we consciously confront life, society and the world. But once this identity is attained, and lived to the full, it is time for us to free the hidden tendencies of desire, and to explore our secret passion for women. This can only make us more gay, since that means becoming more conscious of what we desire and what consistently motivates us.

If the liberation of homosexuality will for many years[52] be a universal problem (which is why today the homosexual 'of strict observance' is

52. Relatively few years, though, in the face of eternity.

still a revolutionary figure, even though the revolution will in due course make this restriction seem in a certain sense perverse), if through the realisation of communism homosexuality will be liberated and lived to the full, we gays, who are the conscious bearers of this seed of liberation, cannot but confront and seek to resolve the problems that relationships with our women comrades impose on us. Thus I believe that totalising gay relationships with women will enable us to discover the reciprocal desire between the sexes, a new reciprocity that is totally different from the asymmetry of traditional heterosexual relations, a revolutionary solidarity. And it is also (and perhaps above all) by deepening our friendships with women that we gay men can liberate our own anima, which unites us with women, and become more 'women' (in a completely different sense than Myra Breckenridge or Raquel Welch!).[53] We can offer women the possibility of new and positive relationships with people of the male sex: women and fags together.

We can hope to see a 'sexual general strike' of women against heterosexual males, and the creation of new totalising relationships between women, the complete liberation of female homosexuality. 'Stop making love with men, let women make love with one another, and with us!' That is our gay proposal to women. And it is a doubly interesting proposition for us, since, if on the one hand we have an interest in deepening our gay relationship with women, on the other hand it is in our interest that all heterosexual males should be at our disposal ... That should be very entertaining. This invitation to women is the first postulate (a dangerous number one ...) of our gay science.

Relations between people of different sex only have a revolutionary sense today when they are gay, i.e. when they are between women and gay men, especially between gay women and gay men. And the heterosexual males? Their arrogant and deficient role is today clearly counter-revolutionary, formed in the image and likeness of capitalist power, and they can only act in a different way with women when they have managed to relate in a new way among themselves. For the time being, from the sexual point of view (and not this alone), they want to do with women what, because of the repression of their homosexuality, they cannot tolerate doing among themselves. They want to fuck women, but

53. [Translator's note: Myra Breckinridge is the titular character of a Gore Vidal novel by the same name, which is the story of a trans woman. She was played by Raquel Welch in the 1970 film adaptation.]

are terrified of being fucked; they like ejaculating against women, but feel horror at the very idea of another male coming over them. This is all part of the heterosexual equation and its absurdity. For the time being, from the standpoint of the revolution, heterosexual males still represent far too greatly capital, the enemy, domination and alienation.

Only the struggle of women can change this. Only our homosexual struggle, only gay pleasure, can make straight men into fags too. And a few men are beginning to understand this, at last: you don't say! … A heterosexual comrade from Quarto Oggiaro wrote the following poem:[54]

A demonstration
of the extra-parliamentary left
is in crisis
a group of homosexual cats
crazy with love for communism
managed to get up close
perhaps too close
to the comrades
who by now are very red
but with embarrassment
with their hands over their assholes
they haven't even got the possibility
of consulting Mao
to settle the argument.

54. Meo Cataldo, *Marciapiede* (Milan, 1976), p. 17.

6
Towards a Gay Communism

Transvestism, Homosexuality and 'Homosexualisation'

> There is more to be learned from wearing a dress for a day, than there is from wearing a suit for life.[1]

As we have seen, 'schizophrenia' sheds light on the transsexual substratum of the psyche, our bodily being-in-becoming (the mind is part of the body, and the body as a whole is far from completely monosexual). We have also established that it is via the liberation of homoeroticism, among other things, that transsexuality is concretely attained; and however much homosexuality is put down by the system today, we gays are among those persons most aware of the transsexual 'nature' that lies within us all. Fantasies of a transsexual character often spring to our consciousness, and many of us have had more or less transsexual experiences.

Which is not to exclude the fact that many transsexuals (and transvestites) today are predominantly hetero. For example, Rachel, the American founder of the Transvestites and Transsexuals Group of the London section of the Gay Liberation Front, defines herself as a 'lesbian', but – from the genital-anatomical point of view – is male. In other words: despite being equipped with sexual characteristics that are both primarily and secondarily coded as male, Rachel feels herself to be, and understands herself as, a woman, and so she acts and dresses as such (her style recalls that of many feminists, and Rachel is a feminist). As a lesbian, she is homosexual, but she is also heterosexual, because s/he likes women, and is even married and only rarely has sexual relations with men, who she finds unattractive in so far as they are usually phallocratic and obsessed with virility. When she lived in London, she was also considered a 'woman' by the comrades of the Women's Liberation Front: as far as I know, Rachel was the only person I know of male sex admitted to the meetings of the English feminists. Judith, her wife, is homosexual,

1. Larry Mitchell, *The Faggots and Their Friends* (unpublished) (New York, 1975).

and, with the exception made for Rachel (but Rachel, in reality, truly constitutes an exception), she has sexual relations only with women.[2]

'Heterosexuals' aware of their transsexuality, however, are at present far less numerous than gays who have undertaken the transsexual trip. This is because heterosexuals, as a general rule, have adapted to their mutilated role of man or woman as something 'normal', obvious and taken for granted, whereas we gays almost invariably experience it as a burden that we have to be exclusively men or women, and suffer from the resistance with which we, and our desire, are opposed by heterosexuals of the same sex as ourselves. The hermaphrodite fantasy, dream and ideal occupy a major place in the gay existential universe.

Society attacks transsexuals or those who might appear as such with special violence: the butch lesbians, the fags, and the 'effeminate' male homosexual bear a greater brunt of public execration and contempt, and are frequently criticised even by those reactionary homosexuals who are better adapted to the system, the 'straight gays' who have managed to pass as 'normal' or heterosexual. These reactionary homosexuals (these *homo-cops*) insist that outrageous queens and transvestites 'trash the gay scene and the image of homosexuality in the eyes of all'. For our part, we outrageous gays see them as queens disguised as straight, as disgraced people who are forced to camouflage themselves, to act a 'natural' life in the role imposed by the system, and to justify their position as consenting slaves with ideological arguments. They wonder 'what it is the gay movement wants, what it is fighting for, because nowadays our society accepts diversity. True, even today we can't make love freely wherever we feel like it, on the buses or on the sidewalks of Via Corso: but then again, not even heteros are allowed to do that. So things aren't that bad. Well, misery loves company …

Many feminists criticise us queens because we often tend in our dress and behaviour to copy the stereotyped 'feminine' fetish that women have to fight. But if a woman dressed like Caterina Caselli or like Camilla Cederna is normal for the system today, a man dressed like Caterina Boratto or Germaine Greer[3] is quite abnormal, as far as 'normal' people are concerned, and so our transvestism has a clear revolutionary character.

2. See Mario Mieli, 'London Gay Liberation Front, Angry Brigade, piume & paillettes', in *Fuori!*, n. 5 (November 1972).

3. [Translator's note: Caselli is an Italian record producer, Cederna a journalist and writer, Boratto an actress famous for parts in films such as Pasolini's *Salò*, and Greer the Australian feminist writer and author of *The Female Eunuch*. Relevant for the

There is no harm in us fags having our bit of fantasy: we demand the freedom to dress as we like, to choose a definite style one day and an ambiguous one the day after, to wear both feathers and ties, leopard-skin and rompers, the leather queen's chains, black leather and whip, the greasy rags of the street porter or a tulle maternity dress. We enjoy the bizarre, digging into (pre)history, the dustbins and uniforms of yesterday, today and tomorrow, the trumpery, costumes and symbols that best express the mood of the moment. As Antonio Donato puts it, we want to communicate by our clothing, too, the 'schizophrenia' that underlies social life, hidden behind the censorious screen of the unrecognised transvestism of everyday. From our vantage point, in fact, it is 'normal' people who are the true transvestites. Just as the absolute heterosexuality that is so proudly flaunted masks the polymorphous but sadly inhibited disposition of their desire, so their standard outfits hide and debase the marvellous human being that lies suppressed within. Our transvestism is condemned because it shows up for all to see the funereal reality of the general transvestism, which has to remain silent, and is simply taken for granted.

Far from being particularly odd, the transvestite exposes how tragically ridiculous the great majority of people are in their monstrous uniforms of man and 'woman'. Ever taken a ride on the underground? If the transvestite seems ridiculous to the 'normal' person who encounters him, far more ridiculous and sad, for the transvestite, is the nudity of the person, so properly dressed, who laughs in his face.

For a man, to dress as a 'woman' does not necessarily mean projecting the 'woman-object'; above all, because he is not a woman, and the male fetishism imposed by capital decrees that he should be dressed quite differently, reified in a quite different guise, dressed as a man or at least in unisex. Besides, a frock can be very comfortable, fresh and light when it's hot, and warm and cosy when it's cold. We can't just assume that women who normally go around dressed as men, swathed tightly in jeans, feel more comfortable than a queen dressed up as a witch, with full-bodied cloak and wide-brimmed hat.

But a man can also get pleasure from wearing a very uncomfortable 'feminine' garb. It can be exciting, and quite trippy, for a gay man to wear high heels, elaborate make-up, suspender belt and satin panties. Once

point that Mieli is making here is that all four were seen to dress and cut their hair in ways considered 'masculine' or severe.]

again, those feminists who attack us gays, and in particular transvestites, for dressing as the 'woman-object', are serving to guilt-trip us for gay humour, the transsexual aesthetic, and the craziness of crazy queens: they introduce a new morality that is, in fact, the very old anti-gay morality, simply given a new gloss by modern categories and stuffed with an ideological feminism, ideological because it provides a cover for the anti-homosexual taboo, for the fear of homosexuality, for the intention to reform the Norm without eliminating it.

Heterosexual feminists fail to hit the mark when they discuss homosexuality. And we queens, moreover, have no intention of being put down by women any more than by men. In the course of our lives, many of the educastrated educastrators we have encountered have been women, and there are certainly far more women still opposed to homosexuality today than there are gay men who are male supremacist and enslaved by the dominant ideology. Many women have abused and do abuse us, they have ridiculed and do ridicule us, they have oppressed and do oppress us. These women cannot but be opposed to us, and we cannot but 'oppose' them, if we intend, from the gay standpoint, to wage a struggle for universal liberation (a struggle, therefore, which involves them as well, fighting against their prejudices, with a view to dissolving all anti-gay resistances). I have already shown how the contradiction between men and women and the contradiction between heterosexuality and homosexuality are intertwined. And so if feminists cannot but oppose the persistence of male supremacy among us queens, we cannot but challenge fundamentally the heterosexual 'normality' with which the women's movement is still suffused, despite the new fashion or ideology of 'homosexuality' that has become widespread in it.

Franco Berardi (Bifo), a heterosexual man, speaks of the 'homosexualisation' of the women's movement, a 'homosexualisation' (the term could hardly sound less gay) which he supports, as a heterosexual male in crisis (but not too much so). And yet Bifo's 'homosexualisation' has little in common with the struggle of us queens for the liberation of the gay desire. The concept of 'homosexualisation' is all too reminiscent, beneath the 'feminist' camouflage of Men's Liberation, of the male supremacist bisexuality of the hustlers. But Bifo will not understand, in fact he cannot understand. To do so, he would have to savour the fragrance of the urinals, and feel in his own person the full weight of oppression that bears down on the shoulders of us gays. For the moment, please, let us speak about homosexuality, we who have come out in the open; homosexual is something one uncovers, not something one becomes. I would like to get her in bed, that Bifo, and confront her 'homosexualisation' with my homosexuality. And this is a gay desire – it is *an advance*,[4] not a concept.

There are also feminists for whom the 'new homosexuality' discovered by the women's movement is not the same thing as lesbianism, which – they hold – is still marked by a male model. Some of them say they came to accept homosexuality after realising the impossibility of going on with relationships with men, and that the homosexual choice is a necessary one for women as long as their struggle has not yet radically changed men and therefore their relations with them. Once again, homosexuality is presented as a substitute choice, a palliative, a surrogate sexual dimension in which the libido withdrawn from male 'objects' is politically channelled.

This is what the new 'homosexual' fashion among feminists amounts to, a fashion that is quickly recuperated by the system (the *Corriere della Sera* has articles about it on its feature page), and which, despite appearances, is simply a new form of the old anti-gay exorcism. The 'new homosexuality' of feminism is worth little more than the 'homosexualisation' of someone like Bifo. It boasts a 'homo' mask, but this actually serves to (un)veil the genuinely latent gay desire, and above all the conscious heterosexual desire that wears the mask. If this mystification is the 'new homosexuality' of women, or at least of certain feminists, then it is quite true that it has little in common with lesbianism. Lesbians are right if they refuse to identify with the general heterosexual atmosphere of the feminist movement, and continue to organise in autonomous ('homonomous') groups.

When there are women who criticise us gays if we dress as 'women', we should not ignore the pulpit from which this preaching comes. I have never been attacked by a lesbian for my make-up, my floral gowns or my silver heels. It is true, of course, that, if for centuries women have been forced by male power to dress up in an oppressive manner, the great creators of fashion, the couturiers, hair-stylists, etc. have almost always been gay men. But the homosexual fantasy has simply been exploited by the system – it still is[5] – in order to oppress women and adorn them in the way that men want to see them. For centuries, the system has

4. [Translator's note: Mieli writes *une avance* in French.]
5. See Chapter 6, section 1.

exploited the work of homosexuals to subjugate women, just as it has made abundant use of women to oppress gays (any gay man need only recall his mother). For this reason, if it is very important for women today to reject certain ways of dress, i.e. being dressed and undressed by men, it is equally important that gays should recapture and reinvent for themselves the aesthetic that they were obliged for centuries to project onto women.

If Marlene Dietrich in her glitter is an emblem of the oppression of women, she is at the same time a gay symbol, she is *gay*, and her image, her voice, her sequins form part of a homosexual culture, a desire that we queens recognise in ourselves. It is true that for a woman today to present herself like a *Vogue* cover girl is in general anti-feminist and reactionary. But for a gay man to dress as he pleases, boldly expressing a fantasy which capital has relegated to the reified pages of *Vogue*, has a certain revolutionary cutting edge, even today. We are fed up with dressing as men. We ask our sisters in the women's movement, then, don't burn the clothes that you cast off. They might be useful to someone, and we have in fact always longed for them. In due course, moreover, we shall invite you all to our great coming-out ball.

There can be no doubt that queens, 'effeminate' homosexuals and transvestites are among those men closest to transsexuality (even if frequently, because of oppression, they live their transsexual desire in alienated forms, infected by false guilt). Queens and transvestites are those 'men' who, even though they are 'men', understand better what it means to be a woman in this society, where the men most disparaged are not the brutes, phallocrats or violent individualists, but rather those who most resemble women. It is precisely the harsh condemnation of 'effeminacy' that sometimes leads gay men to behave in a way that is functional to the system, to become their own jailors. They then balance their 'abnormal' adoration for the male, the tough guy, the hoodlum, with a 'normal' and neurotic anti-woman attitude, which is counterrevolutionary and male supremacist. But the homosexual struggle is abolishing this historical figure of the queen enslaved by the system (the 'queer men' whom Larry Mitchell distinguishes from 'faggots'), and creating new homosexuals, whom the liberation of homoeroticism and transsexual desire brings ever closer to women, new homosexuals who are the true comrades of women, to the point that they can see no other way of life except among other homosexuals and among women, given the increasingly detestable character of heterosexual males. Whenever we gays see 'normal' males discussing one another, or rather tearing one another to pieces, whenever we see them butting against one another, with a profusion of *fucks!*, as if they were fucking, then we truly do think they have understood fuck all, at least if they are still unaware of the homoerotic desire that pushes them towards one another yet confuses them because it is repressed. And if the gay struggle elevates the acidic and put-down queen (acidic even when she's not on acid), transforming her into a *folle*, a gay comrade who is ever more transsexual, it also negates the heterosexual man, since it tends towards the liberation of the queen that is in him too.

Anxiety and Repression. Gay 'Filthiness'

The particular behaviour and fantasies of homosexuals have their counterpart in the blindness and ignorance with which the majority of people respond to the entire sexual question, and the homosexual question in particular. Most of them are still far too unaware of the limitations involved in the opposition between the sexes, even though this may well play a substantial part in their own suffering. Why?

This lack of awareness is the product of the repression they have undergone, and it serves in turn to perpetuate this repression. A severe mental and social censorship conceals what has taken place: their original polymorphous, 'perverse' and undifferentiated erotic disposition was condemned and repressed in the course of infancy, so that the weight of condemnation gradually drags them down into the hell of the adult world, of which the hell of childhood is only the antechamber. Repressed, and thus constricted and deformed, the existence of this tendentiously polymorphous disposition has been relegated to the harsh prison of the unconscious, like the foot of a Chinese woman tortured during imperial times. Restrained by the censorial walls of this prison, each individual has to internalise the sexual values and customs of the heterosexual male model that are imposed by patriarchal society (and in our case, capitalist society in particular). In the words of Norman O. Brown:

> The pattern of normal adult sexuality (in Freud's terminology, genital organisation) is a tyranny of one component in infantile sexuality, a tyranny which suppresses some of the other components altogether and subordinates the rest to itself.[6]

---

6. Brown, *Life Against Death*, p. 27.

The gay movement maintains that the tyranny of genital heterosexuality by no means completely suppresses the polymorphous tendencies of infantile sexuality but simply subjugates them to the yoke of repression. The struggle for the liberation of Eros can release even the most hidden of desires (for example the coprophagous and necrophilic).

In any case, genital tyranny produces anxiety and suffering in us all. The harsher the repression, the stronger the anxiety induced, in our experience, by persons, events and situations which conjure up the wide scope of the repressed contents and tend to disrupt the repression itself. Thus the homosexual is mistreated by the heterosexual because he 'reawakens' in him the homoerotic desire that has been forced to lie dormant for so long. This 'reawakening' is rarely complete, generally taking the form of an unsettling stirring, the presentiment of an earthquake that would threaten the rigid structure of his ego, based as this is on the repression of homoeroticism. The heterosexual insults, provokes and threatens the homosexual because he feels himself challenged by his presence, which besieges his 'normal' equilibrium by suggesting that he might himself be both object and subject of the gay desire.

According to Groddeck, as I have already pointed out, homosexuality is not completely repressed. Rather than repression, it is a question of a daily self-deception, a quasi-repression, a bad faith that leads the heterosexual to present himself as exclusively such, even though he knows in fact that he does have gay desires.[7] It is symptomatic of this that so many men maintain they have never wanted sexual relations with other men; they fear this might please them too much, and that they might become gay themselves ...

As a general rule, the heterosexual views the queer as 'filthy'. This is due, above all, to the fact that the 'normal' individual sees reflected in the gay person the homoerotic component of his own desire, negated and repressed in its anal eroticism, urophilia, coprophilia, etc. 'Normal' people consider 'filthy' any sexual acts bound up with those erotic tendencies which repression has induced them to renounce, giving rise in them – via the induced guilt of their repressed desire – to a particular authoritarian morality, which induces further guilt in its turn. 'Normal' people become maniacs of a certain type of orderliness (of *order* itself), of a certain type of cleanliness and of the police.[8]

---

7. Groddeck, *The Book of the It*, p. 231.

8. [Translator's note: Mieli here plays on a set of linguistic echoes and double meanings: *ordine* means both 'orderliness' and 'order' (in the sense of 'the forces of law and order'), while he sets up a pair between *pulizia* (cleanliness) and *polizia* (police).]

Homosexuals who go out cruising – and almost all gay men do so – know perfectly well that their pleasure very often involves them in breaking the law, disrupting order (even in those countries where homosexuality is not as such a criminal offence). We gays have almost invariably made love in the streets, in parks, in public toilets, in cinemas, museums, churches, in the Tuileries. We have been fucked behind barrack walls, we have sucked each other off kneeling in front of the tomb of Santa Croce, we have held splendid orgies under railway bridges. 'Normal' people can only see it as 'filthy' that we like to eat sperm and be fucked in the ass and that we perhaps do it in the churchyard of the Duomo, at noon, in front of people, and with them. Consider, for example, what the professor Franco Fornari said in reference to a challenge made against him during one of his lectures at the State University of Milan by the homosexuals of the ex-*Fuori!* Autonomous Collective (today called the Milanese Homosexual Collective): 'Homosexuals cannot stop me from doing my job by pretending to have a debate over an argument that doesn't concern my course: it's as if a group of sausage-makers interrupted my lesson to discuss proscuitto and salami.'[9]

From a psychoanalytic perspective, what this reveals is how the association made in this case by Fornari between homosexuals and sausage-makers is far from casual, denouncing in reality his essentially derogatory conception of homoeroticism: if, in fact, the 'proscuitto and salami' are meat from pigs [*porco*], and hence filth [*porcate*],[10] the homosexual-sausage-maker association allows Fornari to assert, indirectly, that homosexuals cannot come interrupt his class on psychology by forcing a debate about their filth. Moreover, the image of the salami obviously symbolizes a penis, while that of prosciutto the rear, the butt. In a word, Franco Fornari cannot tolerate that to his class have come those who want to discuss anal sex, those who are, according to him, *filthy pigs*.

One might note that Fornari, who in the pages of *Corriere della Sera*[11] has written, in spite of his true incompetence, of prosciutto and salami as one does of homosexuality, should at the very least expect to

9. See 'Omosessuali: parliamone in aula', in *Panorama*, n. 502 (4 December 1975).
10. [Translator's note: In Italian, as in English, the word *porco* (pig) can be used to disparage someone who is seen as gluttonous, filthy, and low, although the adjective *porcate* carries a stronger connotation of filth, excrement, and disgust than 'piggish' would in English.]
11. See the articles 'Omosessualità e cultura', in *Corriere della Sera*, (12 February 1975) and 'Il difficile amore diverso', (12 November 1975).

be contested in the university, that place in which he appears publicly, by sausage-makers, who would surely come forward in defence of their own interests and their own real competence in matters of pork.

Lastly, one can't forget that the sausage-maker slices and hacks apart the flesh of the pig. Fornari might therefore affirm: 'How dare those miserable sausage-makers come in to the university and interrupt my class to teach me my own trade of *butchering*?' But he would not say that: because in fact, what has so offended him was not the intervention of sausage-makers, which, beyond the pride of the butcher, could only prove an instinctive solidarity (*the rivalry of the shopkeepers* ...), but rather an intervention by filthy pigs, or rather by homosexuals, by human beings who he can only fathom as if swine, ready for slaughter.

Fear of Castration and the Parable of War

Elvio Fachinelli asks what lies 'at the root of the rejection of homosexuality (essentially of male homosexuality, given that female homosexuality today speaks a language that is very different and less significant, for reasons connected with the historic position of women)'.

It would be interesting to know why Fachinelli sees less significance in the 'language' of female homosexuality. Perhaps because he is a man and is thus concerned above all with his own rejection of male homosexuality. Anyway ... let's see what he says later.

> It is essentially, on the part of the heterosexual male, the fear of losing his masculinity in contact with the homosexual, i.e. something very deeply bound up with his personal identity. For the homosexual, he feels almost as if his very position as a male were being challenged, and hence his individual self-definition; it is as if this proved unexpectedly precarious or insecure, far more so than it generally is. Hence the reactions of rejection and disparagement, hence the various well-known behaviour patterns of aggressive hypermasculinity, which are often surprisingly accompanied by a certain solicitude for the homosexual in as much *as he acts like a woman*. If the homosexual falls into this trap (and falls easily, or willingly), the heterosexual can attack him all the more easily and reassure himself in the process. We can say, therefore, that the homosexual reawakens, as a male who seems to have suffered castration, the fear of castration that is latent in every man. And as simultaneously both male (which he ultimately is) and

> female, he is often experienced by the heterosexual as endowed with a paradoxical castrating and assimilating capacity.[12]

What Fachinelli says here is on the whole a valid interpretation, even if I would see it as risky to consider it an explanation of what 'lies at the root of the rejection of homosexuality'. Heterosexuals, as a general rule, tend to give over-hasty replies to the homosexual question (if rarely anything like as intelligent as this). We can add, however, that, if the homosexual usually reawakens the 'fear of castration' in the male heterosexual, this is also due to the fact that the heterosexual sees his own castration shown up by the gay man, i.e. the castration he has suffered with respect to his homoerotic desire. The heterosexual male fears losing his masculinity, and hence his heterosexual identity, because he knows this is all that remains to him of an Eros that has already been mutilated. And it is precisely because of this castration of his homosexual desire that he does not manage to understand homoeroticism as the totalising, satisfactory, full sexuality that it is, and so fears falling into a void were he to let himself be seduced into a gay experience. Since he knows his heterosexuality to be based on the loss of homosexuality (which does not necessarily mean he is consciously aware of this), the male is afraid of losing his heterosexual identity, should he abandon himself to his unknown homosexuality. In other words, he has internalised the evident if mysterious law of the system: either heterosexuality or homosexuality. Either-or.

According to the Milan *Fuori!* collective, the continuous violence inflicted on homosexuals,

> just like that exercised against women, is indissolubly bound up with the male's fear of losing his power over women. The man who goes to bed with another man is jeopardising his power, betraying the 'solidarity' among males, and this is why he brings all their repression down on himself.[13]

For many heterosexual men, the homosexual liberation struggle is a war waged against their Norm. Now in war, every army seeks ways of aiding

12. Elvio Fachinelli, 'Travesti', *L'Erba Voglio* 11, (May–June 1973), p. 38.
13. *Di omosessualità si muore,* a leaflet published by the Milan *Fuori!* collective on 25 October 1975, just one week before the death of Pasolini.

desertion from the other side. And in these last few years, the number of heterosexual males who desert has steadily grown, experimenting with homosexuality and experiencing the emancipating influence of the gay movement.

In a conflict, however, someone who deserts is generally exposed to a greater risk (at least if the army from which he deserts is not completely and irreversibly in rout), the risk of dying a shameful and infamous death, being labelled a traitor and accused of cowardice. Hence any army that fights intelligently understands the importance of positively attracting deserters from the enemy to its own ranks, and carries out propaganda of disaffection directed at the enemy camp. Propaganda of this kind can prove a deadly weapon, able to destroy a whole army without firing a shot (think of the puppet army of South Vietnam, literally broken apart by desertion).

If, on the other hand, the deserter is uncertain of his fate, and expects to face the inextinguishable hatred of the other side, if he fears risking a cruel death, should he take refuge in the opposing army, or being degraded by deprecation for his cowardice (the fate that his own side would inflict), then he will refrain from putting his planned desertion into practice, however sadly, and remain with his old comrades, continuing to depend on them for his physical survival.

Clearly, any desertion is going to be met with a certain diffidence. It must be, at the very least, individual and unreserved. The deserter will be enrolled in a company of trusty veterans, and certainly not left together with other deserters. Above all, the desertion of an entire enemy unit that wants to maintain its integral character is a cause for suspicion: men's awareness groups, for example, or the gangs of 'neo-homosexual' comrades, if we are to apply the metaphor to the present confrontation between gays and the heterosexual Norm, the deserters being those straight men 'in crisis' who can no longer fit completely into the army of normality and its ideology. Men's awareness groups have no other purpose than to prolong their dithering between the sacred 'normality' of the system and a gay, total opposition to it. We look forward to their dissolution, and to the participation of their former members in the revolutionary homosexual movement, particularly in its pleasures, in our particular pleasures.

To return to the war, given that little boys are so fond of playing at toy soldiers (whereas we queens prefer to be played with *by* toy soldiers). In the case of a group desertion, it is an elementary security measure to *break up* the deserting unit and distribute it in small nuclei among one's front line formations, those most experienced in combat (to put David Cooper in with the Gazolines, for example, or Franco Berardi with Our Lady of the Flowers).[14] More must be expected of the deserter than of any other soldier, just as he needs to be ensured of the fullest support and solidarity of his new comrades.

To give a final example. Let us assume that straight men are fighting in an all too normal colonial army engaged in massacring a colonised (read 'gay') population, who are nevertheless reacting courageously with ever bolder guerilla actions. The hetero colonialist males, despite the fact that their army still controls the main centres and road junctions in the region, and has formidable technical instruments of repression at its command, are unable to carry on. They are sickened by the reprisals which they have had to take part in, and by the atrocities in which they have been accomplices. The last village that they razed to the ground prevented them from sleeping. And so, after having carried out a commendable work of dissatisfaction in their platoon, they decide to desert en masse, bringing all the weapons that they can smuggle out – first among these a perfect knowledge of the mentality and methods of their former army. They venture out into the jungle that surrounds the occupied cities, in which the guerrillas are forced to hide. They are both frightened and fascinated. What holds them back is their uncertainty that the guerrillas will spare them once they reach their camp. In other words, they have deserted from the colonialist army, but they're still afraid of being fucked in the ass.

They take to the hills and begin to fight the colonialist army, and yet they still maintain operational autonomy, undertaking guerrilla actions and sabotage independently from the colonised guerrillas. The latter then have various options. They know very well that the presence of an independent white unit could have a decisive demoralising effect on the colonial army, and they are also aware that acceptance of a united struggle might involve innumerable dangers for the coordination and effectiveness of their actions. On the other hand, however, there is the risk that the deserters, still unrepentant colonialists, might degenerate into simple acts of brigandage against both armies: these are the bisexuals.

---

14. The Gazolines were the most outrageous group of queens and transvestites from the old Paris FHAR; Nostra Signora dei Fiori is a theatrical group within the Milan Homosexual Collective.

It would be opportune for the guerrillas to enter into negotiations with a view to co-opting the deserters. They can certainly agree that these should maintain their autonomy for a certain period of time, as long as they have not sufficiently given proof of their gayness; i.e. to see to what point the bisexuals, absolute heterosexuals until yesterday, are genuine deserters, and form part of the liberation struggle against the Norm.

The solution to this problem lies in the victory of the revolution, in the creation of communism, in the ending of all war, and the definitive withdrawal of all armies. Today, the revolution is being prepared, among other things, by the conflict between the gay movement and the Norm, and by the encounter between homosexuals and deserters from the army of normality. The heterosexual males 'in crisis' must understand that we do not want war: we are forced to struggle because we have always been persecuted, because the policemen of the heterosexual law have repressed us, because we look forward to the universal liberation of the gay desire, which can only be realised when your heterosexual identity is broken down. We are not struggling against you, but only against your 'normality'. We have no intention of castrating you. We want on the contrary to free you from your castration complex. Your ass has not really been amputated; it has only been accused [*imputato*], along with your entire body.

To come over to our side means, quite literally, to be fucked in the ass, and to discover that this is one of the most beautiful of pleasures. It means to marry your pleasure to mine without castrating chains, without matrimony. It means enjoyment without the Norm, without laws. It is only your inhibitions that prevent you from seeing that only by coming over to our side can we achieve our revolution. And communism can only be ours, i.e. belonging to us all, to those of us able to love: why would you want to be left out?

It is capital that still so insistently opposes you to us. What you have to fear is not being fucked in the ass, but rather remaining what you at present still are, heterosexual males as the Norm wants you to be, even in crisis, as if it was not high time to oppose yourselves forever to crisis, to castration, to guilt. As if it was not time to gayly reject the discontent that the present society has imposed on us, and to stop the totalitarian machine of capital in its tracks by realising new and totalising relations: and as we are bodies, erotic relations among us all.

You fear us on account of the taboo you have internalised, and which you still uphold. But this taboo is the mark of the system in you. And we don't want to be led into the catastrophe that is threatening, nor do we want the struggle for liberation, which has only one genuine enemy, capital, to be crippled by your resistances, dogmas and ditherings, by your susceptibility to images and your submission to the Father-system. Your terror of homosexuality is the capitalist terror; it is the paternal terror, the terror of the father that you have not overcome.

There have been wars in which the oppressors, sullied by atrocities, have degenerated to such a point that the only way for the oppressed to conquer has been to eliminate them to a man. In a case of this kind, it is impossible to expect many deserters. We find this in the Biblical wars: God commanded that none of the inhabitants of Jericho should survive the fall of the city. Instead of the 'Internationale', they play the Degüello.[15] They blow the trumpet of Jericho.

But we don't want to play those calls. What we propose is an erotic understanding: we don't want any more destruction, and it is exactly for this reason why we still have to struggle. Revolutionary wars are never anything like the destruction of Jericho.

In 1917 the Bolsheviks and all other revolutionaries proclaimed war on war and preached defeatism in all armies. The Russian revolutionary soldiers fraternised with the German 'victors', they danced together, embraced one another on the occupied Russian soil and shared their bread. Germany was defeated by the revolution brought home by the soldiers. The Red Army that was taking shape was created with the intent to fight war.

Only if the revolution had succeeded in Germany could Russia have been saved. The real loss wasn't at Brest-Litovsk but in Berlin. The French fleet's ammunition saved Russia from allied invasion. Isolated, Hungary, Bavaria, and the Ruhr fell one after another. Russia survived and would assume a new and more perfect repressive role.

We've all been defeated, therefore, in Warsaw. And each of us has their own Kronstadt. But the May that grows within us obliges us now, with gay clarity, to wage real war against capital and no one else. Eros to

15. [Translator's note: 'El Degüello' is a bugle call, most famous for its use by Mexican buglers in the Siege of the Alamo, where it signified that the attacking forces would show no mercy and give no quarter to those in the fort.]

you and to us, captivating sisters and attractive brothers of the universal incest that is announced and impending!

The Sublimation of Eros in Labour

> And meanwhile the proletariat, the great class embracing all the producers of civilised nations, the class which in freeing itself will free humanity from servile toil and will make of the human animal a free being – the proletariat, betraying its instincts, despising its historic mission, has let itself be perverted by the dogma of work. Rude and terrible has been its punishment. All its individual and social woes are born of its passion for work. – Lafargue[16]

According to the metaphysical theory that sees the process of civilisation as the conversion of powerful libidinal forces, their deviation from the sexual aim into labour and culture, repressed Eros may be viewed as the motive force of history, and labour as the sublimation of Eros.

In Freud's words:

> The tendency on the part of civilisation to restrict sexual life is no less clear than its other tendency to expand the cultural unit [. . .] Civilisation is obeying the law of economic necessity, since a large amount of the psychical energy which it uses for its own purposes has to be withdrawn from sexuality [...] Fear of a revolt by the suppressed elements drives it to stricter precautionary measures.[17]

Civilisation, therefore, is seen as having repressed those erotic tendencies that are subsequently defined as 'perverse', in order to sublimate this libidinal energy into the economic sphere (and into the social sphere, too: we have seen how Freud deemed the sublimation of homoeroticism a useful guarantee of social cohesion).[18] This is one of the most interesting hypotheses on the historical imposition of the anti-homo-

16. Paul Lafargue, *The Right to be Lazy* (Chicago: C. H. Kerr, 1975), p. 38.
17. 'Civilization and its Discontents', *Standard Edition* Vol. 21 (London: Vintage, 2001), p. 104. According to the 'mature' Freud, notes Francesco Santini, 'it is not just sexuality that civilisation represses and sublimates in economic activity, but also the death instinct, which is thus also put in the service of the reality principle and externalised in the aggressive conquest of nature. Man conquers and destroys his environment, and in this way avoids destroying himself, prolonging his journey towards death'. See 'Note sull'avenire del nostro passato', *Comune Futura* 1, (June 1975).
18. See Chapter 3, section 7.

sexual taboo, something that cannot be viewed in isolation, but must be considered in relation with other things, particularly the heterosexual Norm, marriage and the family, and the institutionalisation of woman's subjugation to man.

According to Marcuse:

> Against a society which employs sexuality as means for a useful end, the perversions uphold sexuality as an end in itself; they thus place themselves outside the dominion of the performance principle and challenge its very foundation. They establish libidinal relationships which society must ostracise because they threaten to reverse the process of civilisation which turned the organism into an instrument of work.[19]

This is already somewhat out of date, and needs to be revised. Today it is clear that our society makes very good use of the 'perversions'; you need only go into a newsagent or to the cinema to be made well aware of this. 'Perversion' is sold both wholesale and retail; it is studied, classified, valued, marketed, accepted, discussed. It becomes a fashion, going in and out of style. It becomes culture, science, printed paper, money – if not, then who would publish this book? The unconscious is sold in slices over the butcher's counter.

If for millennia, therefore, societies have repressed the so-called 'perverse' components of Eros in order to sublimate them in labour, the present system liberalises these 'perversions' with a view to their further exploitation in the economic sphere, and to subordinating all erotic tendencies to the goals of production and consumption. This liberalisation, as I have already argued, is functional only to a commodification in the deadly purposes of capital. Repressed 'perversion', then, no longer provides simply the energy required for labour, but is also to be found, fetishised, in the alienating product of alienated labour, which capital puts on the market in reified form. Precisely in order to be liberalised – which is to say and marketed – 'perversion' has to remain in essence repressed, and the libidinal energy that is specific to it must continue in large measure to be sublimated in labour and exploited: repressive desublimation is hence involved in the perpetuation of the coerced sublimation of Eros in labour. It is obvious that those erotic tenden-

19. Herbert Marcuse, *Eros and Civilization* (New York: Vintage Books, 1962), p. 46.

cies defined as 'perverse' cannot but remain repressed, as long as people continue to accept the truly obscene and perverted products that capital puts onto the market under the label of 'perverse' sexuality, and as long as there are still those who are content for their 'particular' impulses to be vented in a way that gives them a mediocre titillation from the squalid fetishes of sex marketed by the system. The struggle for the liberation of Eros is today, among other things, the rejection of a sexuality that is liberalised and packaged for sale by the permissive society: it is the refusal of sexual consumerism.

On the other hand, as capital has reached its phase of real domination – i.e. given that capitalist concentration and centralisation, inseparably bound up with the progress of the productive forces and the 'technological translation of science into industrial machinery' (H. J. Krahl) have reduced to a minimum the amount of necessary labour – the maximum portion of working hours now constitutes surplus labour, such that there is what Marcuse calls 'a change in the character of the basic instruments of production'.[20] This process was already foreseen by Marx in the *Grundrisse*:

> In this transformation, it is neither the direct human labour he himself performs, nor the time during which he works, but rather the appropriation of his own general productive power, his understanding of nature and his mastery over it by virtue of his presence as a social body – it is, in a word, the development of the social individual which appears as the great foundation-stone of production and of wealth.[21]

This transformation creates the essential premises for making the total qualitative leap realised in the communist revolution. And Marx adds:

> As soon as labour in the direct form has ceased to be the great well-spring of wealth, labour-time ceases and must cease to be its measure, and hence exchange-value [must cease to be the measure] of use-value. The *surplus labour of the mass* has ceased to be the condition for the development of the general wealth, just as the *non-labour of the few*, for the development of the general powers of the human head. With that, production based on exchange-value breaks down, and the

20. Marcuse, *One-Dimensional Man*, p. 38.
21. Marx, *Grundrisse*, p. 705.

> direct, material production process is stripped of the form of penury and antithesis. The free development of individualities, and hence not the reduction of necessary labour-time so as to posit surplus labour, but rather the general reduction of the necessary labour of society to a minimum, which then corresponds to the artistic, scientific etc. development of the individuals in the time set free, and with the means created, for all of them.[22]

In the face of this qualitative leap, standing as we do before the prospect of revolution and communism, sexual repression is obsolete and only serves as an obstacle. In fact, it maintains the forced sublimation that permits economic exploitation, 'the theft of alien labour-time' (Marx), the theft of pleasure (time) from woman and man, the constriction of the human being to a labour that is no longer necessary in itself, but only indispensable to the rule of capital. Labour, today, serves to preserve the outmoded relations of production, and to ensure the stability of the social edifice that is built upon these.

'Capital', writes Virginia Finzi Ghisi,

> has made use up till now of the erotic nature of labour in order to force man into this, having preventively withdrawn from him any other sexual adventure (relations with the woman-wife-mother in the family circle are no adventure, but only an extended substitution) [...] Heterosexuality becomes the condition for capitalist production, as a modality of loss of the body, a habituation to seeing this elsewhere, and generalised.[23]

The struggle for communism today must manifest itself also in the negation of the heterosexual Norm founded on the repression of Eros and essential for maintaining the rule of capital over the species. The 'perversions', and homosexuality in particular, are a rebellion against the subjugation of sexuality by the established order, against the almost total enslavement of eroticism (repressed or repressively desublimated) to the 'performance principle', to production and reproduction (of labour-power).

---

22. Ibid., pp. 705–6. (Marx's emphases.)
23. Virginia Finzi Ghisi, 'Le strutture dell'Eros', an essay published as an appendix to the Italian edition of the French FHAR's *Rapport contre la normalité.*

The increase in the means of production has already virtually abolished poverty, which is perpetuated today only by capitalism. And if the sublimation of the 'perverse' tendencies of Eros into labour is thus no longer economically necessary, it is even less necessary to channel all libidinal energies into reproduction, given that our planet is already suffering from over-population. Clearly, repressive legislation on the number of children, abortion, and the wars and famines decreed by capital, will not resolve the problem of population increase. Such things can only serve to contain it within limits that are functional to the preservation and expansion of the capitalist mode of production. They serve to increase the war industry and to maintain the Third World in conditions of poverty and backwardness that are favourable to the establishment of capitalist economic and political control. The problem of over-population can be genuinely resolved by the spread of homosexuality, the (re) conquest of autoerotic pleasure, and the communist revolution. What will positively resolve the demographic tragedy is not the restriction of Eros, but its liberation.

The harnessing of Eros to procreation, in fact, has never been really necessary, since free sexuality, in conditions that are more or less favourable, naturally reproduces the species without needing to be subject to any type of constraint. On the other hand, if the struggle for the liberation of homosexuality is decisively opposed to the heterosexual Norm, one of its objectives is the realisation of new gay relations between women and men, relations that are totally different from the traditional couple, and are aimed, among other things, at a new form of gay procreation and paedophilic coexistence with children.

In a relatively distant future, the consequent transsexual freedom may well contribute to determining alterations in the biological and anatomical structure of the human being that will transform us, for example, into a gynandry reproducing by parthenogenesis, or else a new two-way type of procreation (or three-way, or ten-way?). Nor do we know what the situation is on the billions of other planets in the galaxy, many of which, at least, must be far more advanced than ourselves.

If we can thus understand how the repression and sublimation of Eros, and the heterosexual Norm, are absolutely no longer necessary for the goals of civilisation and the achievement of communism, being in fact indispensable only for the perpetuation of capitalism and its barbarism, then it is not hard to discover in the expression of homoerotic desire a fertile potential for revolutionary subversion. And it is to this potential that is linked the 'promise of happiness' that Marcuse recognises as a peculiar character of the 'perversions'.

Finally, let us have done once and for all with the argument that the homosexual question is 'superstructural', and that priority should be given to the socio-economic (structural) level over the sexual struggle. Leaving aside the critique, no matter how important, of the mechanistic, undialectical, and post-Marxist sclerosis demonstrated by many so-called Marxists in their adoption of the notions of 'structure' and 'superstructure', it is nevertheless a grievous mistake to continue to treat the sexual question as only 'superstructural', given that labour itself, and hence the entire economic structure of society, depends on the sublimation of Eros. At the foundation of the economy, there is sexuality: Eros is *substructural.*

Even before this conception of the psychoanalytic matrix of economics and the fundamental function of libido in the process of civilisation, Marxism already affirmed the structural character of the sexual function, even though from a certain historically limited standpoint, since, among other things, its conception was heterosexual and thus partially ideological. As Engels wrote:

> According to the materialist conception, the determining factor in history is, in the final instance, the production and reproduction of immediate life. This, again, is of a twofold character: on the one side , the production of the means of existence, of food, clothing and shelter and the tools necessary for that production; on the other side, the production of human beings themselves, the propagation of the species. The social organisation under which the people of a particular historical epoch and a particular country live is determined by both kinds of production.[24]

Here we can see how the rigidly heterosexual social institutions of nineteenth-century Europe were the condition of the Engelsian idea of sexuality as a determining moment of history only in its procreative role. Engels, in particular, was strongly against homosexuality: in the *Origin of the Family*, he referred in particular to the men of ancient Greece who 'fell into the abominable practice of sodomy and degraded

---

24. Frederick Engels, *The Origin of the Family, Private Property and the State*, pp. 71–2.

alike their gods and themselves with the myth of Ganymede'.[25] Today, the materialist conception has recognised the structural importance of desire, which cannot be reduced to coincide with the procreative instinct alone. And on the other hand, our revolutionary critique must eliminate the prejudices present within Marxism itself, its masculine spirit that would 'ask a proletariat corrupted by capitalist ethics, to take a manly resolution ...'[26]

As for our heterosexual 'comrades', only if they free themselves from their structural fixations, from the mental superstructure that leads them to act in the way that the system allows, will they be able to grasp why the liberation of homosexuality is indispensable to human emancipation as a whole. At the present time, it is above all the repression of their own gay desire and their acceptance of the anti-homosexual taboo so dear to the system that leads them to treat the homosexual question in a capitalist fashion, and essentially to negate it.

The Absolutisation of Genitality, or, Heterosexual Idiocy

In 'Homosexuality and Culture', an article that appeared in *Corriere della Sera* in February 1975, Franco Fornari takes up the Freudian thesis on the origin of male homosexuality, expounded in *Group Psychology and the Analysis of the Ego*.[27] He wrote:

> The homosexual identifies himself with his own mother and imagines his own partner as a substitute for himself as a child. Adapting himself to representing his mother and his partner as the substitute for himself, the homosexual does not just want to recuperate, in an autarchic fashion, the irrecuperable relation of infantile love, but perform this operation through a confusing semantics, analogous to that of Narcissus, who mistakes his own reflected image for that of an other.

Ipse dixit: a Freudian hypothesis is transformed into absolute certainty under Fornari's pen, where it takes on the force of a court judgment on the unequivocally 'confused' character of gay 'semantics'. But the

25. Ibid., p. 128.
26. Paul Lafargue, *The Right to be Lazy*, p. 66.
27. See Chapter 1, section 8.

'semantics' of homosexual relations are 'confused' only to the degree in which they confuse Fornari, who doesn't know fuck all: and on the other hand, it's obvious that only we gays are capable of eviscerating and understanding the 'semantics' of homoeroticism. We homosexuals want heteros to quit condemning manifestations of gay desire, which starts from their own rigorous repression of that desire in themselves. If they censor a part of themselves and are convinced that all is going fine, how can they speak to those who live that part, if not in a prejudiced way?

In any case, before proceeding to examine Fornari's affirmations one by one, it seems opportune to me that we tackle one idea of his theory of sexuality. As Aldo Tagliaferri clearly delineated in his study *On the Dialectic Between Sexuality and Politics*, where he polemicises against the ideology of genitality illustrated by Fornari in *Genitality and Culture*:

> Fornari, with the commendable intent of resolving the antagonism between the natural and cultural, cuts the Gordian (and Freudian) knot of the relation between genitality and pregenitaltiy by cleanly distinguishing the two principles and illustrating the meaning of genital primacy, the 'apex of human development'. He judges pregenitality to be substantially extraneous to coupling and delineates its structure, antagonistic with respect to that of genitality, by following a symmetrical schema that we can therefore outline here. Genital relation is founded on exchange. It gives rise to controlled orgasm: it implies consensus and contractuality. The object reaches maximum valorization. It responds to a correct examination. Meanwhile pregenital relation is founded on predatory infantile appropriation. It gives rise to a pregenital orgasm that is not controlled by the Ego. It presides over the friend-enemy schema. It celebrates the omnipotence of the subject through a drive to appropriate. It is of an illusive nature.[28]

According to Fornari, the genital relation is exclusively heterosexual, while homosexuality re-enters in the pregenital sphere. In *Genitality and Culture*, he writes:

> As reflection hinges on the meaning of the perversions as a confused discourse and on the denial of dependence on the genital object and

28. Aldo Tagliaferri, *Sulla dialettica tra sessualità e politica*, in *Sessualità e politica: Documenti del congresso internazionale di psicoanalisi, Milano 25–28 novembre 1975* (Milan: Feltrinelli, 1976), p. 225.

> the overvaluation of the pregenital object, in reality it refers also to inversion. Ignoring the anal relations that can appear in homosexuals, inversion appears above to be the product, beyond any corporal confusion, as a confusion of persons, both in reference to the self and the non-self.[29]

And here he repeats the old rigamarole about 'introjective' and 'confused' identification of the homosexual with the mother, and the 'projective' and still 'confused' identification, on the part of the homosexual, of their partner with himself.

Before going further, I want to dwell for a moment on the 'anal relations that can appear in homosexuals' (which Fornari indeed ignores). Why *in* homosexuals? Why not *between* homosexuals? Evidently, what preoccupies our psychoanalyst above all, that which one really cannot ignore, is ass fucking:[30] the fact that someone can come *inside* you. But what of heterosexual ass fucking? Fornari leaps over that one too.

Tagliaferri reveals how Fornari extracts and separates genitality from the 'non-genital' or 'pre-genital':

> However, it's truly this that demonstrates the dependence of genitality on pregenitality. That which remains as qualifying as adult genitality is the so-called 'exchange drive'. But the drive is first and foremost elementary, and this elementary involves the unidirectionality of its originary intensity. That a drive could be considered as a component in the project of exchange is quite reasonable, but for this to be so, from its originary state, from its birth state, presenting itself as composite and mediated through the operation of exchange which it will itself lead, is in total contradiction with the very concept of drive. Drive in itself therefore brings us back (both historical and logically) to the intensive and prelogical world of infantile sexuality, which Fornari tries in vain to exorcize.[31]

---

29. Fornari, *Genitalità e culture*, p. 27.
30. [Translator's note: In Italian, the word is *inculare*, which would literally translate as 'to put in the ass', or even more literally, 'to in-ass'. Mieli italicises the prefix of *inculare* to emphasise this sense, which cannot be conveyed by any single English word. He also uses a complex parenthetical – *(inter)venergli* – to suggest that someone coming (*venire*) inside you is also a form of 'intervening' in atomised subjectivity.]
31. Tagliaferri, *Sulla dialettica*, p. 226.

In *Homosexuality and Culture,* Fornari also asserts that those who argue, like Pasolini in a much-discussed article on abortion, that we should encourage homosexual relations so as to confront the problem of population growth – i.e. *more deviancy, less pregnancy* – are pushing for a return of the collective repressed. And up to this point we can only agree with him. However, according to him, this repression constitutes the subconscious 'forest' of the imaginary, concealed in everyone underneath the primacy of heterosexual genitality.[32] Therefore, if only heterosexuality is considered 'normal' by 'culture', this happens because culture is a 'cultivation' set against that 'forest'. According to Fornari, however, to desire the spread of homosexuality is to set oneself against the 'real', opting instead for 'the imaginary in power': 'But while this can be a valid operation when it comes to bringing about a poetic project, entirely subject to human discretion, it certainly isn't when we're dealing with a political project, that's to say, a real cultural project centered on human survival [...] To survive requires that that we procreate', and if we all have nostalgia for those 'maternal waters', reality has taught us that no one would find themselves in those waters if there wasn't heterosexual coitus to create them.'[33]

But the 'reality' Fornari is referring to (that of the 'real' as opposed to the 'imaginary') is not reality in an absolute sense, because absolute reality doesn't exist: just as 'cultivation-culture' today is ideology, custom, and capitalist science, it is 'culture on the side of determined culture that Fornari accepts as Culture' (Tagliaferri). So too the 'reality' he deals with, which is merely the reality of capital, contingent and transitory despite pretending to be necessary and absolution, and against which the revolutionary communist movement fights. We are dealing with the reality that, from the perspective of revolution and human emancipation, must be wiped out forever rather than just altered with partial modifications that pile reality on reality and merely reform cultural 'cultivation'.

On the other hand, it is not in fact true that 'perversions', and in particular homosexuality, do not reckon daily with the reality principle, which certainly can't be reduced to the hypostasis of this determinate reality that Fornari holds to. Aldo Tagliaferri specifies:

---

32. [Translator's note: The word that I have translated as 'forest' throughout this section is *selva*, which might also be rendered as 'woods' or 'woodland'. It is crucial to note, however, that the word shares etymological roots and a general tone with the word *selvaggio*, which means 'wild' or 'savage'.]

33. Fornari, 'Omosessualità e cultura', p. 226.

> The pleasure principle and the reality principle are two abstract polarities that, as such, i.e. as absolute concepts, can be sustained separately only through a ridiculous operation. Fornari uses this radical separation only in order to discredit one of the two. However [...] we might take a specific point of view, that of the dialectical synthesis of the two principles, which conserves the positive sides of their natures. It conserves, I'd suggest, in the pleasure principle the qualification of *ends* and, in the reality principle, that of *means* [...] Both at the existential and the theoretical level, and as can be easily demonstrated, the projects aimed at recuperating pregenitality, other than those of an artistic nature, can be accompanied by a conscious examination of reality. When the reality principle that structures Marxism tries to extend by analogy to the sexual, its examination of reality must consist in taking sex into consideration in its real specificity, through a process of the scientific examination of the reality of the pleasure principle. It is therefore necessary to renounce the effort to cleanly separate, in reality, at least those behaviors that are linked to both principles, and to renounce the accompanying judgment that the pleasure principle must renounce the logic of the real.[34]

As for the 'forest' hidden beneath the actual form of 'cultivation', this is nothing more than a hypothesis that Fornari passes off as absolute truth in hopes of absolutising the actual form of 'reality'. We still know too little of our unconscious and our imaginary to describe it as a 'forest' as opposed to a 'luxurious garden'.

It is true that the psychic substrate which is 'projected' and focussed by 'schizophrenics' appears, above all in the eyes of 'normal' people, to be truly insane (though, at the same time, surprisingly frank and honest): the 'schizophrenic' trip undoubtedly undermines the ideological order. And it's also true that, in the unconscious, one finds 'the primitive man, as he stands revealed to us in the light of the research of archeology and ethnology'.[35] Nevertheless, if the experience of the 'schizophrenic' appears chaotic, that is due to the fact that the 'mad', isolated and marginalised, 'project' their interior universe onto the contorted world of capital, where 'reality' is more precisely the appearance which (un)covers

34. Tagliaferri, *Sulla dialettica*, p. 228.
35. Freud, 'Psycho-Analytic Notes on an Autobiographical Account of a Case of Paranoia', p. 82.

the reality of legal exploitation, of masculine privilege and sexual repression. 'Reality' is today the *appearance* that conceals an absurd and rational irrationality, the true reality of capital. And, vice versa, our interiority is thrown into disorder *insofar* as it reflects the chaotic characteristics and savage repression of the system. To conclude: the real *forest* is capitalist 'cultivation', which protects the heterosexual Norm and strangles all the branches of desire defined as 'perverse'.

We've seen how, if on one hand the perpetuation of the Norm guarantees the repression of Eros and its sublimation of labour, on the other *this* sublimation and *this* labour serve only to prolong the dominion of capital and barbarism. Today, there are above all useless factories that produce useless commodities, and useless and destructive reality (the whole of advertising serves to flog superfluous products). Today, it is a suffocating and cancerous 'cultivation' that dominates: we lack life, lack green, lack houses, lack breath. Our existence and our psyches are largely constructed like the polluted city of capital: too much useless and alienated work, too much absurd reality, too much unhappiness and non-communication that is choking out the human being within each of us, as within the society that is composed of us all.

The movement of communists struggles for the determination of a free future, for the realisation of that garden of intersubjective existence in which each plucks at will and according to their needs the fruits of the tree of pleasure, of knowledge, and of that 'science' that will be a *gay science*. The human being will have won its millenarian battle with nature: and then we will be able to enter into a harmonious relation with it and with ourselves.

Today, the historical premises necessary for the realisation of the 'reign of freedom' (Marx) have developed. Today, we aim to overthrow capital, which, forever uselessly and to its own exclusive advantage, pushes this struggle of human versus nature, and destroys them both. We revolutionary homosexuals are for life. That is, for total transformations. We must rescue humanity from its entire past, from that dark prehistory that weighs heavy inside us all.

Today, as it has always been since the dissolution of primitive communities, the repression of women forms the base of class exploitation which has now transformed into the *real domination* of capital over the species: 'The first class opposition that appears in history coincides with the development of the antagonism between man and woman in monogamous marriage, and the first class oppression coincides with that of the female sex by the male' (Engels).[36] Such oppression constitutes the substrate of the entire *prehistoric* dialectic of the opposition of classes up to our current time, and heterosexuality, or simply the Norm, performs an essential function for such oppression.

If it is true, as Fornari asserts, that we homosexuals identify with the mother instead of the father, it's also true that in this we can see one of the revolutionary potentials of our condition: the negation, however embryonic, of the antithesis of man and woman.

As for the theory of homosexual narcissism, it's clear that only a mentality calibrated by the sense of guilt and remorse linked to masturbation would speak of narcissism in only a negative way. And, if we do find narcissism in homosexual relations, it is in this very capacity to recognise ourselves in others that these relations can bring about a markedly revolutionary disruption, a revolt towards the attainment of communist intersubjectivity and the overcoming of that shimmering illusion of atomised individuality.

So if for Fornari seeing oneself in the other means disregarding the other, for us, on the contrary, it means recognising the other and what is common between us. Narcissus himself thought that he had found an other in that stream: the homosexual discovers himself in others, grasping humanity as such through the diversity that marks individuals. If Narcissus, in reaching to the water and to the world, poetically breaches the walls between I and not-I that are at the roots of the Western neuroses of the opposition between matter and mind, today it is impossible to have a totalising revolutionary reconciliation between human beings without that which we recognise in each other, in nature, in our bodies and the communal communist project. Narcissus, today, may well be taken up as a revolutionary symbol. NARCISO: *Nuclei 'armati' rivoluzionari comunisti internazionalisti sovversivi omosessuali* [Cells of 'armed' revolutionary communist internationalist subversive homosexuals].[37]

But could it be true, as Fornari maintains, that a homosexual sees in their partner a 'substitute for himself as a child?' I don't believe in

36. Friedrich Engels, *The Origin of the Family, Private Property and the State* (London: Lawrence and Wishart, 1972), p. 129.

37. [Translator's note: As is obvious, Mieli's reworking of the Italian name for Narcissus into a revolutionary acronym is largely untranslatable. However, it is worth noting here one specific element of his language: the word *nuclei*, which might be rendered as 'groups' or 'cells', had a particular resonance in the 1970s, as the word

the theory of the substitute, even if I believe that in moments of erotic intimacy, every person, whether heterosexual or homosexual, at times brings out the 'little kid' in their partner, the one that remains in every adult (and that, as the other is revealed at heart to be, so we are reminded of the kids we were and that we still guard within ourselves). Georg Groddeck writes of,

> this childishness from which we never emerge, for never do we quite grow up; we manage it rarely, and then only on the surface; we merely play at being grown up as a child plays at being big [...] Life begins with childhood, and by a thousand devious paths through maturity attains its single goal, once more to be a child, and the one and only difference between people lies in the fact that some grow childish, and some child-like.[38]

When a homosexual makes love with a man much older than him, he can certainly get folded into the role of the child; but more frequently, he'll find 'ghosts' stirred up in him that, if we really want to tie it back to childhood, remind him of adults he knew in the past, when he was a kid.

Love is beautiful because it is various: only Fornari would think to generalise, for all homosexuals, a single type of erotic situation (which, if understood properly, isn't even what actually happens in the terms he has established).

But, in *Genitality and Culture*, Fornari goes even further. In fact, he asserts that after having 'consummated' a sexual relation, gays always experience a sensation of immediate disgust for each other and for themselves. This is such idiocy that I don't think it's worth responding to, even if, when faced with an affirmation of this kind, you can't help reflecting for a moment on what portentous lies our professors pawn off as 'reality' and 'science'. Fornari maintains that the homosexual,

---

was used by far-left groups to mark a horizontal, potentially proliferating form of organisation that would allow the formation of small cadres, rather than a single unified party form. Mieli's imagined group name riffs especially off of Nuclei Armati Proletari (Armed Proletarian Groups/Cells), a radical organisation formed in Naples that was active from 1974 to 1977. Inspired in particular by Frantz Fanon and George Jackson, NAP carried out a string of kidnappings, bombings, and assassinations, and they placed particular focus on the liberation of, and solidarity with, those who were incarcerated.]

38. Groddeck, *The Book of the It*, pp. 18–19.

repeating certain 'distortions of infantile sexuality', hoodwinked by the illusory symbolic equation of 'breasts = butt': in plain terms, the homosexual would exchange their partner's ass for the lost maternal breast if they could. And so,

> in the moment when, during an act of pederasty, a boy or young man becomes a sexual object, the yearning for the maternal-breast comes alive in the illusion of a total possession of those lost breasts, which become part of himself, through parts of a fantastic object that is at once part of him and of the mother. However, the fact that the buttocks, on the plane of the real [i.e. rather than imaginary], are not plausible as containers of milk but are instead containers of faeces, shows the infantile illusions that rest behind the homosexual tendency to collapse after achieving satisfaction, having fallen for the swindle that is implicit in the phrase 'being taken for an ass'. The construction of homosexual libido [...] has to reckon with the inevitable delusion to which anal omnipotence exposes itself, through the way in which it tries to ward off a threatening sensation by forcibly envisioning as an exchange of good things what is in truth actually an exchange of bad things.[39]

As for what counts as those 'bad things', we have to ask Fornari when was the last time he ate shit and found it bad . . . That shit is bad, as Fornari maintains, is a pre-judgment: give it a taste and then let us know (holding aside the fact that coprophilia doesn't have to end in coprophagy).

As for the expression 'being taken for an ass', the meaning of the 'swindle' must be attributed to the 'culture' of male heterosexuality, sex-phobic and anti-gay as it is: for us homosexuals, need we repeat this, to take it in the ass isn't a swindle or scam, but the real deal, so pleasurable and having nothing whatsoever to do with some illusory equation of 'butt = breast'. My ass is mine, and I know damn well that a breast is a different part of the body. So when we desire to fuck someone else in the ass, it isn't because we keep confusing their butt with Mama's breast: and even if this were the case, on some deep level, would that be so bad? We know well how the associations of the unconscious – of everybody's unconscious, including the 'normal' ones – are rather 'original' and bizarre,

39. Fornari, *Genitalità e cultura*, p. 67.

and certainly don't line up with the 'logical' relations of an illusion that Fornari considers as 'reality'. In any case, it would be worth establishing on the basis of what extraordinary intellectual faculty Fornari manages to root out the truth of our interiority better than any of us fags can hope to manage (though we've at least got a little *sense of humour*).[40] By the way: what are we to say about all those men who, during their heterosexual encounters, get a few fingers up the ass from women? Have they confused the finger of their partner for the long-desired dick of the father? Or were they were nursed with a bottle?

Evidently, pawning off these facile interpretations as 'reality' is just the easiest way to disregard *reality*, to deform it and to simultaneously secure yourself a chair of Psychiatry in the capitalist university, along with a little space in the culture pages of *Corriere della Sera*.

For Fornari, then, homosexuality is regressive because it is founded on the desire to recreate in love the lost infantile relation between the mother and son. So what does this therefore say about heterosexuality, that, on the man's part, it is directly centred on the unconscious desire to reenter into the maternal womb, to return to the fetal state? Clearly Fornari seems to have forgotten the Ferenczi of *Thalassa*, that masterful work which for Freud defined the Hungarian psychoanalyst, who had been his disciple, as now his master. But let's borrow from Groddeck again. According to him, it is actually male heterosexuality that is based on the desire to recreate the lost amorous relations with the mother. Moreover,

> A much more important question for me than the love for one's own sex, which necessarily follows upon self-love, is the development of love for the opposite sex. The matter seems simple in the case of the boy. The life within the mother's body, the years of dependence on woman's care, all the tenderness, joys, delights and wish-fulfillments which only the mother gives or can give him, these are so mighty a counterbalance to his narcissism that one need seek no further.[41]

And finally, is it true, as Fornari proclaims, that heterosexual coitus must always precede conception, both now and in the future? It isn't so: many feminists and many homosexuals aren't in agreement with Fornari and

40. [Translator's note: Mieli writes *sense of humour* in English in the original.]
41. Groddeck, *The Book of the It*, p. 234.

see this absolutisation of the world of actual reproduction as phallocentric. It doesn't help to speak of artificial insemination or the like, because it is already difficult enough to imagine what enormous consequences will follow from the liberation of women and Eros. To reiterate: Fornari, skulking in the shadows cast by the dazzle of heterosexual capitalist ideology, tries to assert the absolute hypostasis of a reality, whose future overthrow is, in fact, exceedingly possible to imagine, just as it was possible to theorise (like Ferenczi, for example) the hypothetical origin of the long-ago past of living species.

Heterosexuality is not *eternosexuality*. Heterosexual procreation is not eternal, no matter the obstinacy with which reactionary heterosexuals, Fornari among them, strictly bind the absolutisation of the primacy of their genitality to a use that is arbitrary, anti-materialist, un-dialectic, and derived from a truly obscurantist concept of 'nature'. Again and again, committed heterosexuals hail the dichotomy between 'nature' and 'against nature', as if to assure themselves – it's a small step – that heterosexuality reigns supreme thanks for the grace of God. *Oh my gay God!*[42]

'Normals' Faced with Transvestites. Notes on the Family

So-called 'normal' people are so adapted to the male heterosexual code that they are in no position to understand, as a general rule, the relativity, contingency and limitation of the concept of 'normality'.

Fornari played it well to give them nonsense to swill, from the pages of newspapers to those of his treatises. 'Normal' persons ask for nothing more than to have their own prejudices confirmed by some authority: they are ready to sing the praises of whoever, as long as that person sustains that Science, Culture, and Reality co-validates what the Norm sanctions. The 'normals' search for a tautological relation with 'science': they pretend that those who study predict that which has always constituted the ideological pre-given in which they can see reflected back their identity as 'normal'.

Thus if heterosexuals have always seen homoeroticism as a vice, some psychologist will come along and maintain that homosexuals are 'immature and confused'. 'Perversions' have to be stigmatised, today by a 'scientific' veil made up of the most insolent lies: 'as if they exerted a

42. [Translator's note: this final sentence is in English in the original.]

seductive influence; as if at bottom a secret envy of those who enjoy them had to be strangled'.[43]

'Normal' people do not tolerate gays, and not just because, by our very presence, we display a dimension of pleasure that is covered by a taboo, but because we also confront anyone who meets us with the confusion of his monosexual existence, mutilated and beset by repression, induced to renunciation and adaptation to a 'reality' imposed by the system as the most normal of destinies.

We can observe, for example, the attitude of 'normal' people towards transvestites. Their general reaction is one of disgust, irritation, scandal. And laughter: we can well say that anyone who laughs at a transvestite is simply laughing at a distorted image of himself, like a reflection in a fair-ground mirror. In this absurd reflection he recognises, without admitting it, the absurdity of his own image, and responds to this absurdity with laughter. In effect, transvestism translates the tragedy contained in the polarity of the sexes onto the level of comedy.

It is not hard to grasp the common denominator that links, in a relationship of affinity, all the various attitudes people assume towards queens, and towards transvestites in particular. These reactions, whether of laughter or something far more dangerous, only express, in different degree and in differing qualitative forms, a desire extraverted under the negative sign of aggression and fear – or more precisely, anxiety. It is not really the queen or transvestite who is an object of fear for 'normal' people. We only represent the image that provides a medium between the orbit of their conscious observations and an obscure object of radical fear in their unconscious. This anxiety is converted into laughter, often accompanied by forms of verbal and even physical abuse.

The person who laughs at a transvestite is reacting to the faint intuition of this absurdity that he already has – as has every human being – and which the man dressed as a woman, who suddenly appears before him, externalises in the 'absurdity' of his external appearance. The encounter with the transvestite reawakens anxiety because it shakes to their foundations the rigidly dichotomous categories of the sexual duality, categories instilled into all of us by the male heterosexual culture, particularly by way of the family, which right from the start offers the child the opposition of father and mother, the 'sacred' personifications

43. Freud, 'A General Introduction to Psychoanalysis', quoted by Marcuse, *Eros and Civilization*, p. 45.

of the sexes in their relationship of master and slave. We all form and establish our conceptions of 'man' and 'woman' on the models of our parents, the one as virility, privilege and power, the other as femininity and subjection. To these models, which bind us to them thanks to the hallowed web of family ties that determines our personality, we adapt our conception of anyone who, in the course of life, we encounter or even merely think of. We think only in terms of 'man' or 'woman', to the point that we cannot even imagine anything but 'men' or 'women'. In ourselves, too, we can recognise only the 'man' or the 'woman', despite our underlying transsexual nature and despite our formation in the family, where our existential misery is determined by our relationship to mother or father. The child of the master-slave relationship between the sexes sees in him- or herself only one single sex. This singleness does not seem contradicted by the evident fact that we are born from a fusion of the sexes. And yet we need only look in the mirror (during a trip) to see clearly in our features both our mother and our father. Monosexuality springs from the repression of transsexuality, and transsexuality is already denied before birth. Conception itself, in fact, proceeds from the totalitarian negation of the female sex by the proclaimed uniqueness of the phallus as sexual organ in coitus and its 'power' in the parental couple.

But the phallus does not coincide exactly with the penis, even if it is superimposed on it. While the penis is what distinguishes the male anatomically, the phallus represents the patriarchal absolutising of the idea (of male power) which the penis embodies, an idea that characterises all history to date as his-story. In a world of symbols, the ideal symbology of power assumes a phallic form.

Concretely, this 'power' is based on the repression of Eros, which is a repression of the mind, the body and the penis itself, and above all the negation of femininity. In the present prehistory, it is first and foremost a function of the oppression of women.

From the negation of the female sex in the heterosexual relationship, individuals are born either male or female, the former sexual (as bearers of the penis, the bodily vehicle of the unique sexual organ in the patriarchal phallic conception), the latter 'female eunuchs'. Either, or. The tragedy is that 'normal' people cannot tolerate the transvestite showing up the grotesque aspects of this process, committing an act of sacrilege in confusing the sacred opposition between the sexes, given that he combines in himself both sexes, daring to impose a femininity which has been reduced to a mere appearance onto the reality of a male self. The transvestite sins very gravely, demanding vengeance from the guardians of the phallus.

If the child of the heterosexual relation is a male, he finds himself forced to suffocate his own 'femininity' and transsexuality, since edu-castration obliges him to identify with the masculine model of the father. The son has to identify with a mutilated parent, who has already negated his own 'femininity' and who bases his privilege in the family and in society precisely on his mutilation. The father is unaware of this process, or does not want to be aware of it, but presents as a 'natural mutilation' both the natural difference of women and their mutilation as the work of male 'power', which he, as the guardian of the order, perpetuates. The father negates the mother sexually, a fate to which she was already condemned from birth (since from the patriarchal standpoint she is only a second-class human being, lacking a penis); even before birth, since the repression of femininity and of women has prevailed for millennia.[44] In his sexual relations with the mother, the father generally absolutises the passive role of the woman, her function as hole and receptacle for the phallus with which he is endowed, and which is presented, visibly active, as the sole sexual organ, establishing a symbolic form in which female sexuality – in fact all sexuality – is alienated. The child sees this clearly in all aspects of the relationship between the parents.

If the child is a girl, then the daughter of the heterosexual couple is condemned to view herself in the stereotype of 'femininity', as the negation of woman, and by way of education she is forced to identify with the servile model of her mother. Educastration consists not only in the concealment of the clitoris, but also in the repression of homosexual desire and transsexuality, of woman' s whole erotic existence. Female (trans)sexuality has to be violently repressed so that the woman can appear 'feminine', can be subjected to the male and to the insults inflicted on her by his sexuality, the 'only true sexuality.' On the basis of the Norm, female sexuality cannot exist except as something subordinate. It must not exist in and for itself, but only outside itself, for someone else.

'All this removes any surprise from the fact that historically, femininity has always been perceived as castration, so that according to Freud, at

44. Matriarchal society began to break down in the period that Engels, following Morgan, refers to as 'barbarism' (8000–3000 BC), giving way to 'civilisation'. According to Engels: 'The overthrow of mother right was the *world-historical defeat of the female sex*' (Engels, *The Origin of the Family, Private Property and the State*, p. 120).

a certain moment the child sees the mother as a mutilated creature, and from then on always lives in fear of castration'.[45] Or as Adorno puts it (and these are both only male views):

> Whatever is in the context of bourgeois delusion called nature, is merely the scar of social mutilation. If the psychoanalytical theory is correct that women experience their physical constitution as a consequence of castration, their neurosis gives them an inkling of the truth. The woman who feels herself a wound when she bleeds knows more about herself than the one who imagines herself a flower because that suits her husband. The lie consists not only in the claim that nature exists where it has been tolerated or adapted, but what passes for nature in civilisation is by its very substance furthest from all nature, its own self-chosen object. The femininity which appeals to instinct, is always exactly what every woman has to force herself by violence – masculine violence – to become: a she-man.[46]

In the name of the phallus, the male is forced to deny the sensuality of his ass, and his erotic fullness in general. Ashamed of the ass for being a hole, and yet (in Sartre's phrase) 'the presence of an absence' as much as the vagina and the woman's ass, he comes to conceive it as 'the absence of a presence': i.e. he does not realise that he could enjoy his ass, and sees it as the greatest shame and dishonour to have its sexuality recognised and exercised on himself. The male sentiment of honour springs in fact from shame. The Arabs, among whom male homosexuality is almost universal, paradoxically view it as highly dishonourable for a man to be fucked. They abhor the 'passive role'.[47] This kind of discrimination, and

45. Francesco Santini, *Comune Futura* 1, p. 28.

46. Theodor Adorno, *Minima Moralia* (London: Verso, 2005), pp. 95–6.

47. See Piero Fassoni annd Mario Mieli, 'Marcocco miraggio omosessuale', *Fuori!* (4 October 1972), also 'Les arabes et nous', in *Grande Encyclopédie des Homoséxualités*, pp. 10–27, and the following articles. Very little is known in Europe of the situation of homosexuality among the Arab peoples, and the Islamic nations in general. In fact, homosexuality forms part of the Islamic religious tradition. In a contradictory fashion, this accepts active homosexuality while condemning the passive role. For the *meddeb,* the teacher in the Koranic school, it is quite proper to have sexual relations with his young disciples. Yet this should not give the impression that homosexuality only takes the form of sexual attraction towards adolescents. If this were the case, then the limitation of adults to an active role would be simpler to explain. The ephebe, in the patriarchal view of things, unites the woman and the man, and this

the sexual fascism it involves, is very widespread also among the Italians, the Latin peoples in general, and very many others. 'Double males' are even to be found in Greenland.

Forced to murder his own 'femininity', so as to meet the imperative model of the father, the male child cannot love a woman for what she is, since he would then have to recognise the existence of female sexuality, finding in it a reflection of the 'femininity' within himself. He comes to love women above all as objectifications and holes, and hence does not really love them at all. He tends rather to subjugate them, in the same way that he has already subjugated the subterranean presence of 'femininity' in himself, on the altar of virility.

For him, heterosexual love is the negation of woman, the mutilation of the transsexual Eros. It is a tangle of projections and alienations. 'You are my anima, I am your animus. With you I sense only having overcome isolation. I see nothing of you but that which you do not see of me.' The system sanctions the negation of love, institutionalising it in the heterosexual Norm and hence in that ' normality' which is the law of the sole sexuality of the phallus. And it condemns homosexuality as a rebellion against the subjection of Eros to the order of production and reproduction, and against the institutions (in particular the family) that safeguard this order.

Far from murdering his father so as to espouse his mother, the son rather murders his own 'femininity' so as to identify with the father. He is subsequently forced to blind himself by repressing into the shades of the unconscious, the vision of the tragedy he was forced to perpetrate, so that the 'femininity' he condemned to death will not revive in the darkness of the established patriarchal destiny. For Freud, heterosexuality is the 'normal dissolution' of the Oedipus complex. Homosexuality, which is the inverted solution to the tragedy, the homosexuality which, as Ferenczi put it, is an 'inversion on a mass scale', is condemned and excluded because it involves the risk, for male 'power', that the real version of the tragedy will become clear, to be genuinely dissolved and overcome for ever more. 'Only a particular love', wrote Virginia Finzi Ghisi, 'can perhaps show up the particular nature of the universal relation par excel-

determines his fixation to the passive role. The Arabs, however, are happy to fuck adult men as well, and frequently do so. It is as if the moral blame that their religion ascribes to a man who is fucked does not involve them, although they will often enough suggest the activity.

lence, i.e. the natural sexual relationship, the love of man and woman that reflects in the little magic circle of the family or couple the identical structure both founded on it and founding it, the structure of the big family (the office, factory, community, the world market).' Homosexuality makes possible 'the decomposition of the roles that the generalised natural relationship has crystallised, and the recomposition of new roles, complex and bizarre, and rich in shading: 'All men are women and all women are men.'[48]

Homosexuality is a relation between persons of the same sex. Between women, it proclaims the autonomous existence of female sexuality, independent of the phallus. Between men, even though historically marked by phallocracy, homosexuality multiplies the sexual 'uniqueness' of the phallus, thus in a certain respect negating it, and discloses the availability of the ass for intercourse and erotic pleasure. Moreover:

> In the homosexual relation between both men and women, power and its agency are put in question. Two social victors or two social vanquished find themselves equally forced to abandon and reassemble affection/power/absence of power, they cannot simply distribute them according to the social division of roles. This might seem very trivial, but it puts in crisis the foundations of the distributive order of the present society, its mode of politics, and the structure of political groups themselves.[49]

Repetition Compulsion. The Ghetto. Coming Out at Work.

The union of male bodies, though paradoxically the union of penises, undermines the authoritarian abstraction of the phallus. But male homosexuality can also present itself as doubly phallic, or – in the ideology of the 'double male' – as maximally repressed, an unreserved mimicry of the heterosexual model. In such a case, the sexual relation between men is an alienating lack of communication. Given that homosexuality is considered and socially treated as an 'aberration' – or rather, that passive homosexuality is deemed dishonourable and disreputable, as in the Islamic countries among others – the gay desire, made guilty in this way, can find a certain justification by fully adapting to the laws of

48. Virginia Finzi Ghisi, 'Le strutture dell'Eros', p. 172.
49. 'I gruppi di fronte alia questione omosessuale', *Re Nudo* (5 November 1975).

male 'power', becoming an actual champion of this. Even lesbians can be forced into such behaviour.

It is necessary at this point to remember that the homosexual, just like the heterosexual, is subject to a fixation to norms and values, the heritage of Oedipal phallocentric educastration, and to the compulsion to repeat. Educastration, as Corrado Levi shows, 'tends to predispose and crystallise the libido of us all, by continuous acts of repression and examination, into images and models that subsequently underlie successive behaviours, in the coerced tendency to seek these and act them out'.[50] These images and models are all bound up with the values presently in force in the capitalist context.

> The crystallising of desire onto acquired images tends to lead, and at times in an unambiguous way, to ruling out all other images that are different from these. Only certain images of man and woman are sought (whether heterosexual or homosexual), and we pursue physical types that we have associated with these images: young or old, blond or dark, with or without beard, bourgeois or proletarian, male or female, etc., tending to selectively rule out . . .

one of the two terms. The fixation of behaviour to family models, moreover, determines the type of relationship with the partner: 'as a couple, a threesome, active, passive, paternal, maternal, filial, etc. Only through these filters and diaphragms can we then act, and see both ourselves and those persons we are involved with, who respond in their turn with analogous mechanisms'. Models, images and behaviour tend in general to be delineated in a perspective of male capitalist values: domination, subordination, property, hierarchy, etc., 'and this is connected', Corrado Levi concludes, 'with both the contents of the models followed and the mechanism by which they are pursued'.

Yet if these filters and diaphragms, these mechanisms, are in part common to both heterosexuals and gays, it is also true that, on the basis of the flaw that our behaviour, as a transgression of the Norm, represents for the present society, we homosexuals are in a position to put them in question, by discovering in our own lives a deep gap between the

---

50. Corrado Levi, 'Problematiche e contributi dal lavoro di presa di coscienza del coliettivo *Fuori!* di Milano', 1973 . These quotations are drawn from the printed version of this essay, published as an appendix to *Un tifo* (Milan, 1973).

rules transgressed and the norms still accepted, and by the contradiction this creates in the system of prevailing values. It may well be that the growth of our movement has not yet led us to a complete unfixing of the internalised models and the compulsion to repeat and pursue them. But it has at least led us to question them, developing in us the desire to experiment, and suggesting new and different behaviours alongside and as a gradual replacement for the repetitive and coerced ones. This has happened above all in the USA, where the gay movement is so far much stronger than in Europe, and has brought about a considerable change in the social and existential conditions of homosexuals (in some States in particular), despite the insufferable continuation of the rule of capital. In America above all, we can see the rebirth of sexual desire between gays, which in our part of the world is still to a large degree latent, the fantasy of the heterosexual male, the *bête,* the 'supreme object' of desire, being still very much alive in many of us.

But the situation in the ghetto is certainly far from rosy, in America and in Europe, Japan or Australia. Often, many of us still tend to oscillate between repression and exaggerated ostentation, putting (deliberately) in doubt the genuineness of our 'effeminacy'. This leads to a situation in which all spontaneity and sincerity is outlawed, and replaced by the pantomime of 'normality' or an 'abnormality' which is simply its mirror image. The exponents of such spectacles often end up making the ghetto appear monstrous to our own eyes, not to mention to those more or less scandalised by the far more monstrous heterosexual society that surrounds it.

One particular iron rule seems often to apply in the ghetto. Lack of spontaneity, of naturalness and affection, is often made into a sacrosanct norm, 'communication' taking place by way of a series of witty quips, spectacular entrances and exits, arrows directed with unheard-of precision (unheard-of for heterosexuals). The ghetto queen is a past mistress not only of decking out herself and her apartment, in creating a certain atmosphere, in managing her own mask better than anyone else (which from daily use becomes an identification), she is also mistress of fazing other queens. Many homosexuals today wear the uniform of their persecutors, just as in the Nazi concentration camps. Only it is no longer the pink triangle that is in vogue, but rather a casing that covers the body from head to foot, a mask that conceals the physiognomy, a carapace that constrains the body like a crustacean.

The system has ghettoised and colonised us so deeply that it frequently leads us to reproduce, in a grotesque and tragicomic form, the same roles and the same spectacle as the society that excludes us. This is precisely why we gays can often see through the misery that surrounds 'our' ghetto, and at times with exceptional aesthetic sense and irony. And yet if the present society can come to terms with the ironic finesse that some of us display, and is entertained by the inverted homosexual reflection of its own image, at the same time it does not contain its disgust at the real ghetto (or what it sees of it), and attacks it in a racist fashion.

But the ghetto is not outside the society that has built it. It is an aspect of the system itself. Moreover, the awareness of marginalisation and the sense of guilt induced by social condemnation poison the ghetto, leading it to assume the same distorted sneer as the society that derides it. And if homosexuals are very often not attracted by one another, this is very largely due to the ghetto atmosphere, which is anti-homosexual, precisely because it's held together by a false guilt and a very real marginalisation.

Homosexuals have been so much led always to see themselves as sick that at times they actually believe themselves to be so. This is our real sickness, the illusion of sickness that can even make people really sick. In a similar manner, people shut up for long enough in mental hospitals can end up showing the stereotyped signs of 'madness', i.e. the traces of the persecution they have experienced, its 'therapy' internalised in the form of sickness. Doctors (psychiatrists and anti-psychiatrists alike) are the real plague spreaders, and the real sickness is the 'treatment'.

Often, the illusion of being in some way sick affects the homosexual to such a point that he tries to disguise his own being, a distortion that he is forced to live as a deformation. If we homosexuals sometimes appear ridiculous, pathetic or grotesque, this is because we are not allowed the alternative of feeling ourselves to be human beings. 'Mad' people, blacks, and poor people all bear on their brow the mark of the oppression they have undergone.

But this mark can be transformed into a sign of new life. The face of a transvestite can burn with the gayness of liberated desire, an energy pointing towards the creation of communism. The war against capital has not been lost. Ever more homosexuals today, instead of struggling in silence against themselves, in individual anxiety and the seclusion of the ghetto, are beginning to fight[51] gayly with their eyes open, with bodies open, for the revolution.

It is no time now to conceal our homosexuality. We must live it always and everywhere, in the most open way possible – even at our jobs, too, if we are not to be accomplices of all who still oppress us. Anyone who is afraid of losing his job can come out with moderation, and if necessary, it is possible to maintain a certain reserve without making shabby compromises with the Norm. Things can still be clearly said without using so many words, and one can act in a way that is compatible with one's ideas and desire while avoiding, for the time being, coming out explicitly, if this is impossible without getting sacked. True, the situation is far more difficult for gays in small towns in the provinces. But we can hope that soon the positive effects of the liberation movement will make themselves felt even here.

Given that people are forced to work in factories and offices, it is good that homosexual collectives should be formed here too. Union gives the strength to come out openly, and gay groups in schools and colleges are also steadily on the rise, even in Italy.

I have a friend who works in a bank, where he gets through the good and bad times with wit and wisdom. He recently marched past his colleagues and bosses, mimicking a parade of spring and summer fashions for bank clerks. His colleagues were entertained, and when one of them stupidly asked what the meaning of it all was, he replied: 'I'm crazy', leaving it to the others to wonder whether he really was crazy, or if he indeed takes it in the ass.

In this and who knows how many other ways, the cause of liberation makes headway, without heroism, without even risking the sack. Every queen does what she can, according to the situation in which she finds herself. The important thing is to do one's best (i.e. to work out how one can obtain the best results), and to avoid being trapped by and resigning oneself to the Norm.

To spread homosexuality in one's place of work, today, means spurring people to reject a labour that no longer has any reason to exist, and which largely consists of sublimated homoerotic desire. It is sufficient to enter an office or a factory to immediately sense how the degrading atmosphere of the workplace is pervaded with repressed and sublimated

51. [Translator's note: Mieli once more uses his untranslatable pun, which means both *to fight* and *to cruise*.]

homosexuality. 'Colleagues' at work, while rigorously respecting the anti-homosexual taboo as capital would have them, make sexual advances to each other eight hours a day in the most extraordinary manner, as well as exhibiting themselves as rivals towards women. In this way, however, they only play the game of capital, establishing a false solidarity between men, a negative solidarity that sets them against women and against one another in the purposeless (and hardly gratifying) perspective of rivalry, of competition to be tougher, more masculine, more brutish, less fucked over in the general fucking over, which – despite the label – has no other purpose save enslavement to the capitalist machine, to alienated labour, and forced consent to the deadly repression of the human species, of the proletariat.

If the gay desire among 'colleagues' at work were liberated, they would then become genuine colleagues, able to recognise and satisfy the desire that has always bound them together; able to create, via their rediscovered mutual attraction, a new and genuine solidarity between both men and women; able to embody together, women and queers, the New Revolutionary Proletariat. Able to say 'enough' to labour and 'yes' to communism.

Subjection and the Revolutionary Subject

I believe it follows from the arguments put forward in these pages that only those who find themselves in opposition to the institutionalised Norm can play a fully critical role. In other words, only feminist self-consciousness and homosexual awareness[52] can give life to a vision of the world that is completely different from the male heterosexual one, and to a clear and revolutionary interpretation of important themes that have been obscured for centuries, if not actually proscribed, by patriarchal dogma and the absolutising of the Norm. Women represent the

52. This does not mean that I support uncritically all the feminist and gay groups that presently exist, still less put them blindly on a pedestal; see Chapter 2, section 6. It is necessary to point out the counter-revolutionary aspects of the *politics* of some groups, and to deplore the male supremacy of gay men and the anti-homosexual attitude still current among too many feminists. But a critical analysis of the situations in which feminist and gay groups are debating will precisely demonstrate the immense importance of the issues that they are confronting. Their great merit is to have been the first to raise certain fundamental questions that have been repressed from a very remote time, and they are consequently in the best position to resolve these in practice.

basic opposition potential to male 'power', which, as we have seen, is in every way functional to the perpetuation of capitalism.

And if it is the male heterosexual code that prevents us achieving that qualitative leap leading to the liberation of transsexuality which desire fundamentally strives towards, we cannot avoid accepting the potential and now actual subversive force of homosexuality in the dialectic of sexual 'tendencies', just as we cannot deny the revolutionary position occupied by women in the dialectic of the sexes.

To those anti-psychiatrists who have worked to understand the repressed transsexual nature of desire, I would maintain that the liberation of a transsexuality that has up till now been unconscious cannot be obtained by a male and heterosexual redeployment of the classical psychoanalytic categories (substituting for Oedipus, for example, an Anti-Oedipus), but only by the revolution of women against male supremacy and the homosexual revolution against the heterosexual Norm. And only the standpoint of women and gays, above all of gay women, can indicate the very important nexus that exists between their subordination and the general social subordination, drawing the thread that unites class oppression, sexual oppression and the suppression of homosexuality.

In women as subjected to male 'power', in the proletariat subjected to capitalist exploitation, in the subjection of homosexuals to the Norm and in that of black people to white racism, we can recognise the concrete historical subjects in a position to overthrow the entire present social, sexual and racial dialectic, for the achievement of the 'realm of freedom'. True human subjectivity is not to be found in that personification of the thing par excellence, i.e. capital and the phallus, but rather in the subject position of women, homosexuals, children, blacks, 'schizophrenics', old people, etc. to the power that exploits and oppresses them. This revolutionary or potentially revolutionary subjectivity arises from subjection.

There are here a series of serious contradictions, which have to be overcome so that the true Revolution can be achieved. Still today, in fact, the subversive potential of the majority is held in check by their adherence to one form of power or another. Too many proletarians, for example, and too many women as well, still keenly defend the heterosexual Norm, and hence male privilege and the domination of capital. And yet Elvio Fachinelli can already say: 'We are not far from the day when the peaceful and moderately efficient heterosexual will find himself fired upon by his homosexual comrade'.[53]

53. Elvio Fachinelli, 'Travesti', p. 38.

But Fachinelli knows better than I do that the gun is a phallic symbol. We queens have no intention of shooting anyone to bits, even if we are prepared to defend ourselves as best we can, and will be better prepared in the future. Our revolution is opposed to capital and its Norm, and its goal is universal liberation. Death and gratuitous violence we can willingly leave to capital, and to those still in thrall to its inhuman ideology. Fachinelli, as a good heterosexual, fears gays armed with guns because he fears homosexual relations. It is only to be hoped that this heterosexual fear will be transformed into gay desire and not into terror, forcing us really to take up the gun. I believe the movement for the liberation of homosexuality is irreversible, in the broader context of human emancipation as a whole. It is up to all of us to make this emancipation a reality. There is certainly no time to lose.

8
The End

> As long as women reject or fear the sexual approach of another woman, as long as men are at pains to guarantee and defend the virginity of their own asshole, the reign of freedom will not have been attained; this is the certainty from which the homosexual perspective illuminates the future. – Mario Rossi[1]

I believe that this conclusion does not add anything new to what has been discussed and maintained in the preceding pages. It is simply a concise synthesis of the main perspectives that arise from an analysis of the homosexual situation. Those who have followed me to this point, therefore, will find in these last pages a kind of recapitulation of what they should by now have understood. For those who instead have started by casting an eye at the conclusion (and it's not just a few who do this), the unusual assertions that follow should arouse them either to read the whole book from the first page, or to throw it out of the window, acknowledging in this way that they are not interested (or perhaps too much so ...) in a reading of this sort, of *certain* hypotheses.

From criticism of the ideology of heterosexual primacy and from an examination of the homosexual question and the rich themes inherent in the liberation of Eros, it is possible and indeed necessary to draw hypothetical conclusions – and more than hypothetical – for the future of the human race. These conclusions present themselves as the result of consequences derivable from the present movement of the sexual dialectic in the context of human emancipation: unless – and at this point we have to put forward the contrary hypothesis – revolution and communism do not replace the destruction, war and the biological annihilation of the species, to which capital's lethal rule tends.

1. The liberation of Eros and the emancipation of the human race pass necessarily – and this is a gay necessity – through the libera-

---

1. Mario Rossi, 'Dirompenza politica della questione omosessuale', in Fuori! 12 (Spring 1974).

tion of homoeroticism, which includes an end to the persecution of manifest homosexuals and the concrete expression of the homoerotic component of desire on the part of *all* human beings. *Baisé soit qui mal y pense.*[2]

2. The liberation of sexuality, moreover, includes the complete recognition and the concrete manifestation of erotic desire for persons of the other sex on the part of homosexual men and women, and the realisation of a new gay way of loving between women and men.
3. The (re)conquest of Eros determines the overcoming of the present coercive forms in which both heterosexuality and homosexuality are manifested. This means that the liberation, which is above all a liberation of gay desire, will also lead, not only to the negation of heterosexuality as a heterosexual Norm, but also to the transformation of homosexuality, which today is still in large part subject to the dictatorship of this Norm. The antithesis of heterosexuality and homosexuality will be overcome in this way, and substituted by a *transsexual* synthesis; no longer will there be hetero- and homosexuals, but *polysexual*, transsexual human beings; better, instead of hetero- and homosexuals there will be human beings. The species will have (re)found itself.
4. The freed Eros will be transsexual, also because the liberation of homosexuality and the abolition of repressive heterosexual primacy will have promoted and determined the complete dis-inhibition and liberation of the deeply hermaphroditic nature of desire, which is transsexual (psychoanalysis would reductively say *bisexual*), whether in the face of its 'objects' *or in the subject.*
5. The discovery and progressive liberation of the transsexuality of the subject will lead to the negation of the polarity between the sexes and to the utopian (in the revolutionary sense of *utopia-eutopia*[3]) achievement of the new man-woman or, far more likely, woman-man.
6. But the (almost) mirror-like resemblance, even in difference, between the *object* of transsexual desire and the transsexual desiring *subject* will

2. The Order of the Garter, with its motto 'Honni soit qui mal y pense' – 'let those be shunned who think evil of it' – was according to legend founded by King Edward III (1312–77) in honour of his lover, the Countess of Salisbury, who had let her garter fall during a ball. The King immediately retrieved it and pronounced the celebrated phrase to his courtiers who smiled at the gesture.

3. [Translator's note: Mieli's reference is to the double etymological resonance of *utopia*, as both a non-place (*utopia*) and a good place (*eutopia*).]

lead to a recognition of the subject in the object and in this way to the creation of true intersubjective reciprocity. From the sexual point of view, this will mean the (re)conquest of the *human community*, and the liberated Eros will no longer be separated from other expressions of community. Cured of neuroses, sexuality can be grasped clearly, freed from the sense of guilt, as well as in the social and scientific-artistic forms of its positive sublimation, as now the true Renaissance will take place. Positive sublimation (sublime action) will substitute itself completely for labour understood as alienated and coercive, and for the sterile and self-destructive sublimation in which the greater part of neurotic 'free' time is today lost. All human beings will know themselves, and no longer from an individualistic point of view, which will be overcome, but rather from a transsexual, intersubjective and communitarian one: this consciousness will break down the barriers between Ego and non-Ego, between self and others, between body and intellect, between word and deed.

7. In order that the liberation of homosexuality, transsexuality and human emancipation be accomplished, *the assertion of the revolutionary movement of women is necessary*, as being concrete historical subjects of the universal antithesis to the masculine power presently in force, they will overturn this power, transforming their antithetical position through revolution, bringing about the collapse of the system of repression of Eros that is absolutely functional to it, starting with the heterosexual Norm and the rejection of homosexuality.
8. The collapse of the phallocratic system includes the collapse of the capitalist system, which rests on the masculinist and heterosexual foundation of society and on the repression and exploitation of Eros that together guarantee the perpetuation of alienated labour and hence the rule of capital. The revolutionary proletariat and the movement of revolutionary women are the two faces of the communist/human-community party, and the movement of revolutionary homosexuals is its ass. Like transsexuality itself, the revolutionary movement is *one and multiple*.
9. If the assertion of the movement of conscious homosexuals contributes to making the communist (and) women's movement revolutionary, the progressive liberation of other repressed erotic tendencies will make it ever more gay. The presence today, for example, of a subversive organisation of sadomasochist homosexuals in the USA shows that, from a perspective opposed to the destructive totalisation

of capital, we are moving in the direction of the complete liberation of desire. We cannot imagine the importance of the contribution made to the revolution and to human emancipation by the steady liberation of sadism, masochism, pederasty in the proper sense of the term, gerontophilia, necrophilia, zooerastia, autoeroticism, fetishism, scatology, urophilia, exhibitionism, voyeurism, etc., if we don't move *in the first person* to the dis-inhibition and concrete expression of these tendencies in our own desire, if we don't refer to the practical and theoretical work of those who already live in an open way one or more of the so-called 'perverse' desires, without forgetting that, often, the most 'perverse' are those who get defined as 'schizophrenic'.

In particular, if we aspire to the achievement of transsexuality, we cannot avoid recognising in those who are physiologically or even solely psychologically transsexual today (in the drama of their individual lives, outlawed by the repressive system of the individualist monosexual 'normals' with their enclosed lives) the unique contemporary and concrete expression, always persecuted and far from a free existence, of the 'miraculous' range and scope of desire, of Eros. 'The miracle is that there is nothing miraculous there' (Sartre).

Appendix A
Unpublished Preface to *Homosexuality and Liberation*

Mario Mieli (1980)[1]

Travelling in India and Nepal has made me only too aware how the arguments in *Homosexuality and Liberation* apply even to countries such as these. The repression of sexuality, and of homosexuality in particular, is a fundamental cause of human misery. The serious problem of population increase, for example, would resolve itself naturally with the free expression of Eros, for the determining factor of overpopulation is the genital-heterosexual obsession that I have attacked. The anti-homosexual taboo obstructs true totalising relations between individuals of the same sex, and in this way holds back the human species from the (re)conquest of community. Here, as everywhere, people want to be happy. But immersed in their slumber of resignation, they refuse to open their eyes, content with a mere illusion of life, and turn waking existence into a nightmare, the same as in the West.

Time is pressing. The human race, for the first time in its 'prehistory', faces the risk of self-destruction. Ecological catastrophe is the only alternative to nuclear war, if the capitalist mode of production is not brought to a halt, and completely transformed, by human beings rejecting this suicidal course and taking control of their own lives.

The moment has come when we must either decide openly for life, for pleasure, or else accept the tragic scenario that capital has in store. The moment to realise most sincerely that it is up to us to settle accounts with our fate and establish a better course of action, the best course. Let us hope that we can.

Mario Mieli
Katmandu, 10 December 1979

P. S. The place where the Buddha attained enlightenment is today called Gaya.

---

1. An abridged English-language edition of *Elementi di critica omosessuale*, published by Gay Men's Press, 1980; see 'Translator's Preface', this volume p. xxv.

Appendix B
Translator's Additional Note from Chapter 1

In Chapter 6, Marx describes two phases in the social development of capitalism: the formal subsumption of labour under capital (formal domination) and the real subsumption of labour under capital (real domination). Regarding formal domination, Marx writes:

> The labour process becomes the instrument of the valorization process, the process of the self-valorization of capital – the manufacture of surplus-value. The labour process is subsumed under capital (it is its own process) and the capitalist intervenes in the process as its director, manager. For him it also represents the direct exploitation of the labour of others. It is this that I refer to as the formal Subsumption of labour under capital. It is the general form of every capitalist process of production; at the same time, however, it can be found as a particular form alongside the specifically capitalist mode of production in its developed form, because although the latter entails the former, the converse does not necessarily obtain [i.e. the formal subsumption can be found in the absence of the specifically capitalist mode of production].[1]

This formal subsumption is linked to the production of absolute surplus-value. Camatte writes:

> The capitalist cannot obtain a greater value without prolonging the working day. He has not yet overturned the very basis of society. For the moment, he is limited to substituting himself for another exploiter. Formal domination, therefore, is essentially characterized by this element: from the start, capitalism is distinguished from other modes of production by that fact that it is based not simply on appropriation of surplus-value, but rather on its creation.[2]

1. Marx, *Capital* Vol. 1, p. 1019.
2. Camatte, *Il capitale totale*, p. 100.

Regarding real domination (real subsumption of labour under capital), Marx writes:

> The general features of the *formal subsumption* remain, viz. the direct *subordination of the labour process to capital*, irrespective of the state of its technological development. But on this foundation there now arises a technologically and otherwise *specific mode of production – capitalist production* – which transforms the nature of *the labour process and its actual conditions*. Only when that happens do we witness the *real subsumption of labour under capital*.[3]

It is with the conclusion of the Second World War that we might see the decisive achievement of the passage from formal domination to the real domination of capital in the European and North American zone. This real domination has, as its presupposition, 'a complete (and constantly repeated) [that] revolution takes place in the mode of production, in the productivity of the workers and in the relations between workers and capitalists'.[4] It is based on the production not of *absolute* but of *relative* surplus-value.

> '*Production for production's sake*' – production as an end in itself – does indeed come on the scene with the *formal subsumption of labour under capital*. It makes its appearance as soon as the immediate purpose of production is to produce *as much surplus-value as possible*, as soon as the exchange-value of the product becomes the deciding factor. But this *inherent* tendency of capitalist production does not become *adequately realized* – it does not become *indispensable*, and that also means *technologically* indispensable – until the *specific mode of capitalist production* and hence the *real subsumption of labour under capital* has become a reality.[5]

With real domination, capital manifests the tendency to 'dominate the law of value, exploiting it to its advantage'.[6] In the period of *formal domination*, 'capital dominates the proletariat and its domination is that

3. Marx, *Capital* Vol. I, pp. 1034–5.
4. Ibid., p. 1035.
5. Ibid., p. 1037.
6. Camatte, *Il capitale totale*, p. 103.

of variable capital. It is in the interest of capital to utilize a maximum number of workers in order to achieve a maximum of surplus-value [...] When it passes to a period of real domination, the essential element becomes fixed capital.'[7] There takes place a socialisation not only of production but of the human itself (with both in relation to devalorisation): 'large-scale industry produces the complete worker (*Gesamtarbeiter*) who is the very base of the social human of tomorrow'.[8] After having subjectised all production, capital subjectivises through itself also the means of circulation. Real domination therefore involves, as its characteristic traits: the autonomisation of capital; the expropriation of the capitalists; the full development of interest and credit, and the production of fictitious capital; the absolutisation of capital (its aspirations to eternity and immortality); the autonomisation of forms derived from value. The law of value becomes the law of prices of production.

The real domination of capital manifests itself as 'fascism generalized in all the nations in which capitalist relations of production have developed', writes Camatte.

> The state of capital is presented as guarantor of equitable division among all men. Demands are no longer made in the name of a political ideal, but a social ideal; it is no longer the question of power it had posed, but rather one of structures, understood in the following terms: these structures must be reformed to allow everyone to benefit from economic growth. It is in social democracy that fascism finds its resolution. These assertions cannot be developed in detail at this level of the analysis. For now it is enough to note that the various justifications of capitalist society that were refuted above derive from the autonomisation of social relations and their reification. But: 'It is crises that put an end to this apparent autonomy of the various elements into which the production process is continually dissolved and which it continually reproduces.'[9]

7. Camatte, p. 104.
8. Camatte, p. 106.
9. Ibid., p. 105.

Index